ROBERT RISKIN

ROBERT RISKIN

*The Life and Times of
a Hollywood Screenwriter*

IAN SCOTT

UNIVERSITY PRESS OF KENTUCKY

Paperback edition 2021
Copyright © 2006 by The University Press of Kentucky

Scholarly publisher for the Commonwealth,
serving Bellarmine University, Berea College, Centre
College of Kentucky, Eastern Kentucky University,
The Filson Historical Society, Georgetown College,
Kentucky Historical Society, Kentucky State University,
Morehead State University, Murray State University,
Northern Kentucky University, Spalding University,
Transylvania University, University of Kentucky,
University of Louisville, and Western Kentucky University.
All rights reserved.

Editorial and Sales Offices: The University Press of Kentucky
663 South Limestone Street, Lexington, Kentucky 40508-4008
www.kentuckypress.com

The first edition of this book was published as
In Capra's Shadow: The Life and Career of Screenwriter Robert Riskin.

Library of Congress Cataloging-in-Publication Data

Names: Scott, Ian, 1954- author.
Title: Robert Riskin : the life and times of a Hollywood screenwriter / Ian
   Scott.
Other titles: In Capra's shadow
Description: Paperback edition. | Lexington, Kentucky : University Press of
   Kentucky, 2021. | "The first edition of this book was published as In
   Capra's shadow : the life and career of screenwriter Robert Riskin." |
   Includes bibliographical references and index.
Identifiers: LCCN 2021035833 | ISBN 9780813180526 (paperback) | ISBN
   9780813155463 (epub)
Subjects: LCSH: Riskin, Robert. | Authors, American--20th
   century--Biography. | Screenwriters--United States--Biography.
Classification: LCC PS3535.I82 Z86 2021 | DDC 808.2/3092 [B]--dc23

This book is printed on acid-free paper meeting
the requirements of the American National Standard
for Permanence in Paper for Printed Library Materials.

Manufactured in the United States of America

  Member of the Association
of University Presses

This book is dedicated to my father,
Arthur Scott,
who never got to see its completion
but is there within its pages.

CONTENTS

ACKNOWLEDGMENTS

In writing this new edition of the book I owe a debt of thanks to all the following people for their help, advice, knowledge, dedication, and most of all their patience and understanding. Firstly, to everyone in the English, American Studies and Creative Writing department at Manchester, you have been kind and receptive colleagues for so many years and I'm very grateful for your support.

I want to pay thanks again to those who made the original task of researching and writing this book so much easier. Thanks to Ned Comstock and all his colleagues at the Film and Television Library at the University of Southern California. Ned went out of his way to get materials for me, allowing access to papers when needed, and he provided contacts that transformed the research in ways I couldn't imagine. I would like to thank all the staff at the James R. Webb Memorial Library of the Writers Guild in Los Angeles for their help, attention, and good advice. I wish to thank the staff of the Margaret Herrick Library of the Motion Picture Academy in Los Angeles for similar kindness and dedication. I am extremely grateful to Chief Archivist David Pffifner at the National Archives in College Park, who tracked down memos and papers on Riskin and sent them directly to my front door.

I would like to thank all the staff at the University Press of Kentucky, but especially Sarah Olson, Jewell Boyd, Jackie Wilson, Ashley Runyon, Victoria Robinson and Ann Marlowe for their support and belief in this new edition. I am grateful to the Arts and Humanities Research Council (AHRC) of the United Kingdom for their funding and assistance of this project.

To my friends and family, thank you for all the years of help, patience and tolerance. I owe a significant debt to, among others,

Richard Mountford, Kevin Richards, Steve Bower, Chris Wilson, Justine Stevens, Alan Rawes, Doug Field, Michelle Smith and Ian Shelldrake. To Wendy and Steven, to Pat and Sarah, thank you for your welcome. Finally, I want to say a huge thanks to Karen and Ethan for their love and dedication.

PROLOGUE

The Three-Act Play

In late December 1950, Robert Riskin returned home from work early, complaining of weakness in his left arm and hand. His health had deteriorated over the previous few weeks, and he could no longer concentrate on his screenwriting duties at Twentieth Century–Fox, where he had an office. This latest episode confirmed to Riskin suspicions he'd had for some weeks: that he needed to see a neurologist. There was a dawning realization that he might become incapacitated, and it made him confess his worst fears to his wife, actress Fay Wray. Wray immediately took him to the hospital. "I drove him carefully . . . carefully, believing, crazily, that a sudden stop or lane change might make his condition worse," she observed later.[1]

Once there, various examinations were carried out, including a spinal tap, and Riskin was advised that he needed the attention of the renowned head of neurosurgery, Dr. Tracy Putnam. Dr. Putnam was out of town, and Riskin returned home for the evening, only to lie down in a darkened room with his head throbbing, a side effect of the procedures. The next morning, Riskin and Wray's great friends Flo and Jo Swerling turned up with a limousine, and all four took the drive to Cedars of Lebanon Hospital in Los Angeles. Although Putnam carried out exploratory brain surgery and was hopeful of a recovery, Riskin had in fact already suffered a stroke prior to the operation, and the persistent therapy he received subsequently did little to alleviate a left-side paralysis that was to last the rest of his life.

1

There had been a clot in Riskin's carotid artery, and blood thinning medication, which Fay Wray later remarked could have significantly helped her husband, was simply not available at that time. Years later, Wray recalled how Riskin had drifted in and out of consciousness for ten days after the operation, sometimes weeping with almost unrestrained emotion.[2] On January 7, 1951 he remained awake for fully two hours, conducting a conversation that seemed to recall events from his wartime experiences with the Office of War Information in London. A slow and only partial improvement was beginning to take place. Over the following days and weeks, Wray recorded virtually everything that her husband said and many of the thoughts that flowed through her own mind as well. She wrote, on the same yellow notepads that Riskin had used to created many of his great screenplays, how memory and lucidity returned in a piecemeal fashion, but with a steadily growing accumulation of details and reminiscences.

Although Riskin returned home in the first year after the operation, by the second year he was confined to a nearby nursing home for round-the-clock care. He was now much more physically incapacitated, and a return to normal family life was impossible. He had visits from Edward G. Robinson, Jack Benny, and Irving Berlin, as well as the Swerlings, who came by regularly and always provided good cheer. A long, handwritten letter from Darryl Zanuck to Riskin urged him and Fay to seek consultation with a Swedish neurosurgeon whom the legendary producer knew. Fay had by now returned to work with the intention of raising funds for Riskin's treatment as the family finances began to dwindle in the face of hospital bills and private care costs. She starred alongside a young Anne Bancroft in *The Treasure of the Golden Condor* for Fox and with Jane Powell and Farley Granger in *Small Town Girl* for MGM. A television series for ABC, *The Pride of the Family*, saw Wray team up with Paul Hartman and the sixteen-year-old Natalie Wood, someone she recognized immediately as a Hollywood star in the making.

Despite this regular work, Fay became more concerned about her ability to provide for Riskin's care. There were some reservations about the level and kind of attention afforded him at the nursing home as well. One caretaker ran off with Riskin's car, presumably for some recompense after the man's wife mislaid a fifty-dollar bill and left him desperate. And so Riskin's brother Everett, who had started off with him producing Broadway shows in the 1920s and who was now an established screen producer, decided to meet with the board members of the Motion Picture and Television Country House and Hospital in Woodland Hills. Set up by Jean Hersholt—a notable actor whose career ranged from von Stroheim's *Greed* in 1923 to *Heidi* in 1937 and who had been president of the Motion Picture Relief Fund in the 1940s—the home was a charitable foundation dedicated to looking after those in the profession who had fallen ill or were incapacitated.[3] The service was first class, and Everett and the board soon reached an agreement for Riskin to stay there.

Riskin resided at the home for the next four years. Paralysis of his left side confined him either to his bed or a wheelchair, but he never lost his good humor or humility. Riskin's spirited and voracious desire for life remained firmly intact. Friends and visitors stopped by from time to time, and Fay stayed diligently by his side. Riskin's career had been a glorious one, the sort Hollywood writes into legend as the rags-to-riches kind only it could provide. He had authored his own ticket to fame and fortune in as bighearted a way as he had written his dazzling characters on the page. But filming those characters and embellishing those stories had been in the hands of the filmmaker Riskin worked with almost exclusively through the 1930s and early 1940s: legendary director Frank Capra. Capra had been Riskin's partner and inspiration on so many hit projects. Yet when Riskin got ill and needed his friend most, Capra never showed up.

The Screenwriter as Collaborator

As Marc Norman observes in his history of Hollywood screenwriting, the description "writer" has always been somewhat problematic. "The truth was, the screenwriter dreamed up not only what the actors said, but the reason they were saying it . . . their deepest needs, their greatest hopes, whatever ancient metaphor of mankind they were acting out." For Norman, the screenwriter is really a composer, and when studio executives said they envied those who were often considered the most put-upon people on the lot, what they meant was that screenwriters had the benefit of seeing the movie first, in their heads and on the page. Theirs was the purest form of existence, for "if their work was well-realized [they saw] it perfectly [on the screen], with a beauty and resonance that could bring them to tears."[4]

The love of motion pictures could be encapsulated in the screenwriter's face when their vision ended up realized in the most impeccable form they could imagine. Robert Riskin was fortunate to have that realization happen to him several times in his career. Riskin was also, within his profession, one of the more high-profile and well-paid screenwriters of the era. Such attention brought him acclaim, but it also brought a degree of influence that wasn't typically the province of Hollywood's writing community. Like others, Riskin worked with several writers in his career. He polished other's scripts and one or two helped to refine his. He cowrote some scripts. But Robert Riskin was unusual for a screenwriter of the age because the essence of his writing that ended up committed to celluloid was often similar if not acutely respectful to the intentionality of his scripts as he first imagined them. In a business of many scribes and few Pharisees, Riskin was often in the latter camp.

For all the attention at the time, however, Riskin's career, where it has been characterized, retrospectively affords him no more than a "bit part" and ad hoc status. As this book sets out to clarify and explain, some of the reasons for that indeterminate standing lie with the power and position of screenwriters in Hollywood's Golden Age. Their battle for recognition was Riskin's battle too, though he fought it on their behalf as much as he lined up with his fellow scribes in the trenches, plotting and planning in obscure writers' rooms on the studio lots. They came to him, in other words, and his towering presence as a screenwriter of great skill and tremendous energy was legendary in film circles. He was simply better known, and far more lauded, than many contemporaries with longer-standing reputations. In his heyday in the mid-thirties, for example, it was emerging talents like Billy Wilder who flocked to Riskin's office at Columbia Pictures, eager for tips and advice that he was more than willing to impart. His quietly authoritative presence struck a chord with the fledgling screenwriting guild looking for spokespeople and camaraderie to bond them together. And his writing struck an equally resonant note, with contemporary scenarists as well as theater audiences, because he managed to capture the spirit of the vernacular, the everyday asides that were part of ordinary people's conversation and that brought his narratives to life. Riskin had the gift of knowing what people had to say about life, how they behaved and thought, what their greatest aspirations were, and their worst fears. It was this talent for picking out the foibles of different personalities that endeared his stories to cinemagoers, for they saw in his characters themselves.

But while Riskin's career is an object lesson in the art of the early screenwriter's craft, it is also a cautionary tale of lost opportunities and, even at his elevated status, bypassed credits. Because the other principal reason Riskin found a place in the pantheon hard to come by in later recollections of the studio era is tied up with the director who helped earn him such a glowing reputation. Frank Capra was such a towering figure in American film lore that almost everything he did, and all who worked with him, got sucked into an orbit around Capra's giant sun that then too often obscured roles and missed attribution. Whether you were his longtime cinematographer, Joseph Walker, his set designer Stephen Goosson, editor Gene Havlick, or Riskin and other writers such as Sidney Buchman, Capra's "team" were forever in his shadow. It didn't help, either, that when it came time for Capra himself to write his story, it emerged as entirely entertaining and, quite often, just as mythic and fabricated as the tales he and Riskin brought to the screen.

For Riskin, it is also true that time and tide caught up with his career as Hollywood changed dramatically in the later 1940s. In the short interval between the end of the Second World War and the onset of his illness, Riskin's work never quite recaptured the glories of the previous decade, despite his making some fascinating and unfairly neglected pictures. Desperate to establish control over his material, Riskin ironically never really had as much power of authorization over his scripts, once he was operating from within the production company he formed, as he had managed under studio control at Columbia Pictures, under the spell of Capra and the company's founder and president, Harry Cohn. The almost carefree abandon in his writing during the thirties—the language, settings, and characters juggled and juxtaposed against each other—gave way to tinkering, alterations, and a need to manufacture purpose and presence for his characters when it had come so naturally only a few years before. It would be stretching the judgment to say Riskin fell into a writer's block, for the movies he wrote and contributed to remained captivating and often complex productions. But audiences' tastes were changing, and the long-standing relationship and fabled partnership with Capra, broken up on the verge of war, brought these creative difficulties into sharp relief. Although the association was never tainted by any actual falling-out, its ending in 1941 after concluding production of their hit *Meet John Doe* has been regarded as the long, slow fall from grace for Riskin. In fact, it was anything but, and Riskin's immediate post-Capra work, for the government during the war, was some of the most vital and rewarding of his life. And yet it is precisely that relationship with Capra that has been the camouflage hiding Riskin's monumental contribution to Hollywood writing in the years since. In this respect, a sign of the trouble to come cropped up in 1950, nine years after *Meet John Doe*, and just as Riskin was falling ill.

That year, Capra resolved to remake his and Riskin's 1934 racetrack comedy, *Broadway Bill*, as *Riding High* for Paramount, where the director was now contracted. But as the picture went into production, a dispute erupted that has never truly been resolved. For the first time in over eight years, here was an opportunity for Hollywood's greatest director-writer partnership to reunite. Capra always maintained that he offered Riskin the chance to rewrite the movie. Fay Wray insisted that Riskin volunteered to come on board first but was refused.[5] In the end, Capra attempted to write the picture virtually on his own, though producer Sam Briskin, who was still by Capra's side at Paramount, having guided him and Riskin through the Columbia years, urged Capra to get help. That help came in the form of writers Melville Shavelson and Jack Rose. Although it was clear that Capra was going nowhere with the screenplay on his own and that it was still essentially the tale Riskin had constructed sixteen years previously from Mark Hellinger's short story, Capra then lobbied furiously to get a writing credit for the new version with the Screen Writers Guild. Shavelson and Rose, meanwhile, had to content themselves with a credit for adaptation rights, even though their alterations had shaped the tone of the new picture far more than the director's contribution. Capra appealed directly to Riskin to let him have screenplay credit, but his former partner simply said no.[6] *Riding High* appeared in theaters with Riskin as writer and Shavelson and Rose credited with additional dialogue from Hellinger's original tale.

The die appears to have been cast by this dispute, which harked back to controversial events surrounding the making, and rewritten ending, of the original *Broadway Bill* in 1934. It was never clear, however, that this minor spat over writing credits alone provided the explanation for any cooling of the friendship between Riskin and Capra, certainly not to the degree that one would neglect the other when illness intervened and Capra knew his presence would have provided succor and comfort. At the time, the disagreement around *Riding High* appeared to reveal little more than how much the pair had drifted apart creatively in the intervening years—an artistic separation highlighted by their individual wartime activities that took them in different filmmaking directions.

As the years passed, the *Riding High* dispute took on more significance and the subject of Riskin's relationship to Capra became that much more acrimonious. Discrepancies between their social and professional work surfaced and led to a number of public clashes. As Capra scholars have noted, the director maintained a social relationship with Riskin after the war, but after his friend fell ill and the controversy over *Riding High* had reached a climax, he never visited Woodland Hills, and he telephoned Fay Wray only once in five years.[7]

By contrast, Jo Swerling, Riskin's friend and fellow screenwriter at Columbia, who penned such hits as *Platinum Blonde*—to which Riskin added dialogue—and who was nominated for an Academy Award in 1943 for *The Pride of the Yankees*, stayed by his friend's side throughout. Swerling was also aware of what was going on between Riskin and Capra. On one visit to the nursing home, he paced around Riskin's room complaining that Capra's reluctance to visit his old friend was just not right. In the end, as Swerling got more agitated, Riskin lost his temper, revealing in a flash his deep-seated loyalty to his former partner. He stopped Swerling in his tracks by simply saying, "You're talking about my best friend."[8]

If Riskin's remark suggests a respect and regard that couldn't be broken by each other's actions during their lifetimes, then long after Riskin's passing, in the later years of Capra's life, there appears to have developed a total blindness to the part played by Riskin in what for some was the greatest writer-director partnership in Hollywood's history. As the pair's films came up for retrospective analysis by a new generation of scholars and fans, the subject of Riskin's contribution to Capra's film success came to a head in a series of articles in the *Los Angeles Times* in 1977. The president of the Writers Guild of America, West, David Rintels, wrote a piece claiming that Riskin's scripts were the centripetal force holding together Capra's great movies, including *It Happened One Night* and *Mr. Deeds Goes to Town*. Capra's reply, in a tellingly titled article, "One Man, One Film," set the seal on his view of Riskin. Capra wrote that Riskin was indeed a truly great screenwriter and had been one of his "dearest friends." He went on to claim, however, that Riskin's best scripts were with him, and that anybody who worked on a Capra film, including Swerling, Sidney Buchman, and the Hacketts—Albert and Frances— also produced his or her greatest work when he was at the helm.[9]

Rintels's rebuttal, published on the same page as Capra's letter, dismissed the theory outright. He cited all the success these other writers enjoyed away from collaborations with Capra. The Hacketts wrote *The Diary of Anne Frank* (which won a Pulitzer Prize), *Seven Brides for Seven Brothers*, and *Easter Parade*, while Sidney Buchman penned *The Talk of the Town* and *Here Comes Mr. Jordan*. It was true, Rintels argued, that Capra and Riskin's relationship had a special kind of chemistry. But if Riskin needed Capra, as the director's argument seemed to suggest, then just as often, asserted Rintels, Capra "struck out" when Riskin was not doing the writing.[10]

Capra's argument left a bitter taste. Writing such comments

in the autumn of his life, there was little doubt as to his intentions: he wanted to preserve his reputation and the integrity of *his* films. The success in the early 1970s of his autobiography, *The Name above the Title*, had galvanized Capra into believing that his place in the legion of Hollywood greats was there for the taking, after decades of neglect of his work. Film scholars were beginning to reappraise Capra, too. In an assessment of Capra's movies that appeared around the same time as the debate in the *LA Times*, Leland Poague suggested that Capra's bullish "one man, one film" theory had actually been mapped out by the director much earlier in his career.

In 1936 Capra wrote a series of magazine articles outlining his personal directorial control.[11] Reiterating the point in the 1970s suggested that Capra wanted definitive closure on the subject while he could still make his case. Either that or else he saw an opportunity to position himself firmly in the auteurist film camp which had, thanks to the work of Andrew Sarris, become the key contributory theory among cinematic scholars assessing the individuality of directors in the American industry able to overcome the strictures of the studio system.[12]

It was certainly the case that Capra's pictures had suffered critical deterioration in the politically charged atmosphere of the 1960s and the generational shift toward the New Hollywood characterized by up-and-coming pretenders like Mike Nichols, Francis Ford Coppola, and Martin Scorsese. These and other filmmakers were busy dismantling the system Capra had helped establish. Ironically, though, in among this new generation were admirers of the old school who, as forging young directors, were clamoring for the sort of singular control Capra was laying claim to in his story. *The Name above the Title*, first published in 1971, had begun a recuperation of his reputation, becoming a best seller in the process, and marked Capra's attempts to link his personal "one man, one film" philosophy in print with this wider contemporary movement in Hollywood. But the tone and, frankly, the book's almost dismissive recollection of Riskin's part in the origins of some of the industry's greatest pictures to that point only served to underscore Rintels's argument.

In an interview with James Childs for *Film Comment* in 1972,

Capra carried the autobiography's argument a step forward by responding to a question about his auteurist view of filmmaking quite bluntly. "It is an art form," he said, suggesting that, as with painting or with writing novels or plays, the creative force was singular and individually rooted. As if to reinforce the point, Capra concluded unambiguously, "my films have been one man, one film."[13] It is a position that has been reaffirmed by scholars up to the present era. In her 2020 study of the rise of the Directors Guild of America, Virginia Wright Wexman equates the guild's evolution and influence not simply with the power of authorship as broadly shaped through Hollywood's history, but more specifically with Capra's conception of that auteurism. As Wexman reminds us, the guild's earliest public statement drew on Capra's thinking by quoting his insistence that "What built the motion pictures was individuality."[14]

Even so, for all Capra's long-standing affiliation with the lone artist in other cultural traditions, his duel with Rintels in 1977 was unconvincing. By the time he had finished working with Riskin, Capra asserted, Riskin was the biggest screenwriter in the world: "Yes, Robert Riskin was a giant among scriptwriters—at least when he worked with me. He got his reputation on my films. And if he had been responsible for my success, how come I made better films with other screenwriters?"[15]

This conclusion was uncharitable in the extreme and in many ways not worthy or typical of Capra, in his heyday at least. At the height of his powers, and even allowing for his mid-1930s comments, Capra had acquired little in the way of the extreme auteurist posturing of other directors who were regarded as overtly temperamental or difficult to work with. He was demanding, certainly, and Fay Wray herself asserted such a view. On the set of the one film they made together, *Dirigible*, in 1931, she reported that Capra could be quite cold and aloof with actors.[16] But many people also testified to what film historian Lewis Jacobs called Capra's "sober and judicious" style of filmmaking. "He is a director who displays absolutely no exhibitionism," observed Jacobs.[17] And yet here was someone now in the later years of life who seemed desperately protective of his own work, precious, and even unforgiving in his judgment of others. Joe McBride's sagacious research for his outstanding Capra book, *The Catastrophe of Success* in 1992, attributed at least some of this attitude to Capra's murky postwar links to anticommunism in Hollywood. McBride had uncovered a Security Board file indicating that Capra had supplied the names of screenwriters—significantly not Riskin—to the State Department. Perhaps this affiliation with government made the director dismiss the social and political themes that abounded in his movies for fear that he would be labeled subversive, a word that *was* suggested in his Army Intelligence file. If the pressure of Capra's secret state liaisons had for many years made him defensive and ended up with him blaming his writers for putting in any overtly ideological messaging, then surely Capra was not merely, as McBride reiterated in his 2019 book *Frankly: Unmasking Frank Capra*, "disowning the elements of social criticism [but] contradicting his loudly proclaimed 'one man, one film' theory."[18]

However it was that Capra's conscience saw things, when it came to a defense of her husband's capabilities and the legacy of his friendship with Capra, Fay Wray perceived a very different situation during those difficult years at the start of the 1950s. She produced a terse, and interestingly unpublished, reply to the exchange of views that had filled the pages of the *Los Angeles Times* in 1977. She succinctly set the record straight concerning those years looking after Riskin and what the extent of his relationship with Capra was by that time. The implication was clear: regardless of Riskin's comment to Jo Swerling that suggested a loyalty to Capra that was unwavering, of the many friends who visited her husband during the years of his illness, Wray said, Frank Capra was not among them.[19] That decision seemingly told her all she needed to know about Capra's later reluctance to share the credit for their incredible success.

In her own memoirs, published in 1989, Wray seemed to relax her tone a little, perhaps out of loyalty to two great friends, possibly with a desire to tell her part in Riskin's life with as little fuss as possible. Certainly her comments are a good deal more reserved in the postwar story of the drifting apart of one of American cinema's greatest teams, choosing to relay only the happy times Capra and his family had with her and Riskin, and never really accounting for Capra's no-show in those last years. The episode concerning *Riding High* and its screenwriting ownership does not appear at all in Wray's account. Nevertheless, in the long list of visitors for Riskin that she recites in the book, particularly in the first year after his stroke, something of the dispute's legacy haunts her account, as does Capra's conspicuous absence.[20]

The Screenwriter as Icon

The debate over Riskin's place in Capra's firmament continued long after the 1977 series of exchanges concluded. McBride's 1992 biography not only unveiled a postwar legacy for Capra that was entirely at odds with his films' social progressivism, but also consciously redirected the artistic force of the writing in the relationship away from Capra and toward Riskin. It became an account that divided both critics and fans of the director. What they saw revealed in McBride's analysis was a determined propaganda effort on Capra's part to write Riskin out of the story virtually from day one of their partnership. And even in the summer of 2002, when Hollywood brought forth its first real attempt in thirty years to remake a Capra-Riskin classic—the Steven Brill–directed *Mr. Deeds,* starring Adam Sandler and Winona Ryder—discussions of input to and responsibility for the original's brilliant premise and conception once more filled the pages of newspapers and movie magazines and began to divide critics all over again. Such exercises confirmed that, for a long time, Riskin's life story in film remained Capra's story, the two forever linked by a run of critically and commercially successful films from, essentially, *American Madness* (1932) to *Meet John Doe* (1941) that remains virtually unparalleled in Hollywood's history. But Riskin's tale, his screenwriting genius, and his legacy within movies, is so much more than the sum of his collaborations with Capra.

The partnership was immense, and while the later controversies complicated the pair's achievements, they also served to conceal individual successes for Riskin that deserve far more attention than the footnotes he was assigned in appraisals of

Capra's career. Thus the argument here is somewhat less concerned with refuting Capra's indifference to Riskin's contribution –whether it was intentional from the start or after the fact—than with spotlighting the harmonious symbiosis at the heart of their relationship. Capra might claim better directing on his part without Riskin, and even that is debatable, but one is hard pressed to find better examples of collaborative filmmaking, of the director and screenwriter working so perceptively in tandem that each enhances the other's craft.

Equally important is the claim that Riskin's writing had a life of its own, in movies with and away from Capra, where recurrent and profound themes continued to stake their place in his narratives, be they social and political undercurrents, constructions of gender, or themes of urban and rural dislocation. This authorial, production, and directorial work sans Capra has barely been contemplated in any analyses, whether of the pair together, of Riskin by himself, or within the context of the wider studio era of the 1930s and 1940s.

But there remains a third element to this investigation. In his excellent history of screenwriting, *FrameWork*, Tom Stempel lays out the reasons for a wave of playwrights, journalists, and short story writers making their way to Hollywood, principally from New York, in the late 1920s and early 1930s. They were looking for money, quite naturally, asserts Stempel. With the onset of the Depression, which hit New York before it made its way farther west, the effect on jobs and assignments for these scribes was noticeable. Then there was the fact that the studios were attracted to some of the most famous literary figures of the age, believing that their presence would bring even more glamour and prestige to the movies than had been stored up over nearly three decades of silent film. By the start of the 1930s, actors needed lines, voices demanded dialogue, and the sharper and wittier the words, the better.

For writers who did not quite belong in the literary pantheon with Faulkner, Fitzgerald, and the like who went west to try their hand at screenplays, there was still the small matter of anonymity in Hollywood behind the studio gates, which meant that their work was not subject to the same kind of critical scrutiny it had to endure in New York. Film reviews, they realized, generally spoke of directors and producers long before they ever, if at all, made mention of writers.[21]

Stempel's point is that this combination of circumstances led to ongoing and accepted myths about screenwriters. First was the myth, backed in fact by considerable evidence, that few either enjoyed or made the transition from "New York writing" to "Hollywood writing." Second, and again not entirely without foundation, was the idea that even those writers who did establish themselves felt that they were in some ways prostituting their talent. After all, writes Stempel, "they were paid large sums of money for the privilege of having their work changed."[22]

The context of this situation, and the argument about adaptability to the Hollywood routine, provides the route by which a significant minority of individuals did garner a reputation for themselves in the Southern California film community. Riskin was as prominent among these individuals as anyone. Like Ben Hecht, Jules Furthman, Clifford Odets, Philip Dunne, Nunnally Johnson, and many, many others, Riskin found his artistic niche in screenwriting, but he did so having already dabbled in other parts of the movie business. Promoting Riskin ahead of these great scenarists is not the intent here—significantly, Riskin himself would have refuted such a claim anyway—but there was something unique about the style, subject matter, demeanor, and outlook of Robert Riskin that did differentiate him from other writers. And some of that originality stems from the context Stempel writes of. Riskin was a mildly successful playwright, had been a budding journalist, but felt little in the way of loyalty to, or commonality with, the literati of New York society. As the screenplay for his and Capra's 1936 masterpiece *Mr. Deeds Goes to Town* testifies, Riskin was more than happy to ridicule on screen the so-called Algonquin Round Table of Manhattan's self-proclaimed literary elite.

He also never felt that New York was the only place to be for a writer. Consequently, he displayed no great artistic affinity for the city, even though it was his hometown. But neither was he interested in simply taking the money and running from Hollywood. He went to Los Angeles in the early thirties with a career in mind, not a paid holiday. Anonymity was not a watchword for him, either. Riskin liked the lifestyle and the attention that film-making afforded by the mid-thirties, and he liked to promote his work. But what was crucial and different about Riskin was that he liked to promote the work of *all* writers. What he maintained that others couldn't was a way of dealing with the struggle for recognition and attention that screenwriters had to endure in the system that Hollywood had concocted, and then thriving once that recognition was secured. And Riskin dealt with celebrity when it finally arrived as he did with producers, directors, and especially studio heads like Columbia's Harry Cohn: in the same calm, firm, but unfussy manner. In other words, Riskin's background and early career prepared him for self-promotion in Hollywood, but he never moved into self-aggrandizement.

It was a sense of individuality in a collective system and the relaxed, seemingly effortless way he carried out his work that not only bore comparison with his fellow writers—some of whom were far more excitable and critical of the lies and fabrications of Hollywood as they saw it—but that also deserves efforts to detach him from the partnership he has been forever associated with. It is not just that Riskin was a great writer; he was also a surprising, contemporary, and even radical writer. Many of his peers, including those cited above, might be described as far more liberal, progressive, and perhaps daring in their work. Richard Corliss, in his notable book on screenwriters, *Talking Pictures*, reserves special mention for writers like Ben Hecht, whom he saw as the personification of Hollywood. "A jumble of talent, cynical and overpaid; most successful when he was least ambitious; often failing when he mistook sentimentality for seriousness, racy, superficial, vital and American," claims Corliss.[23] By contrast, Corliss's description of Riskin largely rests upon the man's "quiet conviction and self-respect."[24]

Riskin's writing then, rather like his demeanor and contributions to the screenwriting guild organization and, later, to documentary propaganda, never dealt in extremes. His politics, his social examinations, and his wit never screamed at you from page or screen. Instead they worked subtly to drag you into his worlds and into a style that was the epitome of nobility and integrity.

But Riskin never forgot his East Coast political roots or progressivism, and Franklin Roosevelt's New Deal response to the Depression was never far from the surface of his scripts. In the very first scene of his and Capra's breakthrough hit, *Lady for a Day* (1933), street vendor Apple Annie (May Robson) meets a fellow down-and-out on the street. "Everyone's broke," says the man to Annie, there's no money to be made. "Ah, stop your yapping," she says. "Didn't yer hear the president on the radio?" The film's opening coda about confidence and optimism in the depths of the Depression directly references the contemporary, and novel, fireside chats that FDR embarked upon right at the outset of his administration just as the film found its way into theaters. Annie's remark barely needs repeating in the rest of the movie; *Lady for a Day*'s endorsement of Roosevelt's mandate is made concrete in one apparently innocuous line. But with Riskin, few lines were ever innocuous. Little wonder that the trade paper *Variety* in its review of the picture stated: "While not stinting a full measure of credit to director Frank Capra, it seems as if the spotlight of recognition ought to play rather strongly on scriptwriter Robert Riskin."[25]

Riskin's career thrived on challenges naturally, but one gets the impression that the secret to his success in Hollywood was that the test was not always in the next script but in adapting to, and keeping up with, the Hollywood culture itself. A succession of moves throughout his career prepared him for adaptability and new goals. It also made him accept the contradictory nature of the film community as an exaggerated but necessary form of what it was: a constructed, socially engineered dreamland. In other words, Riskin was a much more original contributor to the era by virtue of his scripts *and* career trajectory than has ever been recognized. But also, significantly, he demonstrates as much as any of his fellow scribes how costly has been the neglect of the screenwriter in Hollywood's history. Riskin was an example of the type of true polymath who held together a variety of dimensional narratives and themes in this era, whose contribution to the routines and craft of the industry should therefore have been far more instrumental in many more retrospectives of Hollywood than has ever been the case.

Employed first as an office manager for a New York shirt-maker, followed by a stint writing comedy shorts, only to begin producing Broadway shows with his brother before scripting a series of Hollywood classics in the 1930s and then heading off to direct operations for the Office of War Information in Europe, Riskin moved seamlessly from one post to another in his life, effortlessly commanding artistic and cultural projects few would dare to take on. Along the way, failures ensued—not least his first and only attempt at directing a picture, *When You're in Love* (1937)—but Riskin drew on wit, humility, and an easy simplicity with stories and characters that masked a multifaceted individual at work, navigating the boundaries of an intricate economic and creative community. It wasn't just that this classic rags-to-riches tale provided an apposite rejoinder to the Hollywood mythmaking process, it was that he revealed a depth and sensibility to the industry that complicates the picture of its often merciless ambition.

Robert Riskin was a Hollywood icon, but one who could never be easily pigeonholed. Riskin was not shy about indulging his whims and playing up to the glamour of the movie colony, and yet he never allowed the glitz, the deceptions, or the temptations of Hollywood—the vices that felled many others—to bury or conceal his vision and ambition. On one level, the assortment of Hollywood starlets and, later, more established actresses that Riskin was photographed with out on the town, the social whirl he was very comfortable with, seemed to confirm the man's reluctance to take seriously the industry's political battles within, as well as outside, the film community. And yet his principled stance in support of the key faction within the emerging Screen Writers Guild, as well as his strenuous efforts to build a filmmaking unit out of the government's wartime propaganda machine, not to mention the significant features of screenplays as singularly and socially articulate as *American Madness* and *Meet John Doe*, signaled how acutely aware Riskin was of the political and cultural responsibility of his position. His story and his contribution to an astonishing cinematic age have, for too long, revolved around Frank Capra's considerable achievements; thus his legacy, such as it stands, has been built on the foundations of his and Capra's original use of film as an art form.

Riskin's career is certainly the story of Hollywood's adolescence within the medium and the industry's manipulation of that artistic form for its own ends, but it is also about the forging of political, social, and cultural links that have kept American cinema, from that day until this, close to the center and reaches of power. Most of all it is the story of a screenwriter who forged his own identity and made his own lasting stamp on filmmaking in the studio era: an individual account not, until now, relayed through the individual.

Therefore, the thesis of this book is stark in its aims. The intention is not to privilege Riskin over Capra in redrawing the history of their relationship in ways that, for instance, Joe Mc-Bride's work has already done. The point of this book is to privilege Robert Riskin, period, and through him to stake a claim for the screenwriting fraternity and their munificent legacy. In one sense, the book sets out to do no more for Riskin than might be expected for any other screenwriter from his generation or after. It aims to set the record as straight as it can be—for accreditation is an ongoing process that has recognized more and more screenwriting contributions, especially since the beginning of the twenty-first century, and still has much to do—and to mention all the films that Riskin worked on. It is also the aim, through Riskin, to articulate the reasons why screenwriters in general, and this screenwriter particularly, were so important to Hollywood's classic era. But Robert Riskin's career is also an irresistible tale, one that wraps up his inestimable contribution to wider cultural and political channels within American society in a narrative that is worthy of his most revered screenplays. It is a tale too integral to the period to ignore any longer.

CHAPTER ONE

THE MIRACLE MAN

Robert Riskin was born on the Lower East Side of New York City on March 30, 1897. He was one of five children born to parents Jakob and Bessie, émigrés from tsarist Russia who had escaped to America so Jakob could avoid conscription into the army. Jakob's aversion to tsarist rule developed out of a way of life that saw him steal horses from the army only to sell the same animals back to the military for a profit. Riskin's father became a committed socialist and was proud of it. His fervent belief in socialist values acted almost as a personal religious creed. Riskin and his two brothers, Everett and Murray, and two sisters, Essie and Rose, all spoke Yiddish, and their upbringing was conventionally Jewish, but this induction into the faith came from their mother rather than Jakob. Bessie insisted on Jakob's, as well as the children's, attendance at temple once they had settled in America. The family moved around in Riskin's early years, from New York to Baltimore, on to Philadelphia, and finally coming to rest in Brooklyn. As strict attention to faith waned due to these upheavals and the children grew wary of the need to assimilate into American society, religious commitment settled on the Friday night family dinner. Bessie always insisted on attendance, even after the children had grown up and left home.[1]

Riskin's mother was a dedicated and fiercely protective parent to all of her children. She held family life to be sacred and kept a close-knit and, importantly, happy household together. Humor was an enduring trait of the Riskin family that served the young Robert well in his early years. It had to. Riskin knew he needed to toughen up very quickly in an environment where the merciless taunts of the Irish and Italian kids in his neighborhood were an everyday occurrence. He and Everett sold the *Saturday Evening Post* to earn extra money for the family—something of an irony given that, later, critics would often compare his work to the paper's wholesome and sentimental short stories. At thirteen, Riskin dropped out of school to be an office boy at a textile company owned by Joe Golden. Golden both spotted Riskin's preoccupation with writing and taught him his first harsh lesson in failing to grab an audience. Realizing that Riskin wrote poetry at lunchtime, Golden offered him a promotion if he would write a love letter cum marriage proposal to Trixie Friganza, a girl in the office whom Golden was too shy to approach himself. Riskin's letter failed to grab the necessary attention and light a fire under the relationship between his boss and Trixie, and he was duly fired. Riskin became a victim of the kind of casual employer-employee relations that could be taken for granted in the burgeoning industrial culture of early-twentieth-century America.

Undaunted and clearly with a resilience born of the Lower East Side, Riskin moved on and eventually found work with the company that would alter the direction of his life. Heidenheim and Levy were well-known New York shirtmakers who swiftly assessed Riskin's potential. As film writer Joseph McBride describes it, "Riskin's bright, glib personality made a quick impression on the partners, who made him their office manager."[2] More important, Heidenheim and Levy had a sideline in movie investment. They pumped money into a company in Florida that made silent comedy shorts for Famous Players–Lasky, later to become Paramount Pictures. The partners showed some of their scripts to Riskin, and in his already well-rounded, ebullient style, he quickly dismissed them out of hand. Although his opinion did not initially seem to count for much, when Famous Players–Lasky rejected the comedies, the partners, it is safe to speculate, panicked, then recalled Riskin's judgment, and in desperation decided to send their opinionated seventeen-year-old office manager down to Jacksonville to run the company.[3]

Riskin did not have even the first idea about what a movie company did or how it operated, let alone the kind of material it might churn out, but he did have some knowledge of theater. From a young age, he had sneaked his way into vaudeville playhouses in the nearby neighborhood of Flatbush to write down

A young Riskin in navy uniform, circa 1917.
(Photograph courtesy of Victoria Riskin.)

jokes and sketches. It was here that Riskin had learned Pitman
shorthand, which allowed him to copy down literally hundreds
of jokes and routines, a skill that continued to serve him well
throughout his career. Long after he became famous, Riskin
would comment self-effacingly that, with a touch of polish, he
was still using the same gags from those early years.[4] His enthusiasm for the stage would seem to be the only explanation for
how and why he hired Broadway comedian Victor Moore and
his wife, Erma Littlefield, to star in a new series of shorts called
the Klever Komedies for Heidenheim and Levy's company.[5] Together they made dozens of one- and two-reel skits—some esti-
mates suggest over a hundred—with Riskin becoming a virtual
one-man band of writer, producer, and director to ensure that
costs were kept as low as possible. None of these films now exist,
but the quality of Riskin's writing and his ability to spot a gag are
apparent in Famous Players' approval of the scripts and in the
profits the movies generated. In 1917, Riskin was twenty years
of age and had $6,000 earned from the Klever Komedies.[6] His
opening dalliance with movies was all too quickly interrupted,
however, when the First World War belatedly caught up with
the United States. Riskin enlisted in the navy, although his status

and participation in the American war effort are sketchy to say the least. He never spoke very much about his experience in the service, and it is unlikely he ever saw any real action.

After the war was over, Riskin found himself back in New York, but without a job. It has been suggested that he took courses at Columbia University, but no records survive.[7] Later accounts of this time have Riskin trying to sell linoleum and then working in a business selling spark plugs.[8] Certainly he had caught the writing bug and was hanging around newsrooms and toying with the idea of becoming a playwright. He was also living a pretty meager existence. He had become part of a down-on-their-luck bunch of artists that included Jimmy Hussey, Edward G. Robinson, and Lee Tracy, all of whom inhabited a garret at the Green Room Club, a poor man's cultural den in the heart of the city at Forty-seventh and Broadway. As Fay Wray describes it in her unpublished memoirs of Riskin, this was a four-story building with dormitories that happened to have a tavern attached to it where the denizens could hang out and swap stories.[9] It is apparent from these living conditions that the money Riskin had saved from the Klever Komedies had dwindled away; the loss of finances was an occurrence that would come back to haunt Riskin at the end of the 1920s. He lived a hand-to-mouth existence at this point, but the burden of poverty, together with the stimulus of social interaction generated by the Green Room Club, produced a creative template for Riskin's later screenwriting that was patented in some of his best rakish, semiautobiographical characters, particularly newsmen such as Stew Smith in *Platinum Blonde* (1931) and Peter Warne in *It Happened One Night* (1934).

Meanwhile, Riskin's brother Everett saw the opportunities that Riskin's prewar operation had afforded, and he pushed for the two of them to set up an office rather grandly presenting themselves as movie producers. Riskin looked to his brother to put all the money into the venture up front. The jobs did not exactly pour in, however. Two principal productions are often cited as about the only things that kept the Riskin brothers afloat at this time. The first was "Facts and Follies," a series of shorts described as "muscle-building as a way of meeting and marrying the prettiest girls."[10] By all accounts, these were third-rate comedy routines dressed up as social commentaries.

With "The Riskinettes," their second foray, Bob and Everett created a puppet series where inflatable characters moved about by having air blown through their rubber bodies.[11] Neither of these creative efforts made much money, nor did they light up the New York movie scene with dazzling reviews or offers of further work. So the brothers turned their attention to Broadway. Riskin was by now writing short sketches with the serious intention of becoming a playwright. But nobody was brave enough to finance his efforts for the stage, and so, with no one else to put on his dramas, Riskin's logical and only next step seemed to be producing them for the stage with his brother.

Ironically, the plays that the brothers initially put on were generally not Bob's work. The first Riskin brothers production to draw any attention at all was not even a comedy, a form that Bob was at least familiar with. In 1925, the *New York Times* reviewed *The Mud Turtle* by Elliot Lester, a tale of agrarian struggle, not a million miles from the subject matter that Riskin would later inject into some of his most famous screenplays. The play lasted fifty-two performances, which was not bad for the cutthroat world of Broadway producing in the twenties, and Bob and Everett now had at least name recognition to build upon. The following year they produced *She Couldn't Say No*, an all-out farce starring Florence Moore and written by B. M. Kaye. Moore played a lawyer trading on false credentials, a character Riskin took some components of for his own later screenplay, *Ann Carver's Profession*, a film with a female lawyer at its epicenter. *She Couldn't Say No* proved to be the Riskins' longest-running show, with seventy-two performances. Further productions followed, including the restoration comedy *A Lady in Love* and, most notable, a revival of a play made famous by Henry Irving, *The Bells*.

Then, in 1927, Bob met up with the playwright and theater impresario John Meehan. The brothers were going to produce one of Meehan's plays, but in the summer of that year, Riskin was struck by an idea as he and Meehan were returning home from one of the most famous heavyweight boxing matches of the era, between Jack Dempsey and Jack Sharkey at Yankee Stadium in the Bronx. On the way home, Riskin spotted a well-known evangelist, Uldine Utley, preaching in a tent near the stadium.[12] Riskin immediately said that he and Meehan ought to write something topical about a fake preacher exploiting people's beliefs. Both had read Sinclair Lewis's latest novel, *Elmer Gantry*, about an ex–football player following pretty much the same path, so the idea was not completely unique. In addition, Utley's more famous contemporary, Aimee Semple McPherson, who is often cited as the inspiration for the character the writers concocted, was already a nationally known figure. Still, it is not clear that Riskin and Meehan meant to give their lead character, Mary MacDonald, the same manner of charismatic elucidation that made McPherson a national phenomenon from the very start. Indeed, the controversy that engulfed McPherson's career was still ahead of her at this point; the country was not yet privy to her salacious private life then beginning to unfold. Only later did the public gasp as she went through three husbands and toyed with the country's moral turpitude.

Nevertheless, the way the idea formed in Riskin's mind—religion and capitalism fused—was an early example of his ability to extract real life from the streets and translate it onto the page. What seemed to interest Riskin was the secular social inclusiveness of evangelism that allowed people from varying backgrounds and circumstances to become absorbed in the rhetoric of causes. From very early on, class and social divisions, those shrouded enigmas of the American experience, seemed to tantalize and torment him, a legacy perhaps of his father's and grandfather's political beliefs. The dilemma of his modest upbringing and later personal wealth was a contradiction that inspired Riskin's best writing yet kept him as wary as he was proud of being a prime exhibit of the American Dream.

With evangelism, Riskin was clearly fascinated by the language of religion and the call to a kind of devotionalism, as well as the ability not only to engross but also to deceive people. Despite the subject matter, however, there is no real evidence to suggest that Riskin's emerging thematic concerns had any personal religious fervor attached to them. He did not practice his Jewish faith in any precise or meaningful way throughout his life. But this should not be confused with a cynical dissatisfaction. Later, when he arrived in Hollywood, Riskin joined the Jewish Country Club in Los Angeles in order to play golf and, more important, to socialize within Jewish society. There were in fact few other choices available in Los Angeles at the time for Jewish people who wanted to associate with one another, and joining was an important signal of Riskin's attitude to his faith. While he had been conscious of the need to assimilate into "mainstream" American society as he was growing up, Riskin always reminded himself, and later his own family, that "being a Jew was a club you couldn't resign from."[13] If Riskin therefore appeared ambivalent about religion much of the time, the faith that was measured by this statement, and that emerged through his characters, should indicate that belief in some fashion remained strong and credible throughout his lifetime. The preacher-of-the-street story line in his and Meehan's drama was but one example that helped to create a cross-fertilization of social classes within Riskin's tales, and together with a concern for belief and ideals, specifically American ideals, this theme set up a cognitive layout for his writing that would be important to him time and again.

Riskin was so taken with the ideas that had been inspired by seeing Uldine Utley that he and his new partner decided to put aside Meehan's present work and concentrate on writing their drama. Meehan roped in an experienced producer-director, George Abbott, to polish some of the dialogue, and by December 1927 a new play had duly arrived on Broadway with Riskin as cowriter: *Bless You, Sister*. The drama, starring Alice Brady as Mary, was the tale of a minister's daughter who becomes so disenchanted with religion following the death of her father, who is little missed by his congregation, that she turns to the dishonorable racket of saving souls on the street for money. The *New York Times* review of the play spoke significantly of religion being treated as any other commodity. It also made reference to both *Elmer Gantry* and *Bride of the Lamb*, two stories that the review correctly spotted as having been on Meehan's and Riskin's minds. The review in the *Times* concluded with the somewhat backhanded compliment that the play was good but might have been great. Indeed, *Bless You, Sister*, while enthusiastically endorsed by most audiences, found a generally mixed reception among critics, who thought the satire amusing but the final-act conversion and romantic finale a little strained. Riskin's later downbeat assessment of the play testified that he took such comments to heart. One positive aspect that recurred in the reviews, however,

Riskin as an aspiring
dramatist in New York,
1920s. (Photograph
courtesy of Victoria Riskin.)

was the praise reserved for the performance of Alice Brady in the
lead role, a significant sign that Riskin's construction of female
protagonists was to become a major force in his stories.[14]

Despite the initial audience enthusiasm, *Bless You, Sister* lasted only twenty-four performances. But the play demonstrated
not only Riskin's growing obsession with people's positions in
society, their calling in life and attraction to causes, but also his
penchant for putting ordinary folk in extraordinary situations—
two narrative and ideological preoccupations that would emerge
perpetually in his later screenplays.

As with a number of parts of Riskin's early life, the period from 1927 until he turned up in Hollywood in late 1930 is
somewhat vague. Pat McGilligan's assessment of this moment
in Riskin's career asserts that it was clearly a time when, flush
with confidence over having a coauthored piece on Broadway,

Riskin devoted a great deal more time to his writing. It is certainly known that he teamed up with fellow writer Edith Fitzgerald in this era in order to assemble more material for the stage. She was Riskin's companion over a three-year period, and an intense working and romantic relationship developed as a result, though she never became his wife, as was often reported in the press at the time and later.[15]

Riskin and Fitzgerald's first effort at writing for the stage never made it into a theater, but their second proved to be a major breakthrough. *Many a Slip* had Riskin writing and coproducing with Everett and Lew Cantor, and the play marked his directorial debut with a no-holds-barred comedy starring the major Broadway actress Sylvia Sidney, who at twenty was already well on her way to becoming a Hollywood star. The trademark Riskin characters and plot undulations were now emerging into view. Here, a newspaperman called Jerry, living in a Greenwich apartment, gets tricked into marriage: his girlfriend Patsy's mother concocts a phantom pregnancy in order to get him to commit to the one thing he has always sworn against. The show opened at the Little Theatre in New York on February 3, 1930, and ran for fifty-six performances. It is hardly a stretch to conclude that Jerry and Patsy had something of Bob and Edith about them, and certainly Jerry's attitude to marriage was an outlook Riskin adhered to for a long time. That he managed to claim some delicate aspect of his personal life and turn it into a witty diatribe about relationships and modern life confirmed a detached observational style inherent in Riskin's writing that would serve him well. His willingness to parody his own story additionally created a personal edge to his characters that was a cut above most of Riskin's other dramatist contemporaries. Patsy and Jerry were thus an early incarnation of successive fictional couples whose banter and slapstick became shorthand for their romantic allure, never more so than in the later characters of Peter Warne and Ellie Andrews in *It Happened One Night*. Although once again, as with *Bless You, Sister, Many a Slip* did not receive universal acclaim, the dialogue and some of the play's funniest scenes clearly made an impression with critics, and eventually it was proclaimed one of the top plays of the 1929–30 season.[16] Riskin and Fitzgerald added at least one more major credit to their résumés in 1930, when fellow

Lower East Sider Eddie Cantor, who was about to embark on a successful radio career as well as a career in the movies, starred in their play *Her Delicate Condition*.

With these achievements under his belt, Riskin could finally claim a name in Broadway theater. Whether he really saw Hollywood as the next port of call is uncertain, however. Two things helped to convince him: One was the Wall Street crash and its impact on his finances. The second was that Hollywood came calling for him even before he had time to pack his bags and head west.

First Impressions at Columbia

Riskin's attitude to money was a contradictory force within his life. Clever, witty, and often shrewd in so many of his dealings, he was nevertheless adventurous with money, as the loss of his profits from the Klever Komedies testifies to. Yes, there was much generosity with friends and associates and always an innate willingness to help those around him who were in difficulty, but Riskin also played cards, went to the racetrack, and most damaging of all in 1929, dabbled with investments on the stock market. When the Wall Street crash occurred in October, Riskin lost a lot of money but was also farsighted enough to realize that the economic downturn would result in many Broadway stages falling dark for quite a period of time. More minor plays, like the ones he and his brother had until now put on, were unlikely to survive their first week in the new financial climate. Hollywood was therefore a way to retrieve cash, and thankfully for Riskin, motion pictures already had an idea of what to do with his material.

The studios had recently begun a long trawl through the Broadway scribes in their search for talent and stories that could fill the demand for that revolutionary new trend that was clearly here to stay: talking motion pictures. According to McGilligan, the other major group that descended on Hollywood at this time, journalists, fared much better than playwrights, who, initially at least, considered movies to be beneath them. Hacks—who were used to deadlines, to the snappy concision that journalistic styles brought—fit into the studio mentality very quickly. Playwrights either hurried on back to New York in the early days of sound, confident that the future of drama still lay on Broadway, or grumbled their way through assignments, seeking the pastoral pleasures of polo, bars, and the beach in between.[17]

Riskin's advantage was that he traversed both these camps, for he had an attraction to journalism as much as he felt a calling to drama. Richard Corliss compares Riskin's later style and outlook in movies to those of his fellow "playwright-journalist" Ben Hecht. Corliss identifies in both an ability to manufacture degeneration in some of their principal characters, delivered with acerbic, often colloquial venom.[18] Both sensed the way that quick-fire vernacular language could aid narrative construction while being lyrical and poetic as well as coarse and humorous, all in the same moment. Screenplays didn't have to read like Chekhov, thought Riskin and Hecht, but they shouldn't face the strain of flat, overly pronounced dialogue either. The compositional affinity of the two surely helps to explain how their paths crossed a number of years later, during World War II, when they worked indirectly with each other on government propaganda films. Their commitment to this cause was easy to surmise, for both had climbed out of humble origins and knew the value of liberty for what it had brought them to. Like Riskin's, Hecht's parents emigrated from Russia and strove to build a new life in New York, and from these luckless origins, both Riskin and Hecht went on to transform their lives in the mythological likeness of the American Dream. Hecht, for his part, became an immediate success in Hollywood with his first script, the gangster epic *Underworld* (1927), directed by Josef von Sternberg.

Riskin did not arrive in Hollywood to write a first script until three years after Hecht's spectacular first success, but he sold his first play adapted to script to the studios before he even got to California. Riskin had sent *Many a Slip* to the Warner Brothers office in New York and received an invitation to turn up there and conduct negotiations for selling the play as a screen story. Warner offered Riskin $10,000 on the spot, more money than he had ever known on Broadway. The studio's attorney, pressing him for a quick sale, presumably because he knew Riskin needed the money, said that was the offer and no more. Riskin got up, headed for the elevator, and pressed the button to go down and leave the building. As the elevator doors opened, the attorney ran out of his office; Riskin was offered $30,000 for the play. He accepted.[19] *Many a Slip* was bought by Warner Brothers in 1930, was turned into *Illicit* by the studio's contracted scribe Harvey Thew, and was directed by Archie Mayo, a Warner perennial throughout the decade. Starring Barbara Stanwyck, the picture was released in 1931. Columbia Pictures, meanwhile, purchased *Bless You, Sister*. With a script by Jo Swerling, it was transformed into another vehicle for Stanwyck, also in 1931, called *The Miracle Woman*. The film was to be directed by Frank Capra.[20] Riskin actually turned down an offer to work on his adapted stage play almost as soon as he arrived in Los Angeles, but little did he know that his rejection was about to change the course of his movie-writing career.

By mid-1930, Riskin had arrived in Hollywood. He, Edith Fitzgerald, and Everett had all headed for California with the promise of jobs at Columbia. While Everett eventually settled down to become a longstanding and successful staff producer, and Bob immediately began scriptwriting, Edith parted company with the Riskin boys. Maybe she thought, if marriage was not an option for her and Bob, like Patsy and Jerry in their breakthrough play, what was the point of continuing the romance? For whatever reason, the relationship came to an end there. Fitzgerald hung around Hollywood for quite a few years, making three reasonably successful outings as a scenarist: for Greta Garbo in *Inspiration* (1930) and *The Painted Veil* (1934), and for *Riptide* (1934) starring Norma Shearer. Fitzgerald married the tennis star Elmer Griffin and actually became California women's tennis champion herself in 1934, but she ended up back in New York as a playwright, though not before making a final intrusion into Riskin's life some while later.

Riskin arrived at Columbia with a considerable reputation for his plays, though he and Everett had made hardly any money on Broadway in their few years producing and writing and had only a handful of really decent reviews to their names. Riskin's name, however, had already become synonymous on the West Coast with the "boy prodigy" moniker, and as Hollywood was a young person's game, so the feeling went that he ought to be their type of writer.[21] In retrospect, it was fortunate that Riskin's talent, which might have lain dormant at some studios, was nurtured in good surroundings at Columbia. The studio was the perfect stopping-off point for the brothers; its small-time, parsimonious operation, with its production-line technique of running off movies to order, was the symbiotic accompaniment to their Broadway existence. Certainly Riskin never fell into the trough of self-flagellation that afflicted writers at other studios. The 1930s were probably the peak of guilt and paranoia among screenwriters, many of whom felt their lives—and talent—were wasting away on such trivialities as movies.[22] Riskin, however, never succumbed to these artistic afflictions and fit neatly into a studio collective where writers had an identity. "Let the writer talk" became Harry Cohn's refrain at story conferences, and Columbia, as a result, it is not too ambitious to suggest, became the Brill Building of studio screenwriting in the thirties.[23] From Riskin to Swerling and Sidney Buchman, on through Hecht, Virginia Van Upp, and Donald Ogden Stewart, there was a respect for these talents and their many successes, even if Cohn's insistence on making a deal, not to mention his volatile temperament, meant that financial reward and artistic credit for their efforts were not always the first things on the studio's agenda.

From the very beginning, it also helped that Riskin's sense of sleek, tight dialogue was a perfect match for the emerging sound era and the need to tell stories with an economy of effort. He had to learn this lesson quickly, however: the very first script that Riskin turned out for Columbia ran to two hundred pages, not because it was long-winded but simply because Riskin had thrown "everything, including the kitchen sink" into it, as he later confided. Harry Cohn had a rule that scripts should never be more than ninety pages long, and producer Bennie Zeidman, who was looking after Riskin, got fired.[24] It was a harsh introduction into Hollywood's structured world, and though he felt shocked at the punishment for Zeidman, Riskin didn't stop offering his views, telling it straight to directors, studio heads, or whoever else would listen. He saw no point in doing otherwise, for not saying anything, making no impression, as far as Riskin could make out, would offer the same result: the studio would show you the door. Right away, during one of his first story meetings at the studio, Riskin got to use this tactic of no-nonsense talk and inadvertently shaped the course of his life.

At what might now be described as an almost mythically predestined screen conference, Riskin arrived late one day to hear a conversation about a movie well into preproduction. In a room full of other freshman scenarists, he asked the person next to him who the guy at the front was telling the story . . . badly! "That's Capra," came the reply to an obviously unimpressed Riskin. It was then that he began to notice the plot of the film, and it slowly dawned on him that this was *Bless You, Sister*. When Capra finished, Harry Cohn immediately pressed Riskin, whom he introduced quite deliberately as the writer, for suggestions.

The denunciation of his own work that followed was either a very calculated gamble by Riskin to elicit attention or a brutally honest assessment of his early writing and a sharp reminder of those reviews that had dwelt on the play's shortcomings. He made the point that the drama had, to all intents and purposes, been a flop and asked why anyone would want to turn a flop play into what was likely to be a flop film. "I wrote that play," he said. "My brother and I were stupid enough to produce it on Broadway. It cost us almost every cent we had. If you intend to make a picture of it, it proves only one thing: You're even more stupid than we were."[25] Once the shock of the writer's tearing up his own work wore off, it became apparent to all in the room that Capra—the star director, at least on Columbia's lot—was getting increasingly annoyed with Riskin, who continued his diatribe by suggesting that the play's concern with religion had been just too heavy a topic, and if Broadway audiences found it difficult to stomach, then movie audiences were sure to feel the same. When the confrontation was over, Capra and Cohn went ahead and made the picture. Jo Swerling—who was also in the room that fateful day—wrote it, and Riskin maintained his brave, many thought foolish, stance of having nothing to do with it whatsoever.

Even as early as 1931, Frank Capra was in such a strong position as a director at Columbia that he had the weight to carry forward projects like *The Miracle Woman*. Since joining the studio in 1928, he had already directed thirteen features for Harry Cohn, seven of those in his first year. In Charles Maland's assessment of the director's career, Capra's rise from the late twenties is linked with the economic fall from grace experienced throughout America from that time until well into the thirties. The popularity of a host of Capra's movies derived from the fact that, as Maland argues, the films "provided audiences with psychic escapes from their pressing burdens."[26] With comedies like *Ladies of Leisure* (1930), detective stories such as *The Donovan Affair* (1929), and especially action-adventures like *Flight* (1929) and *Dirigible* (1931), Capra gripped audiences with his fast-paced, realistic, and modern stories. In fact, because of its newly crowned star director, Columbia as a studio made the same dramatic leap in status during the early thirties as it moved, in Ethan Mordden's words, from "minor to major player."[27] At its helm, Cohn maintained independence and managed to keep the studio compact. Cutting costs was a state of mind ingrained in all the staff on the Columbia back lot in Gower Gulch. Even Capra referred to the studio as a "riffraff of a place," but he secretly knew the discipline was good for him; the demand to bring pictures in on budget lit the twin sparks of creativity and originality.

It was virtually Capra alone, between 1928 and 1931, who created the platform for the studio to rise through the rankings, and Columbia's and Capra's successes as major players were thus inextricably linked between 1931 and 1935. The only thing preventing the director from acquiring the title of absolute auteur in this second period of his career at the studio was to be the writing of Robert Riskin. For Mordden, Riskin's position in the Capra firmament was a key facet because, unlike contemporaries such as von Sternberg and Ford, for whom "iconography of character" was all, Capra knew that plot and dialogue mattered in his movies.[28] Maland, on the other hand, perceives the director as searching during the early thirties for a "voice" in his work, which subsequently found its truest expression, he argues, only in Capra's most famous pictures, such as *Mr. Smith Goes to Washington* and *It's a Wonderful Life*—ironically, two films in which Riskin had no input and yet ones that, understandably, remain linked with the writer.[29]

Long before these two films came along, however, Capra fine-tuned his style in a set of early-thirties melodramas, sometimes but by no means always comedic, that were reeled off seemingly at will for Columbia. These were presented to an increasingly captivated audience having to come to terms with the worst effects of the Depression. It seems obvious in retrospect to link Capra with economic despondency and the political climate of the time. Andrew Bergman, in his influential study, describes the emergence of what became known as the "screwball" comedy film as an important concealment of the most divisive effects of the financial collapse. And the man he assigns as the progenitor of this screwball style and its later, more socially conscious, form is Frank Capra.[30]

What is interesting, however, is that until Capra made *The Miracle Woman*, the real constant in his filmmaking was the visual style and sophistication he brought to the screen, rather more than content and certainly more than any social construction in his stories. *Submarine* and *Dirigible* were action films that wowed audiences with their audacious sequences in the air and underwater, but their topics were very different from the kinds that Capra would tackle after he teamed up with Riskin. Once in harness with the writer, Capra discovered something else that went hand in hand with his reflexive sense of pace and timing, something that came from Riskin's outlook and persuasion. It may now be the easiest and most obvious observation to make, but after *The Miracle Woman*, Capra's films did begin to say something about contemporary American life (even in the fantasy-adventures *The Bitter Tea of General Yen* and *Lost Horizon*). But, as Ray Carney's illuminating theory about Capra tries to display, the early-thirties movies also offered something more illusory and philosophical, something that captured the essence of people's hopes and dreams.[31]

Platinum Blonde (1931), *American Madness* (1932), *It Happened One Night* (1934), and *Broadway Bill* (1934) all shaped the emergent Capra philosophy on film, and all increasingly divested themselves of the concerns and constraints that were being played out in Depression-riddled America, whether those concerns were to do with money, power, authority, or trust. And the films were all produced with the writing and creative input of Riskin. Indeed, from 1931 until *Mr. Smith Goes to Washington* in 1939, Capra made only two films without Riskin's brilliant, individual, and intuitive contribution: the social melodrama *Forbidden* (1932), starring Barbara Stanwyck and Adolphe Menjou, which was written by the director himself and Jo Swerling, and *The Bitter Tea of General Yen* (1933), from a screenplay by Edward Paramore, again with Stanwyck in the leading role.

So the emphasis in Capra's work on plot and dialogue identified by Mordden, together with his search for a "voice" in Maland's assessment, did metamorphose into something like the director's classic, formative style much earlier in the relationship than previously acknowledged. And Riskin's contributory impact on the choice of material did have an immediate effect, as is shown by a comparative analysis of *The Miracle Woman* and the follow-up *Platinum Blonde*. Until 1931, each picture Capra made for Columbia had earned a little more money than the last, and each had enhanced the director's reputation in Hollywood for quality filmmaking on a shoestring budget. From the comedic drama of *Ladies of Leisure* to the action-adventure of *Dirigible*, Capra had largely struck gold. In 1931, by these already high standards, *The Miracle Woman* was his first real failure, and Riskin's self-deprecating judgment of the project seemed to be vindicated.

It wasn't that the picture was bad, just that its message was laid too thickly across the narrative. If anything, Capra's film carried over too much weight and anxiety from Meehan and Riskin's play. From the very beginning of production, the film troubled Columbia's front office, particularly Cohn's partner, Joe Brandt. The studio sent the script to various clergy, and as a result, one or two of what were judged snide religious quips were omitted from the final cut.[32] But, to his credit, Harry Cohn knew where the heart of the film's message lay, and protests about the lead character's key line—"Religion's like everything else; it's no good if you give it away"—went unheeded; the line stayed in the picture. Religion went hand in hand with consumerism, the film opined somewhat controversially, because consumerism had accumulated its own devotees. Thus material accumulation, *The*

Miracle Woman daringly suggested, had become the new religion of twentieth-century America.

"The film is about the psychology of the masses, about the gray mob that follows an opinion leader," writes Vito Zagarrio of Capra's adaptation, taking up this theme about the selling of mass belief. It is a significant statement, for Zagarrio's description could apply to a number of Capra-Riskin films further down the line, not least their last true collaboration a decade later, *Meet John Doe*. The trouble was that the masses would find "no hope and no utopia" in *The Miracle Woman*'s finale, only a heroine looking to purge her evil incarnation.[33] This was an abrupt lesson for a country that had altered in a very short space of time. The America of 1931, when the film was released, was not the America of 1927, when the play was written and first performed. In a nation of opulence, exploitative evangelist Mary MacDonald of *Bless You, Sister* came across as nothing more than an impostor with a cause to sell who ultimately discovers the folly of her "operation." In the desperate times of the early thirties, Florence Fallon of *The Miracle Woman* (why an alliterative but different name was used is not clear), even with her redemptive rejection, in the conclusion, of all that she had done in conning people out of their money, appeared to question the foundations of honesty, trust, and faith at the very crossroads of social interaction.

Many years later, Capra interpreted his own conversion to the picture as similarly dramatic: he saw *The Miracle Woman*'s moralistic statement as a kind of revelatory vision that offset man's simpler pleasures and desires with the promise of spiritual completion.[34] He admitted quite readily, however, that his introduction of a new character to the film, the greedy, unscrupulous Hornsby (Sam Hardy), diluted the power of Fallon's fall and reconversion. Hornsby's death in a road accident, which prompts Fallon's awakening from her sideshow, is a convenient contrivance rather than a sincere shock of guilt on her part, the latter being the reaction that Depression audiences perhaps hoped for. As a result, the film failed to move cinemagoers and critics alike, but it did signal the characteristic nuances, even one screenplay removed, that Riskin's ideas would impart to Capra's direction.

Whether Riskin's principled stance and accurate premonition

of the film's fate prompted Capra to call for him to work on his next project is not known. More likely, Swerling, who had also been impressed by Riskin's honesty, pushed Capra and Cohn to allow Riskin to work with *him* and the director. Swerling and Riskin had struck up an immediate friendship at the studio. Swerling, too, had tried his hand at writing plays and had been a journalist as well as a comic-strip artist before making the journey to Hollywood. His family, too, were Russian émigrés. Swerling had an easygoing affinity with writers and directors that made him popular and respected, and his style, humor, and enjoyment of life were entirely consistent with Riskin's outlook.[35]

While Riskin and Swerling were becoming acquainted, Capra was already in the process of making his next picture, *Forbidden*, with Stanwyck, Menjou, and Ralph Bellamy, as well as another movie at virtually the same time. They premiered barely three months apart, partly due to contractual disputes involving Capra's leading lady and Cohn. Capra had started *Forbidden*, but when Stanwyck held out for better pay in her battle with the studio chief, and thus held up production, he laid it aside for *The Gilded Cage* starring Jean Harlow. This was the film's title until its final trade review in early October 1931, when it became *Platinum Blonde*.[36]

Capra and Swerling had story credit for *Forbidden*—an original screenplay—while a whole mixture of people had gone to work on *Platinum Blonde*. Capra wasn't even penciled in as the original director of the movie, but thanks to studio politics and a little luck, the Capra-Riskin liaison was about to be born. While the story for *Platinum Blonde* was credited to Harry Chandlee and Douglas Churchill and the adaptation was by Jo Swerling, credit for dialogue, for the first time on a Frank Capra picture, went to Robert Riskin.

Entering the Gilded Cage

Platinum Blonde is "a far less polished film," in Ray Carney's view, than some of the movies that Capra was about to undertake. Carney suggests a hasty and rather contrived series of events in the plot that seems sloppy and tentative in comparison to the tightly wrought stories that Capra and Riskin subsequently brought to the screen.[37] Soundman Edward Bernds, who worked on the picture, shares the feeling that the story was not exactly unfamiliar in Columbia's roster. "Robert Riskin's structure of scenes and his sharp dialogue, however, were new," writes Bernds, significantly emphasizing Riskin's contribution over Swerling's. He goes on to pinpoint how Riskin managed to convey leading man Robert Williams's character perfectly on screen, even claiming that this set the platform for Columbia's advance into romantic screwball comedy as the thirties developed.[38]

The picture is often compared to *The Front Page* in its outlook and swiftly executed narrative drive. Originally appearing as a stage play by Charles MacArthur and Ben Hecht—who, in the three years since his arrival in Hollywood, had become the hugely influential author of not only *Underworld* but also *Scarface*—the first film adaptation of *The Front Page* was also produced by Columbia, directed by Lewis Milestone.[39] It appeared in 1931, the same year as *Platinum Blonde*, and Capra admitted later that he and Swerling had effectively swiped one of the stories featured in the stage play, now picture.[40]

Within Milestone's film, MacArthur and Hecht dealt with the real concerns of racism, politics, and city corruption that they perceived as endemic to their setting, Chicago. The urbanity of the piece was what Swerling and Riskin took from the stage play and laid onto Capra's film. *Platinum Blonde*'s influence thus derived from, but was not interested in communicating explicitly, the ideas of reciprocity and institutional machine authority. The "little man from the small town" was the typically convenient phrase always bandied about as a description of Riskin's work. In fact, far more of his screenplays operated within urban environments than rural backwaters, and the rural idyll, whenever it appears, say in *Mr. Deeds Goes to Town* or *Meet John Doe*, is rarely on screen for very long.[41] In addition, Riskin's interests always extended beyond his central character, innocent, naïve, and agrarian or otherwise, to further players who epitomized the modern metropolitan condition: ambitious, career-oriented, time-consumed people looking for inspiration and/or answers to their lives.

Platinum Blonde revealed these traits right from the beginning of the partnership, but it also managed to be a neat little character piece of all the individuals concerned. Capra, Swerling, and Riskin embodied the characters in the movie, whose concerns and tribulations almost mirror the director's and writers' own experiences. The crack news reporter in the film, Stew Smith (Robert Williams), for instance, is trying to become a playwright, just as Riskin and Swerling were once striving to do, but he can't decide between the wilds of Siberia and the sophistication of Madrid for the setting and theme of his play. Finally he takes some good advice and begins to write about experiences close at hand, in contemporary American society. The events in the play Smith writes are, in effect, his experiences at what Riskin would call being a "Cinderella man." He marries a rich socialite, Anne Schuyler, played by Harlow, but discovers her privileged world is not for him. Ultimately he confesses his love for down-at-heel newspaper gal Gallagher (Loretta Young), who has, of course, always been hopelessly besotted with him. The clever, modern dialogue—especially the long explanation about "puttering" that is inserted into a scene between Smith and the Schuylers' butler, Smythe—the witty social commentary, the romantic optimism of the film, and in particular the hero's questioning of ideals and values within his life: each element, every little attitude and idea, had an interchangeable component of Capra, Swerling, and Riskin about it. All three, for example, felt uneasy about the segmentation of the classes and the dos and don'ts of society's elite. Riskin's dialogue divulged much of the film's interest in social standing and graces by holding a light to the aspirations and thoughts of the characters. Smith wakes up from a Schuyler society party soon after his marriage to Anne only to be confronted by his new valet, Dawson (Claud Allister). "Was I very drunk? I must have been to hire you," he jests, throwing the notion of somebody's being there to help put his pants on into sharp relief. In the film's finale, Anne's father, Michael Schuyler (Donald Dillaway), visits Stew at his flat after he has left Anne and escaped the "gilded cage." "Do you know why I am here?" inquires Schuyler senior. "No, not unless some of the silverware is missing," retorts Stew. One-liners of this quality show both Riskin's capabilities as a writer and his cynicism toward positions of class. He had an innate ability to summarize social and cultural attitudes while making the audience laugh out loud. This was the great difference between *Platinum Blonde*'s lively social repartee and *The Miracle Woman*'s almost maudlin, confessional dialogue. What Capra and Swerling had in terms of story and character, Riskin built upon with various shades of comedic enlightenment.

In addition, Riskin helped Capra and Swerling to assemble Jean Harlow's enduring screen persona in this movie, even if it wasn't quite as sassy and overtly sexual as some of her later roles would turn out to be. The late alteration of the title to *Platinum Blonde* from *The Gilded Cage* was, however, an important signal of this creation for Harlow's brief career. As Richard Maltby observes, the very title of the picture was a headline phrase, already passing into the vernacular language of the time, that had advertised Harlow's first major screen appearance, in Howard Hughes's *Hell's Angels* the previous year.[42] Riskin's writing for Harlow's character steered the title phrase into a whole new set of interpretations, not all of them virtuous, and very nearly defined the actress's tragically short career in movies. Anne is vacuous and yet desperate. She exists for the wealth that she inherits and yet craves feeling and experience. To desire to live life beyond the "gilded cage" and yet be too scared to leave its confines was a heady mix of social engineering and characterization that Riskin was building toward even this early in his screenwriting career. *Platinum Blonde* is, in essence, a preview of the character types and gender constructions he was to pursue for the remainder of his career.

Carney asserts, in respect of this point, that Smith's final clinch with Gallagher, rejecting the provocative and alluring gaze of Anne, is Capra tempting his audience with the mysterious addictions of imagination and desire.[43] But though the camera is Capra's in this game of spectacle, the mind at play is Riskin's. He doesn't allow a neat romantic summation between Stew and Gallagher but plays out their betrothal in the context of Stew's play and the reactions of the characters in the final act. Says Smith, bringing Gallagher close to him, "He goes to the little O'Brien gal and he says to her—in some pretty words of some kind—something that you can write—he'll say—'Darling, I'm sorry. I've been a fool all my life. I've always loved you, only I didn't sense enough to see it. As quick as I can get a divorce from my wife, I want you to marry me.' Then he'll kiss her or something."

Platinum Blonde confirmed that Riskin's romantic imagination could make a love story come alive with trysts like this, but the picture also said something about the nature of aspiring professionals, such as reporters, that came to fixate both Capra and Riskin in their films. Robert Williams's portrayal of Smith is filled with the laconic timing that only a star of vaudeville, which the young sensation had been, could bring to the part. "Which country is this library in?" he asks Anne when first making his way through the labyrinthine Schuyler mansion. Williams was the type of actor, joined to the type of role, that Riskin found easy to write: wisecracking, fiery, unsure how to veer between hard-boiled and sentimental. Williams knew exactly how to deliver a line that witty. Riskin surely would have written more for the star but for Williams's untimely death following an emergency operation only days after the film's premiere.

The picture's close companion of the time, *Forbidden*, had Barbara Stanwyck also playing an ace reporter, but this time caught up in an affair with a politician. Reporters and politicians became staples of Capra's stories, both with and without Riskin. Again, one might surmise that, in these worlds at least, the reporter could act as the intellectual artisan, the middlebrow consumer and arbiter of taste, money, and power between the well-to-do and the down-at-heel. But there is a fundamental difference between the reporters in the two pictures that emanates from Riskin's creative consciousness; we know it is his doing because he repeats the feat time and again in later films. The difference is that, in *Forbidden*, Stanwyck's character, Lulu Smith, can find no hope or reconciliation in a double life trapped with two men she cannot love or save. In *Platinum Blonde*, however, Riskin allows Stew's double life with Anne the socialite and Gallagher the homespun girl to offset material pleasure with philosophical enlightenment. As Carney suggests, the end of the film, in which Stew has sacrificed all of his worldly goods, his clothes, and even his space—adopting a cramped studio apartment when once he

roamed the halls of the Schuyler mansion—is done for the benefit of an "enriched consciousness." Stew's imagination takes over
as he tries to write that play, the one that is now about his life and
experiences, his worldly desires and feelings. He is becoming,
asserts Carney, no longer the heir to the Schuyler fortune with
Anne, or a mere reporter as he once was, but a playwright.[44]

As Leland Poague has claimed, there are, in the collaborative
partnership of Capra and Riskin, constant themes of reinvention
and of characters recreating their lives with their own words
and deeds, and no more so than in the case of Stew Smith.[45] The
films that followed *Platinum Blonde*, particularly *It Happened One
Night*, *Mr. Deeds Goes to Town*, and *Meet John Doe*, all feature hard-
bitten reporters who discover the redemptive practices of rewriting their histories and trying to carve out different lives for themselves. The inclination to associate such concerns with Capra
seems natural; with Riskin, overwhelming. His lifestyle and outlook went through drastic alterations during the early thirties.
From struggling for a pittance on Broadway with the threat of
financial ruin hanging over him after the crash, Riskin was soon
earning $1,500 a week in Hollywood as a contracted screenwriter.
His characters took on a moral fortitude that seemed to question
the location and desire of money, love, happiness, and the spiritual. This change in Riskin's circumstances partly explains his
decision to get involved with union activity in 1933. He helped
to found the guild for screenwriters that, although initially loyal
to producers' motives in Hollywood, became more progressively
liberal after it formally broke away from the playwrights in 1936.
Riskin was set to become one of the star union men of the era and
a major spokesperson for the Screen Writers Guild, but he was
also far and away one of the highest-paid screenwriters working
in the industry at the time. The contradiction never left him. The
need to feed one's conscience with social responsibility crept into
the minds of his fictional protagonists almost unconsciously, and
they were nearly always left with undesirable and/or morally
determined choices about their lives and futures.

Whether these turbulent machinations in his mind really contributed to Riskin's being the social conscience at the heart of
Capra's movies after *Platinum Blonde* is less of an issue at this

time than whether he was actually persuading Capra to *think* about the darker and less appetizing aspects of life, especially in the Depression. *The Miracle Woman* certainly suggests this, although it is interesting to note, for example, that Capra was later far less enamored of *Forbidden*—a film Riskin was not involved with—than some of his other early-thirties films. Yet on reflection, and even allowing for characters that seemed more dour and burdened by what life had dealt them than Riskin's, this too was a powerfully constructed melodrama about weight and responsibility in society. Though Jo Swerling's script has often been described as wordy, the conclusion to the film, in which Lulu Smith shoots her domineering and violent husband, Al (Ralph Bellamy), and then walks away from her dying lover, Bob Grover (Adolphe Menjou), is still a forceful and emotive finale.[46] Lulu tears up the letter from Bob that would have given her financial security, and then she dissolves into the masses on a depressing, rain-sodden street, an eerie visual coda for the mood of the times.

Capra's reaction against *Forbidden* was, however, as much tied up in his obsession with Barbara Stanwyck as it was in the film's paling against *Platinum Blonde*'s effusive story line. Joseph McBride describes the period on set as a time when Stanwyck finally rejected Capra's romantic advances and stayed with her none-too-reliable husband, Frank Fay. But McBride also remarks that Capra somewhat downplayed *Platinum Blonde*'s considerable financial success and cinematic accomplishments and, hence, the artistic role of Riskin.[47] In truth, Capra probably looked on both films as a singular period of reflection and reassessment tied up in his romantic involvement with Stanwyck. Riskin's role was not so prominent as dialoguer that any overall shared credit for the picture would come his way in any event. Capra's disappointment and exhaustion after a dual-film working schedule showed in his decision to leave for Europe soon after *Forbidden* was completed, to take time to think and recuperate. Therefore he no doubt lost sight, retrospectively, of the importance that *Platinum Blonde* played in establishing a rapport between him and Riskin: a rapport that engaged his astute visual composition with the writer's lean, articulate dialogue. When Capra returned, however, the first film he took on developed that burgeoning re-lationship with Columbia's newest aspiring writer and demon-strated that Capra would no longer be a stranger to topical social issues. With an original screenplay by Riskin initially entitled *Faith*, the two were about to achieve their first hit together with the film *American Madness*.

CHAPTER TWO

THE BIG TIMER

By 1932, Riskin had already begun to establish himself as a key figure in Hollywood screenwriting. He had immediately demonstrated his credentials as a writer of smart dialogue and witty rejoinders on Frank Capra's *Platinum Blonde* in 1931, and in the course of the following year, Columbia head Harry Cohn set Riskin to work on a whole series of projects. The very first screenwriting job he undertook after the Capra film immediately drew attention to his work. In Jerry Hoffman's adaptation of the Augustus Thomas play *Arizona* (1931), Riskin modernized the dialogue and gave a more contemporary feel to the tale of a girl who is discarded by her West Point cadet sweetheart, only to marry his superior officer for spite and then begin to fall in love with the older man. In an effort not to confuse the picture with a Western, the studio released it under the title *Men Are Like That*. The film's first trade reviews, as well as a longer appreciation in the *Los Angeles Examiner*, praised former silent star Forrest Stanley in the lead role and even remarked on the impression made by an up-and-coming young actor named John Wayne.

But the *Los Angeles Examiner* review reserved its highest praise for Laura La Plante as the female lead. Once again, just as reviews of his Broadway dramas had, the comments served notice of Riskin's ability to construct women's roles with depth and sensitivity, allied to punchy, emotional dialogue.[1] The resilient female protagonist appears again and again in these early narratives, spurred on by an idiomatic portrayal of early-thirties society as well as the influence of Columbia's leading female scribes. Riskin quickly prospered in the studio's budget-restricted and time-constrained atmosphere, contributing some words to

William Beaudine's *Men in Her Life* (also 1931), from a Warner Fabian story, and then being credited as dialoguer on Beaudine's *Three Wise Girls* (1932), the script having been adapted by one of those female Columbia writers, Agnes Johnson. These two writing slots in particular were valuable experiences, for they paired Riskin with one of Hollywood's most legendary and prolific early directors and taught him quickly how to shape dialogue on screen without wasting words. Having struck up a friendship, Riskin and Jo Swerling wrote *Shopworn* (1932) for director Nick Grinde, from a story by Sarah Mason. Riskin went on to contribute words to Grinde's *Vanity Street* (also 1932). The output of Columbia, and the swift turnover of its projects, is brought into sharp focus by the fact that, still in 1932, Riskin followed all this with the script for *Night Club Lady* for stock Columbia director Irving Cummings and penned *The Big Timer* with Dorothy Howell for Edward Buzzell, as well as the film *Virtue* for the same director.[2]

Night Club Lady came from a Thatcher Colt story about a police commissioner (Adolphe Menjou) desperately trying to protect a nightclub owner (Mayo Methot) from a bunch of crooks chasing a handsome bounty. Riskin delved into the seedy underworld with vigor. This tidy mystery thriller concerns itself with the way the crooks manage to get to the lady of the title, Ida, despite all the police protection. For those who would later think of Riskin as nothing more than a sentimentalist when it came to his closures, this film demonstrated that hard-edged, nail-biting dynamics were also his trademark, if need be.[3] *The Big Timer*, on the other hand, revealed Riskin's instincts as a sports fan, telling the tale of a cocky, big-shot boxer aiming for fame and fortune, with Ben Lyon and Constance Cummings in the lead roles. The narrative harked back to Riskin's experiences with friends like John Meehan, watching title fights in New York in the twenties. Riskin authenticates time and place very neatly in *The Big Timer* by having as the opening scene an advertisement for the well-known boxer James J. Jeffries in one of his fights of the time. The photographic fragments of contemporary time and events passing by the fictional protagonists succinctly confirm Riskin's desire to maintain social and cultural authenticity, and they highlight his identification with a working-class audience whose desires and pursuits were realized directly by his characters on screen.

Similar techniques are brought to the fore in *Virtue*, where an ex-prostitute, Mae (Carole Lombard), attempts to hide her past, including time served in jail, while building a future with her taxi driver husband (Pat O'Brien). The film teamed up Riskin with his longtime production colleagues Joe Walker and Edward Bernds, the soundman who noticed Riskin's potential on *Platinum Blonde*. *Virtue* provided the writer with a real opportunity to insert crackling dialogue and cultural rejoinders into one of his earliest full-length scripts. In the opening scene, for example, in which a magistrate orders her to leave New York for good, Mae gets into a conversation with fellow inmate Lil. Mae remarks that if she doesn't obey the order to leave, she will have to spend time in the Danbury penitentiary. "Isn't that where they make hats?" asks Lil. "Yeah, I'd have gone," replies Mae. "But I got a hat." Lil says that she remembers being there once and exclaims, sarcastically, what a great town it was. "They never bury their dead," she mocks. "Just let 'em walk around." These sly comedic swipes at dead-end towns provided immediacy, poignancy, and recognition for an audience watching the outside world on screen and looking for hints of forgiveness and optimism in its relentless hardship. Scenes like these were starting to bring the young writer's scripts attention and plaudits. There had been reports that some at Columbia were disaffected with Riskin's writing after he arrived from New York and before *Platinum Blonde* became a big hit for the studio. But a three-year contract signed after that film demonstrated that the demand for Riskin's scripts was growing considerably, and his subsequent efforts, with dialogue as sharp and subtle as this, illustrated why.[4]

Riskin had met Columbia's leading female story editor, Dorothy Howell, while working on *Platinum Blonde*. As it turned out, Capra's film and *The Big Timer* provided a convenient passing of the torch, as Pat McGilligan describes it, of principal Columbia screenwriting duties as the thirties progressed. Howell had been the studio's chief scenarist and Capra's main collaborator on films like *Submarine* (1928), *The Donovan Affair* (1929), *Rain or Shine* (1930), and *The Miracle Woman* (1931). After 1932, her name disappeared entirely from Capra's films, and Riskin became the screenwriter of choice.[5]

While the partnership was cementing itself, however, Riskin

continued to maintain allegiances to other Columbia directors. For instance, he worked with Buzzell again on *Ann Carver's Profession* in 1933, perhaps his most famous work at the time outside the Capra collaboration. The film marked something of a peak in Buzzell's directing career. He had been a Broadway musical comedy star in the 1920s and had gone on to appear in a number of early talkies at the end of the decade, including *Midnight Life* (1928) and *Little Johnny Jones* (1929). But he acquired a decent reputation at Columbia soon after these appearances by directing and starring in comedy shorts for the studio, twenty-six in all. Buzzell's first major feature was *The Big Timer*, complete with Riskin's script, and he went on to make moderately successful B pictures at Universal, Paramount, and MGM, as well as Columbia. Although he would direct a couple of lesser Marx Brothers movies later in the decade—*At the Circus* (1939), produced by Mervyn LeRoy, and *Go West* (1940)—*Ann Carver's Profession* could rightly be judged the height of his critical fulfillment.

But while Buzzell was becoming merely a minor director around the studio lots, screenwriter Riskin was carving a niche for himself as an artisan who could transform films with prescient dialogue and relevant social comment. The Ann Carver of the title is a go-getting career woman who sparks jealousy in her husband when she becomes a successful, breadwinning lawyer. The *Herald Tribune* in its review commented on the timeliness of the movie's challenges to traditional roles, and the *New York Times* thought the film modern and daring in its attempts to show how women coped with career and home life.[6] Ironically, the eponymous lead role was played by Riskin's future wife, Fay Wray, though they didn't know each other at this point and it is unlikely that they ever met in preproduction or on the set. Unfortunately for the film and the actress, the movie was somewhat cast adrift by Wray's spectacular starring role in *King Kong* that same year. But interest in *Ann Carver's Profession* remains, especially in the shooting script, which demonstrates the greater extent to which Riskin was already becoming involved in the filmmaking process itself. His own comments on various scenes, penciled in next to the dialogue, indicate changes to camera angles and a number of new camera shots that were needed, as much as the addition of new scenes and words.[7]

Even as Riskin was cutting his teeth working for a number of other directors at Columbia, he had also been writing a full-length story for the screen that would daringly combine romance, melodrama, gangster narrative, and social consciousness. In its infancy the screenplay was entitled *Faith,* and although Riskin neither had it in mind nor knew all its ramifications, the film version was about to become the first full-blown Capra-Riskin collaboration.

While culturally topical films were by no means unknown, and Capra's fascination with religious evangelism in *The Miracle Woman* was a good example, studios' willingness in the early thirties to tackle the worst effects of the Depression, as well as politics, law and order, and economics, was another matter entirely. Ian Hamilton's account of screenwriting in the classic studio era cites *The Gold Rush* (1925), *Greed* (1923), and *The Crowd* (1928) as three silent-era movies that "politicized" events and issues on screen and had considerable impact on audiences. Although they arguably paved the way for a more socially conscious outlook in the thirties, all three were authored by significantly powerful creators—Chaplin, von Stroheim, and King Vidor, respectively— and when screenwriters or directors of a more mortal persuasion wished to get their message across, the restrictions were lengthy and numerous.[8]

In 1930, the Motion Picture Producers and Distributors of America instituted the Production Code for films, a form of self-regulation that was famously overseen by Will Hays. But the code had a number of incarnations, and its far more rigorous enforcement was reserved for films made after 1934. Between 1930 and 1934, some of the studios, Columbia and Warner Brothers being principal among them, took their chances and came up with a set of pictures, in a number of different genres, that were often gritty, daring, sexually provocative, and with no little violent content.

In his study of Depression-era films, Andrew Bergman cites shyster movies, fallen women pictures, and, in particular, gangster flicks as hugely influential treatises about America, the audiences, and the filmmakers themselves during the period. Movie houses, he surmises, "were important places in the 1930s."[9] The onset of the Depression concentrated the mind and focused the attention of Hollywood on the economic and political turmoil in American society. Especially in the genre cycles of prison and gangster movies, the penal system, urban environments, and the persistent undertow of sexual mores bore down heavily on the likes of *Scarface* (1932), *I Am a Fugitive from a Chain Gang* (1932), and *Wild Boys of the Road* (1933).

As a writer, Riskin never felt entirely at home with such downbeat, often cynical and plaintive narratives, but it is a measure of his confidence and ability to transcend cyclical trends in popular cinema that his script for *Faith* confronted the contemporary economic situation in the United States in a manner no other writer dared attempt. Ben Hecht, Sheridan Gibney, and others who were responsible for the kinds of films mentioned above brought the disadvantaged and the dispossessed onto theater screens for audiences to contemplate and share their suffering. But *Faith* bravely tackled the fiscal calamity head-on by having as its central character and resolute hero not an outsider but an establishment figure: a banker. The man in question, Tom Dickson (played in the film by Walter Huston), was to be a caring individual who makes loans on the basis of character rather more than credit; who puts his trust in his own, and America's, financial institutions; and who has faith in the people. Dickson's faith is challenged, however, when a robbery at the bank, compounded by rumors of how much money was stolen—a whispering campaign initiated by one of his own indiscreet secretaries—starts a run that threatens to destroy everything he has built. Seeking help from his skeptical board members, who have never liked his methods of loaning money, and trying to prevent his ex-con bank teller, Matt (played by Pat O'Brien), from taking the rap for the robbery, Dickson races against time to save the bank and his friends.

Prescient or not in the midst of the banking crisis of 1932, Riskin's story did not look like the kind of fable that would immediately find sympathy with audiences. Who was going to want to watch a movie about a bank manager as upholder of American ideals when bank managers were being denounced as liars, cheats, and scoundrels in the worst pockets of economically ravaged America? It has long been speculated that the film got made only because Dickson was a composite portrayal of Columbia's chief financial backers of the time, the brothers

A. H. "Doc" and A. P. Giannini, who ran the Bank of America.[10] A *Collier's* profile of Riskin in 1941 even cites his visit to one of the brothers in preparation for the writing of the script.[11] This story ties in, though far from conclusively, with offhanded claims that Riskin was assigned *Faith*, rather than dreaming up the story all by himself.[12]

What Riskin instinctively achieved with his screenplay, cleverly deflecting attention from the central concerns of financial institutions and those who ran them, was to draw on audience interest from across cinematic genres and hence to appeal to a wide base of film devotees across social and economic classes. In the picture, Tom and Phyllis Dickson (Kay Johnson) are a middle-aged couple who bring melodrama to the fore by dealing with career, home life, and a woman's place in modern society. Bank teller Matt Brown and secretary Helen (Constance Cummings) act out the youthful romantic subplot in the story, while Cyril Cluett (Gavin Gordon) gets to be both the philandering, upwardly mobile cad about town and the story's connection to a gangster subplot that involves robbery and murder. Looking back at the film now, it is easy to be underwhelmed by Riskin's acute sense of characterization, particularly in constructing the hoodlum types who terrorize the weak-willed Cluett—who owes them money—to allow them access to the bank vault. Neither this story nor the following Capra-Riskin effort, *Lady for a Day*, has any real place in the gangster milieu that grew up around classic, iconic pieces of the same era, like *Scarface*, *Public Enemy*, and *Little Caesar*. One might even accuse Riskin of assembling one-dimensional characters who lack the attitude and authority of the personalities in those pictures. Yet the two Capra-Riskin films that portray gangsters do so with entirely opposite character and narrative constructions. In *Faith* the hoodlums are straightlaced, uncompromising, and, in their actions if not their poses, just as menacing as Muni, Cagney, or Robinson in their brutal shooting of the bank's night watchman. But in *Lady for a Day*, Riskin had the idea of turning the gang into pussycats, playful caricatures who carry heroine Apple Annie through her wonderful concoction of a privileged life for one day, all for the benefit of her visiting daughter and her fiancé. It was a skillful manipulation of type that Riskin would re-employ manfully just a few years later, in John Ford's *The Whole Town's Talking*, in which he and Ford would get Edward G. Robinson to ape his own gangster persona from *Little Caesar*.[13]

Lary May argues in *The Big Tomorrow* that this ethos of what he calls "interpenetrating opposites" permeated genres and formula films considerably in an era associated with traditional American myths. Major cowboy stars of the thirties and forties like Gene Autry and Roy Rogers incorporated the values of the rugged cowboy with the urban singer of swing ballads. Soviet filmmaker Sergi Eisenstein saw Disney characters as popular because "they evoked a vision of wholeness to counter the deep fragmentations of the modern world." Disney mixed animal traits with human emotions and came up with moral lessons and interpretative social values.[14]

The political message in examples like these, argues May, was that by incorporating into the self the desires of outsiders, be they gangsters, fallen women, or cartoon animals, the new citizen carried into the civic sphere the capacity to cooperate with outsiders and to reinvent oneself and society. Nowhere was this more in evidence, he believes, than in the movies of Frank Capra. Committed to both composite personality and generic film formula, Capra and Riskin created conversion narratives that focused on competing views of cultural authority. The villains' view of life was complete and closed to new ideas, suggests May, and thus what Capra importantly achieved was to evoke the myths of American traditions in his films as agents of change, to critique and alter the present state of society.[15]

While Capra's vision is interpreted as the touchstone of these ideas, Riskin's construction of his ensemble cast was all-important in this process. He simply had that uncanny ability to frame character according to taste and plot requirement and yet, crucially, make it seem believable, smart, and funny all at the same time. His script for *Faith* matched melodrama and comedy with Capra's cinematic eye for movement, atmosphere, and pace. Columbia picked up the story as a matter of course, Capra—eventually—came on board, and the project acquired a new name, but all this barely begins to relay the background, story, and importance of *American Madness*.

From Faith Comes Madness

How the script for *Faith* came to be filmed and renamed *American Madness* goes to the heart of the dilemma that grew up in the relationship between Frank Capra and Robert Riskin over the next twenty-three years. In his autobiography, Capra states quite clearly that "Riskin and I concocted a wild story about a bank president who is filled with youthful optimism and a cheerful trust in men."[16] Capra gave an interview in 1973 in which he claimed that he had been influenced to write the story by the "life of Giannini." Rochelle Larkin's account of the history of Columbia Pictures, written in the mid-1970s, also affirmed that Capra had thought up the story line.[17] Yet this was patently not the case. The script was already in some draft form long before it came into Capra's hands, and it seems clear now that he was not even slated to direct the movie as it went into production.

Subsequent investigation has shown that the experienced Allan Dwan began filming scenes for *Faith*, and even after that, another director, Roy William Neill, replaced Dwan before Capra took the helm. Joseph McBride explains that Capra, returning from a trip to Europe, had already announced that he intended to do an adaptation of Joseph Hergesheimer's novel *Tampico*, about an oil-drilling tycoon in Mexico. And yet it seems somebody at Columbia, be it Capra, Harry Cohn, studio manager Sam Briskin, or some other executive, already had ideas about a Capra-Riskin collaboration, because *Faith* began filming without Capra but with his production team, including cinematographer Joseph Walker and sound mixer Edward Bernds. Both, according to McBride, had less than complimentary things to say about Dwan, and he fell victim to Cohn's occasional tactic of throwing directors off pictures very early to shake up the back lot and keep people on their toes.[18] In those first few days of filming, by all accounts, Dwan was making Walter Huston look bad, and that was a tough thing to do. But Dwan had a pretty big reputation, having directed Fairbanks and Swanson, among others, in the twenties, and having had his first talkie hit, *While Paris Sleeps*, just prior to beginning work on *Faith*. The story goes that Cohn got rid of Dwan, reputation or not; the director moved to Britain soon afterward to make three pictures and did not return to Hollywood until 1934. It is possible that he got an offer and hence opted to abandon Riskin's script and Cohn's tyrannical rule, although the financial reward in the British film industry, likely not as big as that in Hollywood, seems not to have been the sole reason for the switch. Neill's all-too-brief flirtation with the picture is also hard to fathom. He was mainly a B-movie director, more closely aligned to mystery and adventure (he would later direct a number of the Sherlock Holmes mysteries for Universal) than the kind of pointed social comedy he was dipping into here.

In any case, soon after, Capra gave up on *Tampico*—it passed to Irving Cummings and became *The Woman I Stole*—and joined *Faith* well into the production process, with very little time to overlay his own ideas and vision, though he did have the inspired idea to rebuild the whole set. What was clear in this early forging of the partnership between writer and director was that, just as *American Madness* brought the combination of Depression politics, banking crises, and mob behavior to the forefront of Hollywood ideals for the first time, it also paved the way for a harder-edged, more discursive style in Capra's later films, those with as well as those without Riskin. The director would claim in his autobiography that *The Miracle Woman* showed he was not afraid to tackle "idea" films,[19] which remains a persuasive view, but *American Madness* brought these ideas into the social and political realm and catapulted his vision into the maelstrom of institutional, economic, and elite forms of power relations in a way the earlier films had not suggested was possible for Capra.

For Richard Corliss, *American Madness* remains the definitive Capra-Riskin film, by which he seems to mean the one film from which so many other strands of plot, character, scene-setting, style, humor, and social construction arise. Indeed, Leland Poague talks of *American Madness*'s many influences upon Capra and Riskin's later, oft-described landmark social comment film, *Mr. Deeds Goes to Town*. Poague cites certain similarities in casting and allusions to particular states of mental distress as further evidence of the earlier film's status as prototype.[20] In one scene, for instance, Matt Brown, the ex-con whom manager Dickson has trusted with a job at the bank, is questioned under duress by the police inspector (Robert Emmett O'Connor) about the previous night's robbery, for he suspects Brown is the inside man who has given the thieves access to the money. The inspector pulls in his chief witness, Brown's landlady, Mrs. Halligan, who is a sweet but dotty old woman very much akin to twin sisters Jane and Amy in *Mr. Deeds*, who think Longfellow Deeds is "pixilated." The woman questioned by the inspector even mentions two patrons of her bed and breakfast lodging, the Dooley sisters, a pair of outlying characters one could imagine filling very nicely the roles of the siblings in the later film. "It was a half hour after the Dooley sisters," claims Mrs. Halligan, trying to pinpoint when Matt arrived back at his room. Asked whether it could have been one o'clock, Mrs. Halligan replies that it could have been, but not earlier. "Yes I know," retorts the inspector. "'Cause the Dooley sisters weren't in yet."

"No," she says. "Because the clock struck four, and when it strikes four, it's one." The comic effect breaks the mounting tension but doesn't distract the audience from the dilemma Matt is facing. Even Mrs. Halligan's warped logic is condemning Matt as an accomplice, and Riskin offers this moment of comedy to the audience to show that only the truth can unravel the concoction of deceit and blackmail within the narrative.

In a scene further on in the film, Tom Dickson sits alone in his office while, outside, a bank run threatens to write off his life's work, and his gaze turns toward a gun that sits patiently in his desk drawer. Poague sees parallels between this scene and Longfellow Deeds's lonely vigil in his prison cell, waiting for that film's climactic trial over his alleged insanity to begin. What is more important, however, than these ringing chimes of similarity between scenes is something pertinent to all the Capra-Riskin films and, especially, to the screenwriter's narrative and idealistic preoccupation: Riskin's treatment of gender politics, a feature that, as already intimated, had begun to develop long before this film appeared.

Phyllis Dickson (Kay Johnson), a key player in *American Madness*, reveals traits and feelings not commonly attributed to female characters of the time. Yes, there was Jean Harlow (in Capra's own film, no less), as well as Dietrich, Garbo, and Mae

West, all of whom played with sex, flirtation, and titillation, not to mention prostitution in the likes of *Blonde Venus* and *Faithless* (both 1932). But Phyllis is all common sense and middle-class maturity, and she originally appears a dutiful wife to bank manager Dickson, hoping, early in the film, that her arrangement of a dinner engagement will remind him of their wedding anniversary. When an emergency meeting in Philadelphia crops up that Dickson feels obliged to attend, Phyllis, in her disgust, resorts to some rather cheekily progressive flirting with a younger man, bank assistant Cyril Cluett. "You know, there ought to be a Congressional Medal for men like you. America's comfort to misunderstood wives," she asserts. Cluett, however, simply wants to use her as an alibi for his involvement in the bank robbery, having been forced to play a part so he can pay his gangland creditors. Phyllis gives the audience cause for concern by playing the coy, liberated older woman to perfection until, arriving at Cluett's flat after a night on the town, she and Cluett discover that Matt has shown up to try to persuade Mrs. Dickson to see the error of her ways. Thus Matt's loyalty to Dickson explains why he has no satisfactory account of his whereabouts for the policeman the next day: he doesn't want to reveal to his boss where he was or what he knows about the relationship between Phyllis and Cluett.

Poague states that Capra had a deep affinity with Phyllis Dickson, and we might attribute that simpatico to Riskin. Her presence and attitude are those of a woman excluded from the life of her husband and longing for the plaudits that he bestows upon others.[21] Here Riskin is considering the constraints imposed by society upon women of the 1930s. But Phyllis has what Riskin always admired in his real life—female companions—and what differentiates his female protagonists from so many others is their nagging sense of independence and personal conviction. His heroines on the page, almost without exception, fight patriarchal legacies and traditions and continue to make their way in a man's world. Future characters like Babe Bennett, Ann Mitchell, and Mary Peterman (in the postwar *Magic Town*) are all professional, go-getting newspaper hacks in the male tradition. But they all seem to crave the intellectual, social, and sexual duel of partnership and the stimulation of male companionship, and they do so with very individually defined personalities.

One is drawn to analyze Riskin's writing in the context of film studies work on feminism and spectatorship. Eric Smoodin's research into the reception of Capra's movies (largely an investigation of the director's extensive correspondence with fans) refers to definitive assessments by the likes of Laura Mulvey and Jackie Stacey.[22] But the "narrative gaze" identified in Smoodin's analysis of female characters, especially those in Capra's early pictures (*Flight* and *Ladies of Leisure* particularly), is associated rather more with Stacey's connection between female spectators and stars than it is with Mulvey's take on patriarchal observation both in and regarding the text. Smoodin aligns these early Capra films with Columbia advertising campaigns, for instance, in which a star like Barbara Stanwyck would court the "intensity of [female audiences'] identification with female stars while watching a movie."[23] Riskin's screenplays, on the other hand, from *Platinum Blonde* onward might be seen to engage with, if not contest, Mulvey's assertion of the male gaze that "projects its phantasy onto the female figure."[24] Mulvey's and others' psychoanalytic readings of texts, inspired by Freud and Marx, deserve a wider review within Riskin and Capra's work than is possible here, but at the level of identification and position—within the narrative as well as society—Riskin's female protagonists do periodically challenge and subvert the male gaze and patriarchal dominance, as later chapters will testify to.

Riskin could not really be accused of pursuing a feminist line of inquiry in his films, however, and the phallocentric examination of the "lack," so often discussed in feminist film readings, remains a feature that could be read into a number of his screenplays. In real life, women intrigued Riskin, which contributed to a somewhat stereotypical vision of him as a genial playboy. His emergence as Capra's chief collaborator in the thirties saw him acquire the title of one of Hollywood's most eligible bachelors, and Riskin was certainly up to the challenge. He often went out on the town courting beautiful actresses, but Riskin's longer relationships tended to be with women at once feisty, independent, and more than a match for his quick-witted interplay. If one were harsh toward Riskin's female characters—utilizing Stacey's thesis—one might accuse them of being the kind of character female moviegoers wanted to be but didn't know how to become in their own world. And yet, conversely, they also had the kind of impregnable personality that predated a Hollywood era filled with the likes of Bette Davis, Joan Crawford, and Angela Lansbury, all of the mold Riskin loved and could have written so much for in time. Instead, he helped to make even bigger stars of Barbara Stanwyck, Jean Arthur, and Claudette Colbert, and did so by bringing out the unique traits of each, extolling their consciousness as actors, and, in the process, consolidating their status as female icons rather than just adulated starlets.

American Madness demonstrated Riskin's flair for constructing intricate associations between his characters and underpinning a film with social change at the same time. Themes of loyalty and sacrifice, which would later become associated with classic Hollywood narrative interplay, were intrinsic to movies of this time, but Riskin instituted these themes on many different levels of interaction within one film: between husband and wife, between young lovers, between the desperate and depraved, and, simply, between friends. And each interaction hinted at the tensions endemic in thirties society: between the privileged and the poor, between the criminal and the law-abiding, between institutions and the masses, and, yes, between men and women.

And yet not only have Riskin's worlds rarely been credited with such spirited, progressive, and intriguing ideological tendencies, they have often been directly criticized for them. "There was a breed of screenwriter notorious for sticking stilettos of social comment between the ribs of Hollywood's most bourgeois of films. Predictably, the handles still stuck out. Robert Riskin, Dudley Nichols, Joseph L. Mankiewicz, and Dalton Trumbo could all write entertainingly—and more convincingly—when they relaxed and let the characters lead *them*, instead of trying to collar the moviegoer and lead him down the road toward some fashionable 'ism.'" So states Richard Corliss in describing some of the marvelous panoply of scenarists discussed in his seminal 1974 book *Talking Pictures*. Corliss grouped the above writers, and a few more besides, into a chapter entitled "Themes in Search of a Style." In many ways, Corliss's regard for the "still fresh" *American Madness* at the start of Riskin's screenwriting career becomes the stick to beat his later writing with, especially Riskin and Capra's last collaboration, *Meet John Doe*, in particular its closing sequence.[25]

To Corliss, the message became the medium with these writers. He identifies an almost obsessive desire among them to make the personal, confessional, social statement their careers had been destined for, whether it was *Sister Kenny* (Nichols, 1946), *The Barefoot Contessa* (Mankiewicz, 1954), or *Johnny Got His Gun* (Trumbo, from his own novel, 1971). In Riskin's case—and Corliss focuses on only three of the main films, *It Happened One Night*, *Mr. Deeds*, and *Meet John Doe*, before moving on—his final film with Capra is the climax of his chase for the ultimate ideological deposition. Whether this theory is correct or fair, of Riskin or of the other writers here—Herman Mankiewicz seems to get in only by virtue of writing *Citizen Kane*—is less the point than Corliss's focus on character as theme. Elsewhere he has written that Riskin's personality, his "quiet conviction and self-respect," suggests where the inspiration for characters occurred and which plots were more to his liking. He was better, thinks Corliss, on high-pressure bankers (*American Madness*), newspapermen (*Platinum Blonde* and *It Happened One Night*), Broadway sharpies (*Lady for a Day*), and racetrack touts (*Broadway Bill*) than fantasy (*Lost Horizon*, *The Miracle Woman*—presumably as *Bless You, Sister* originally—*Mr. Deeds*, *Meet John Doe*), criminal gentility (*Mister 880*), split personality (*The Whole Town's Talking*), or Broadway adaptation (*You Can't Take It With You*).[26]

Certainly, it is hard to argue with the view that Riskin's characters seemed more comfortable and were often at their best when they were wisecracking reporters, ambitious business moguls, or institutional authority figures. But if such characters did ring true with audiences and critics, it was because they also anticipated the mood of modernism, corporatism, social engineering, and control that twentieth-century American society was entering. *American Madness*, with Tom Dickson attempting heroically to fight these tendencies, displayed this social framework as well as any film of the early thirties. And rather than simply make a character like Dickson unflinchingly cocky in his utilitarian stance, Riskin instituted doubt and apprehension in places, whether over money, career, or, particularly, love. Riskin liked dialogue that sparked competition between his star-crossed lovers and left unresolved sexual tension lingering in the air for just as long as was necessary. More than this—and here lies a facet of Riskin's work that not only has been underappreciated but is also not easily observed in the contemporaneous work of other writers of his quality—there is evidence that he had a vision of what needed to go on screen and how these ideas could be communicated cinematically, not simply through character and dialogue. No film provides clearer realization of this aspect of Riskin's work than *American Madness*.

After Allan Dwan left *Faith* as it began filming and Roy Neill passed up the opportunity to direct, Capra persuaded Harry Cohn that the set for the film had to be reconstructed to provide more space and to act as a focus for action and movement. Ray Carney's argument about Capra's cinematic vision centers upon his tactic of using large, expensive sets for a majority of his action, so that audiences remember his central characters as "living and acting within specific institutional and social spaces."[27] Those who observed both directors' interpretation of the script, like Walker and Bernds, soon marveled at Capra's ability to inject life and pace into the narrative. Capra's orchestration of his players and Walker's cinematography are two brilliant factors at work in the movie. Indeed, the director offered a touch of genius by literally speeding up the film. As he himself described, in addition to deviating from the trend of the time, which used dissolves between scenes, Capra quickened the picture by first timing scenes and then having the actors crank up the dialogue to about one-third faster than the scene's original speed.[28] It is not hard to see how the film, at this rate, came in at less than eighty minutes long and served to define the construction of classic Hollywood narratives in the early thirties.

With the fluid movement of camera and actors, crowd scenes, and dialogue interjected over other conversations and in between the hum and noise of the bank floor, as well as the authentic creation of location, the bank vault in particular, Capra created a tapestry of increased restlessness and frustration culminating in the story's set-piece scene: the run on the bank. But what is interesting about this cinematic realization of potential economic ruin and mob action in *American Madness* is that Riskin already had written many of these ideas into the script. He had already visualized how the run should look, where the camera might pan, how unruly the mob might become. He even had a sketch in his notes for the montage of whispering between switchboard operators and bank customers about how much money has been stolen, which precedes the panic on the floor of Dickson's establishment. The montage, superbly filmed, would become a signature feature of Capra's movies—later with the aid of Slavko Vorkapich—but Riskin was part of its creation. Joseph McBride endorses the point, observing, "Capra followed Riskin's story and dialogue to the letter, and he also adhered closely to the screenplay's unusually detailed visual plan."[29]

The Capra presentation of characters confined to certain locations, overseen by towering edifices, emphasized the central structure of Riskin's writing: the three-act drama. The players were location-specific in a way that made the action theatrical, composed, and cultivated. It was a perfect match for a filmmaking team that was unusually technical and sophisticated for the time. Carney makes the point in his analysis of Capra's films that, although Orson Welles and his cinematographer Gregg Toland would take many plaudits for their use of depth of field in *Citizen Kane* a few short years later, Capra, Walker, and Riskin were ahead of the game. They had established their own visual composition of creating elaborate patterns on screen, particularly following from *American Madness* in *The Bitter Tea of General Yen* and *Lost Horizon*, but also in *It Happened One Night* and *Meet John Doe*.[30]

American Madness contravened the rules of Depression cinema in 1932. Tom Dickson, the banker turned savior, proved a big hit with audiences, and Capra got rave notices for discovering a powerful platform from which to discuss life, social issues, and economic change. Riskin, even in the most generous of assessments, hardly got a look-in. The *Hollywood Reporter* did talk of the "perfect script and dialogue that is a treat to hear," but other reviews that focused on the boldness of the piece chose to reflect more on Capra's considerable skill behind the camera than on Riskin's writing prowess.[31] *American Madness* had no contemporary copies in a Hollywood looking to reflect and reassure its audience that the Depression could be overcome. Within a year, Ben Hecht's story *Hallelujah, I'm a Bum* (1933), written for the screen by S. N. Behrman, had Al Jolson as a singing mayor uniting the unemployed, while Columbia's own *Man's Castle* (1933) featured Riskin's later companion, Loretta Young, finding romance with another New York down-and-out, played by Spencer Tracy. Poverty could be a source of "carefree pleasure" in pictures like these, according to Colin Shindler.[32] But these films didn't make audiences stop to think about their nation's social and economic malaise, and they proved to be poor box office fare as well.

Riskin's story, on the other hand, weaves romance, comedy, and melodrama into a subtle tale. His script had cultural cohesion and social references; his politics suggested hope but warned of needing to remain strong. Yet later, the film would become Capra's sole creative preserve, and he would go on to claim credit for the name change as well, even though *Faith* remained the title until the picture was getting trade reviews in May 1932. MGM executive producer Harry Rapf actually suggested the alternative title to Cohn after one early preview, and it was Cohn who seems then to have foisted the idea upon Capra.[33]

It is easy enough to surmise that Riskin was getting a poor deal from Capra, Cohn, and the studio in general. But there is plenty of evidence to suggest that Capra only retrospectively developed this attitude to his authorial vision and that he gave Riskin credit at the time. After all, in interviews and later, when separation and illness took over, Riskin remained incredibly loyal to Capra and never had anything but generous words to say about his direction. The blunt truth is that Riskin wasn't that much removed from any other screenwriter working in Hollywood at the time. All that *American Madness* demonstrated was that screenwriters were talented enough to work up their own story lines, and inculcated enough in the process to put the film, as well as the story's words, down on paper. With the likes of

Orson Welles and Billy Wilder, as well as many others, the league of writer-directors was about to infiltrate Hollywood to a much greater degree. Riskin would have his chance to join this coterie but would quickly realize how little it suited his style of working. Does this mean that he could not have directed *American Madness* as well as Capra did? In a technical sense, possibly not, but in setting and atmosphere, Riskin knew how good a story this was and how well he had laid the foundation for Capra's visual presentation.

The biggest disappointment emerging from the *American Madness* project was that Riskin, who must have longed to write another screenplay like *Faith*, never did, perhaps because he never got the chance. Columbia imposed a constricting outlook by demanding swift and repeat success. Although he later coauthored both *The Thin Man Goes Home* and *Magic Town*, he and Capra, at least, would work again only on adapted stories. Three would follow very quickly in the course of the next two years.

Politics and the Columbia Way

American Madness had laid the groundwork for, but had not truly cemented, the Capra-Riskin partnership in 1932. Their next film together, *Lady for a Day*, in 1933, did all this and more. Capra had worked his way through *Platinum Blonde, Forbidden,* and *American Madness* with little recognition from the Motion Picture Academy. He freely admitted in his autobiography, and others have confirmed, that he sought remuneration for his work through Oscars, but his films, while much admired and devoured by audiences, were not getting any acknowledgment in that area. The extent to which Capra thought awards would cement his place at Columbia, and in Harry Cohn's affections, is not clear, and whether he wished for recognition as a means to solidify the studio's position as an emerging player in Hollywood is even more open to speculation.

The relationship between director and studio chief was tempestuous, to say the least. It changed significantly after 1932, altering the dynamics of the Capra-Cohn-Riskin triumvirate. That year, Cohn established singular control of the studio in Los An-

geles, a unique management structure for the Hollywood industry at that time: no other studio had one man running the whole
show. It should be noted, however, that all the other studios were
considerably bigger than Columbia and therefore were unlikely
to have the type of hands-on operation Cohn conceived of. Harry
had in fact run Columbia with his brother Jack and their partner,
Joe Brandt, until 1932. Brandt decided to sell his stake in the company, and though Jack appeared to be the most likely to succeed as
chief executive, Harry suddenly stepped up with a $500,000 buy-
out that left him in sole control and Jack as merely vice president
and treasurer. Harry acquired the money from A. H. Giannini and
the Bank of America, A. H. and his brother A. P. having been the
apparent inspiration that year for *American Madness*.[34] Whether or
not art and life mixed as coincidentally as it seemed, Harry Cohn
rarely made financial or positional slipups. Attilio (A. H.) even
nudged the confluence of movie success and studio takeover by
writing a letter to Cohn after the film's completion, expressing
his hope and belief that the picture would renew people's faith in
their financial institutions, exemplified, presumably, by the Bank
of America's continued backing of Cohn and Columbia's moviemaking vision.[35]

American Madness also signaled a very important structural so-
lidification of the team that put together one of Columbia's most
popular films of 1932. The "Capra unit" would, from *American
Madness* onward, work as Columbia's first-run feature unit—in
other words, its principal big-budget team for the studio's leading
productions.[36] The unit that had gone to work on *Faith* at the start
of the year, without Capra, was, it seems, already being groomed
for Cohn's ascendancy and the beginning of Columbia's move up
the Hollywood pecking order. It would be the only first-run unit
at the studio during the thirties, and that Riskin's story and original script united them should not be seen as coincidental. Cohn's
pronouncements on his team's films over the next couple of years,
as laid out below, set the tone for a consistent fixation with story,
script, and dialogue that Riskin, as well as colleagues like Jo Swerling and Sidney Buchman, would revel in. If, as Thomas Schatz
surmises, it was possible to discern what Cohn's "aesthetic" actually was, then an early interview that mentioned "novelty, hu-

man appeal, humor and pathos" in his studio's films confirms a belief coming to fruition in 1932 that working as a team, with writer and director in close harmony, was the Columbia way.[37]

Capra's ambitions in 1933 stretched at least as far as personal recognition and reward for his increasingly popular work. The director quoted Cohn himself, however, as saying at the time that only "arty junk" got nominated for Academy Awards, a signal that this was not the type of picture Columbia made.[38] Derogatory though Cohn's description might have been, Capra had half-hoped that *American Madness* would fall into that category. But nothing was forthcoming from the nominating committee, and the experience may have told Capra how unfashionable a studio Columbia was for the fledgling movie awards. So its leading director resolved to make an arty picture, and while Riskin worked on *Ann Carver's Profession* with Eddie Buzzell, Capra ingratiated himself with producer Walter Wanger, who was about to bring an adaptation of Grace Zaring Stone's novel *The Bitter Tea of General Yen* to the big screen.

The two experiences could not have been more different. Riskin was now establishing a name for himself in Hollywood circles and with Cohn. Following the success of *American Madness*, Columbia's emerging screenwriter realized that he had a voice to offer and a position to defend from within the industry. A piece by James Whale in the *Los Angeles Herald* in September 1932 suggests that writers were nothing more than rented scribes who were reproducing the ideas of executives, producers, and directors on demand. Riskin published a reply directly repudiating Whale's arguments. "The producer and director who expect the writer to turn it on like a water faucet are bound to be disappointed in originality, if not in quantitative output," he countered. Riskin continued that the job of the writer—to turn around in two weeks an idea that has just been concocted from a title—is "an obstetrical feat that is nothing short of a miracle."

Pointedly, Riskin pleaded for time and consideration for writers. He said that Whale's comparison of films to stage dramas was just not appropriate. There was little time for the screenwriter to act as artist, to compose and consider his or her story, unlike the dramatist, who could write when inspiration came, he insisted. While talking pictures were not the great mystery everyone thought they were, he concluded, too many financial considerations and demands went into productions, with too little credit for writers' contributions.[39] Riskin's observations, of course, emerged from his experiences in his first two years at Columbia. He had served an apprenticeship doing all the things—churning out dialogue, constructing story lines at breakneck speed—that he felt damaged creativity and the collaborative process. The article served notice of Riskin's intent to use his initial success to create a working environment he was comfortable with, and it cultivated Harry Cohn's opinion that stories and dialogue were what made great movies. It was a position Riskin would defend several times and with increasing fervor as his career progressed. But it also signaled that he was in Hollywood for the long haul. Unlike other scribes from the East Coast, Riskin would never find his patience tested by the film colony to the point of resignation and retreat.

Riskin's output helped to back up his public declaration: he spoke from a position of strength precisely because he was already being enveloped by the Hollywood game that he sought to criticize—that is, producing scripts to order so as to rise up the ranks and achieve some degree of control over his writing. It was being leaked by the press, and talked about all over town, that Columbia was now linked with a number of Riskin's own screenplays, all conceived in quick succession as his credit rose within the studio. Cohn was reported as being on the verge of buying Riskin's original story *The Bottom of the Sea* for Jack Holt to star in, though the film was a comedy rather than an action-adventure the likes of which Holt had done previously for Capra.[40] A *Los Angeles Evening Herald and Press* report in the late summer of 1932 predicted that Columbia's chief was "sure to approve" the purchase of Riskin's dramatic treatment of Jimmy Starr's play *Confield*, about 1890s gambler and cultural bon vivant Richard A. Confield. At the same time, James Mitchell in the *Los Angeles Examiner* was claiming that Riskin already had a script in preparation called *Bouquets for the Living*, based on the eminent physicist and savant Dr. Robert Millikan. Riskin was attracted to men of greatness, claimed Mitchell, because, as he quoted the writer, they "must have lived an intensely dramatic life to achieve their greatness."[41] While these treatments and dramas never did surface on the Columbia roster, partly because of Riskin's emerging partnership with Capra, older stories were being revitalized. Notable among these was a remake of *Illicit*, put out as *Ex-Lady* (1933) starring Bette Davis by Warner Brothers, which had bought Riskin and Edith Fitzgerald's play *Many a Slip* and released the original picture only three years before.[42] Rather like Capra on the directing side, Riskin was creating a reputation for himself within the confines of Columbia's small backwater as the writer to be seen with.

Capra meanwhile "pleaded"—his word—for the chance to direct *The Bitter Tea of General Yen* and got his way, casting his favorite leading lady, Barbara Stanwyck, in the role of Megan Davis. *Bitter Tea* is a tale of love across racial divides: an American missionary falls for a powerful Chinese warlord. The film, not unexpectedly, proved controversial and was nearly banned in Britain and other Commonwealth countries for its too-blatant portrayal of "relations" among different nationalities.[43] No Academy Award nominations followed, and *Bitter Tea* lost money in the United States, only the second disappointment of its kind for Capra, after *The Miracle Woman* two years earlier.

Capra quickly changed tack, thinking that if art couldn't get him recognition, old-fashioned Cinderella stories just might. What appears certain is that in taking on *Lady for a Day*, Capra was making a major play for Academy recognition. He picked up the story cheaply, but again, retrospectively, he claimed Riskin was not involved in its production until Cohn put pressure on the director to come up with something and Riskin suggested a new title for the Damon Runyon short story.[44]

In fact, once more, what appears an open-and-shut case of the partnership's coming to fruition with this production is in fact a tale of claim and counterclaim, with a little bit of fact thrown in for good measure. Joseph McBride's detailed reading of the gestation period for *Lady for a Day* is instructive in this regard. Far from having Capra and Riskin slogging away on the screenplay for months, McBride points out that, in his memoirs, Capra mistakenly recalls the period after *Lady for a Day* as the one when he was loaned to MGM to make what would have been the most provocative film of his career had it not been shelved. Entitled *Soviet*, the story was of an American engineer and Russian commissar who work together to build a massive dam in the USSR. The project had floated around the studio for some time, but with Capra now personally recruited by Irving Thalberg, the film had gained a fresh impetus and a new script written by Jules Furthman. All this development, however, took place at a slightly different moment than Capra remembered; the director was in fact loaned to MGM between the making of *Bitter Tea* and *Lady*. McBride is quick to speculate that the sequence of events Capra recalls only aids the conspiracy against Riskin's contribution to *Lady for a Day*: Capra forgets the writer was toiling away for a good four months on his own while he, Capra, was preparing a completely different picture.[45]

The most telling contribution to this saga, however, comes from a statement Capra made in an interview with Eileen Creelman of the *New York Sun* in September 1934. The article was a brief portrait of Capra's recent success with *It Happened One Night*, his disappointment at failing to complete *Soviet* and his hope that it could be revived, and his reflections on *Lady for a Day*. Capra said that he had read Runyon's story four years before making it and just hadn't thought it could be transformed into a picture. And yet Riskin's screenplay not only achieved the transformation but also made the movie a stunning success.[46] Capra's statement was an unqualified admission that Riskin and he were a team and generous with each other's talents, as well as an acknowledgment that his writer deserved the praise for the script. But it was also the sort of comment that would make Capra's later statements concerning his authorial authority all the more frustrating.

What is even more significant is the acclaim the screenplay drew from Columbia's chief. After *Lady for a Day*'s successful opening, Harry Cohn gave Riskin focused attention that built on a philosophy confidently set in train by his takeover of the studio. In a March 1934 interview for the *New York Telegraph*, Cohn famously said, "We believe here that writers are more important than either star or director. . . . Look at *Lady for a Day*. . . . More credit is due to Riskin for that picture than to Damon Runyon, who wrote it as a magazine story. Another studio [Fox], which has first call on stories in that magazine [*Cosmopolitan*], passed it up. But Riskin saw something in it—the basic story idea—and liked it. He showed it to Frank Capra, who also liked it, and they went to work."[47]

Cohn's statement could easily have been seen as undermining Capra's authorial dominance among Columbia's directors as well as punctuating Riskin's rise through the ranks. It could also have been one of a long run of digs that Cohn loved to toss out in interviews like unexploded grenades, waiting for his biggest players to blow up in the face of putdowns or public humiliation. In fact, Capra had confided in Cohn his reservations about the film just as it was about to go into production. But Cohn had $300,000 invested in the picture—virtually the highest amount the studio had put into a film up to that point—and besides, he believed in the story. He told Capra to go ahead anyway.[48] For all Cohn's wildly unreliable state of mind when it came to things artistic, he was right that Columbia aimed for stories with character, warmth, and a sense of originality, all of which had to come initially from the writing. Cohn stuck his neck out for Riskin as much as for Capra, and as his *New York Telegraph* interview showed, *Lady for a Day*'s success meant that he could afford to be generous to Riskin and to the picture, for it accentuated the new status that the studio craved and put the Columbia mogul almost side by side with Hollywood's big players.

Lady for a Day made a huge impact with audiences because, as Ray Carney has observed, the film fused "visionary dreaming and pragmatic scheming."[49] The picture was not radically different from *Bitter Tea*; the central character of each movie, Megan in *Bitter Tea* and Annie in *Lady for a Day*, experiences a dramatic and, to a degree, exotic transformation, realizing, for a short time at least, a lifestyle she could before only aspire to. Yet Capra wondered in retrospect, given the greater success of *Lady for a Day*, whether the very exoticism of *Bitter Tea*'s setting distracted the audience from the characters' motivations and desires. It was a first sign that he doubted whether his talents could be expanded into other genres of film, and in truth, Riskin's story interests kept Capra on familiar ground through most of their critical and commercial peak, with the one notable exception in 1937 of *Lost Horizon*.

Riskin, for his part comfortable and confident on home turf with his New York setting, adapted Runyon's taut little vignette, "Madame La Gimp," into an engrossing fable of Depression wish fulfillment set in the heart of the American city. Apple Annie (May Robson), a fruit seller down on her luck, learns that her daughter Louise (Jean Parker) is engaged to a rich European socialite and is bringing him and his father, Count Romero (Walter Connolly), to New York to visit her. To shore up her credibility and make sure Count Romero agrees to the marriage, Annie pretends to be living the high life. She engages not only some well-meaning hoodlums but also the city's political establishment, including the mayor, to help her create an alternative existence for just one day so she can entertain her daughter and future husband as matriarch Mrs. E. Worthington Manville.

Riskin's adaptation, although quite different from the original story, pleased Runyon to no end. He lavished praise on the screenwriter in his newspaper column and in private correspondence.[50] The secret was again in adapting but not overextending the mix of character, sentiment, and narrative, as Donald Willis has argued. Willis regards *Lady for a Day* as the near-perfect Capra-Riskin film: the fairy tale virtually comes alive for the audience, partly because the picture seems to represent a collaborative effort by cast and crew, and partly because the casting is perfect.[51] Riskin's overall involvement in the film signified the amount of influence he now wielded, with Cohn as well as with Capra. Not only in story and dialogue, for Capra ended up filming Riskin's fourth draft of the story virtually intact, but in casting as well, Riskin made a very telling contribution. He even had his girlfriend of the time, Glenda Farrell, play the part of Dave the Dude's mob moll, Missouri Martin.[52] Capra rather dryly dismisses this move in his memoirs by saying only that they looked no further than Farrell for the role.[53] This hints that Riskin may have gotten approval elsewhere, but Capra's comment probably shouldn't have too much meaning read into it. Casting was an imprecise venture even at the best of times.

Riskin's confident, increasingly sophisticated style of writing is apparent from the very first scene of *Lady for a Day*. Apple Annie and her friends are struggling to eke out an existence on the streets of New York as the mass of humanity sweeps by them. Meanwhile, in the opulence of the Hotel Marberry, wealthy mob boss Dave the Dude (Warren Williams) gambles on which piece of sugar a fly will land on. Riskin confounds the audience's expectations about this opening juxtaposition of wealth and poverty by matching Dave and Annie. They know each other because Dave buys an apple from her every time he is about to make a big deal; she is his good luck charm. More than this, Dave, we discover, has also paid for a doctor to look after Annie and warns her of the dangers of the cheap liquor that she plies herself with. It is this relationship that drags Dave into the plan to help Annie out of her dilemma when her bellboy contact at the up-market Marberry gets fired. Preceding the comic attraction of a group of hoodlums trying to act like upper-class denizens, Riskin once again invites the audience's sentimental attachment to his female lead by making her position seem desperate at the outset. "Laugh, why don't you," Annie pleads to Dave, mocking the gruesome irony of having her daughter find out she begs a pittance on Broadway by selling apples. "Oh, why don't you laugh?"

Capra, too, complements the fairy tale by capturing the atmosphere of Depression society and the tensions of social dislocation. When Annie is forced to enter the Hotel Marberry, where her letters are being sent to her alter ego, Mrs. Worthington Manville, the director fashions a distant world of opulence, service, and hushed tones, a hermetically sealed comfort of wealth where Annie cannot find any sympathy. Her raucous presence is not desired in the hotel's lobby; she is rebuffed by the silent displeasure of the staff and patrons. It is a marvelous signal that Annie's later transformation will fool her daughter and revolutionize her own social status, a conversion that will be confirmed by the presence of the mayor and governor at her reception in the movie's finale.

But Riskin's script goes even further than this, establishing a political power base within early-thirties society that is far more exacting than that in many other light, romantic scripts of the time. Annie's adventure is actually the trigger for institutional disruption. The police lieutenant and commissioner, mayor, and governor head up successive levels of bureaucracy that are unnerved by Dave's plan for Annie, which they take to be some racket. Only when they accept and then agree to participate in the illusion do they experience an enlightened realization that working together for the common good is a much better ploy than trying to score political points off each other. Beginning with what is virtually Annie's first line in the film, in which she reminds one of her down-at-heel pals that things are sure to improve soon because she has listened to the president on the radio (a forceful endorsement of Franklin Roosevelt's fireside chats only six months into his presidency), Riskin seamlessly injects social banter, brilliant vernacular dialogue, and contemporary political issues into the picture, superbly stage-managed by Capra's peerless direction.

Ned Sparks's performance as Dave the Dude's right-hand man Happy McGuire is a joy to behold and gives Riskin the opportunity to crank out one-liners virtually at will. When the mob borrows an apartment at the Marberry to set Annie up in her fictitious world for a week, Happy comments that the letter handing over Mr. Rodney Kent's place stipulates, "I don't care what you're doing as long as you don't leave moustaches on the paintings." When Dave suggests that Happy act as Annie's husband, Mr. E. Worthington Manville, the retort is swift: "I got a wife who doesn't like me to go 'round marrying people," he says deadpan. "She's fussy that way." Riskin even allows Happy a little dig at the narrative's rapidly approaching sentimental resolution: "I had a tough time as a kid believing in Santa Claus," Happy professes.

As a result of its humor and pathos, the touching and satirical *Lady for a Day* was a major box office triumph for Capra and Riskin. It also achieved that which no other Columbia film had yet been able to: it made the breakthrough with the Academy judges. The film was nominated for three Oscars: Capra as director, May Robson as actress, and Riskin as screenwriter. It did such good business for Columbia that the studio virtually repeated the movie a year later. With Jo Swerling writing, David Burton directing, and Robson nearly reprising her role, the similarly named *Lady by Choice* is about an exotic dancer (Carole Lombard) looking for respectability in the shape of a transformed grande dame (Robson), who she hopes will help her to marry the man she loves, against the wishes of the man's overbearing mother.[54] Swerling found at times that he could do no better than refer to Riskin's screenplay.

It was true that *Lady for a Day* paraded the writer at his most effortless. Edward Bernds comments in his memoirs that the script was "brilliant" and "a delight to read" in its own right.[55] The film became one of Riskin's personal favorites. Its qualities are shown up by Capra's attempt to remake the picture nearly thirty years later, in what was to be his last directorial effort. *A Pocketful of Miracles* ran fifty minutes longer than the taut, perfectly constructed *Lady for a Day*. The new film only fleetingly recaptured past glories and paled in comparison with its delightful predecessor.

Politics, the Guild, and the Major Breakthrough

Lady for a Day picked up none of the awards for which it was nominated at the Academy dinner of 1934, and Riskin remained somewhat eclipsed at the event by his director and star. At this time, the screenwriting and story categories were linked, and there remained a strong feeling of afterthought in rewarding writers. Screenwriting was, however, becoming politicized in 1933, and Riskin helped to lead the charge. The scenarists of Hollywood had been members of clubs and associations, even a prototype of the Screen Writers Guild, for many years, but these groups lacked power, particularly any bargaining position for better wages or conditions. In 1927, Louis B. Mayer had helped to incorporate a writers division into the Academy of Motion Picture Arts and Sciences, but it clearly acted as a representative of studio interests.

In February 1933, as *Lady for a Day* was going into production, a group of ten screenwriters met at the Knickerbocker Hotel in Los Angeles with the intention of revitalizing the Screen Writers Guild and making it a powerful source of ownership and publishing rights for screenwriters' material. By April, more than two hundred writers, Riskin among them, had left the Academy and joined the new guild under the leadership of its first president, John Howard Lawson. This set in motion a long period of lobbying for recognition. Talk among the writers looking to establish the position of the guild and give some clout to its members switched to motions of amalgamation with the major New York writers' guilds, the Authors Guild and the Dramatists Guild. The studio moguls, who had themselves made their way from the East Coast, some from its theatrical enclaves in New York, regarded this coming together of writers' groups as a pact between communists, anarchists, and who knew what other kind of radical malcontents. But they really interpreted the move as an act of disloyalty, a sign of lack of respect for those who were part of the "family."

Riskin had trouble with the guild's stance as well. He freely admitted that he was somewhat ambivalent toward its politics in the period between 1933 and 1935 and said that he just went about minding his own business, a phrase that he put into an entirely different context when the battles within the guild became more heated and accusatory.[56] It seems inconceivable that Riskin was not hearing stories or being asked his opinion of developments, but it is entirely consistent with his character that he chose to keep his own counsel for as long as he did. As for his colleagues, it was widely assumed among the more experienced and conservative writers of Hollywood that the Screen Writers Guild was acting as a mouthpiece for activist forces and hotheads in their midst, a view Riskin didn't entirely endorse but feared the accuracy of. Herman Mankiewicz, attuned to a Depression much of Hollywood was still quarantined from if not in denial about, summed up the feelings of his screenwriting generation in typically acerbic fashion.[57] "You'll go out on the streets carrying big signs," he said. "'Help! Help! We're only being paid seven and a half a week.' And everybody will say, 'How about those poor guys? Seven dollars and fifty cents a week.' And then somebody else says, 'No seven *hundred* and fifty *dollars* a week.' And then duck because you'll all be stoned to death."[58]

As the year moved along and Franklin Roosevelt's presiden-

cy took off through the spring of the one hundred days that introduced the New Deal to America, the confrontation between
the studios and the new union became a standoff. By November
1933, MGM announced a new contract for its writers whereby
each would be engaged for the length of the one movie he or
she was working on, and then laid off at the close of the film's
production. Talk of threats and intimidation was rife. A rival
organization of the guild was cultivated among conservative-
minded scenarists, even moderate figures like Irving Thalberg,
who transformed himself into one of the fiercest critics of the
Screen Writers Guild in this period.[59] For more than three years,
the battles raged back and forth. Riskin became drawn into the
conservative enclave, particularly by colleagues and friends like
Philip Dunne, who convinced him that, as a recognizable and
respected public figure with a record of public endorsement of
improving writers' conditions (in the *Los Angeles Herald* article he
had written), he was one of the men who could make the writers
and producers see sense and come to a satisfactory accommo-
dation for all concerned. But Riskin had also spent much of the
twenties scrimping and saving in a decade of excess, and he now
found himself on the other side of the fence in a time of misery
and hardship. After the success of *It Happened One Night* in 1934,
in the middle of this war of attrition, Riskin was becoming one of
Hollywood's highest paid screenwriters at $1,500 a week. While
he supported the intent of the Screen Writers Guild, he sympathized with the position Mankiewicz had laid out: the union had
to represent those who had more money than they knew what to
do with as well as those struggling to break into the industry. The
result of such a dichotomy was that either the rich campaigned
for the poor in some kind of outreach program, or else they all
stood together and campaigned on the same platform from very
different positions in the Hollywood food chain.

The Screen Writers Guild proposed an embargo on new material for the screen until 1938 if amalgamation with the New York
guilds was not allowed to proceed. Riskin, allied with the conservative forces looking for a sensible compromise, seemed to be on
the right side of the argument, but that very same conservative

faction was about to jolt him out of his complacency and force him to make a very tough choice about the future of the guild.[60]

While the Screen Writers Guild struggled with its identity, Riskin's place in the film community was now being automatically aligned with Capra's. Over the course of the previous two years, there had been moments of divergence between the two—as each suggested and then went to work on differing projects—and never an outright declaration that a clear partnership was being forged. But by 1934, the partnership appeared to be a given, and the histories of the two men seem to accept nothing less. Charles Maland states that they set to work together on their next project largely without delay.[61] Both McGilligan and McBride describe a sense of urgency among the team—Walker, Bernds, and the rest, as well as Riskin—to make something quickly and inexpensively to carry forward the weight of momentum that had been building since *American Madness*.[62] This clamor to have a new picture in the can as soon as possible was apparently effective, as the next Frank Capra–Robert Riskin movie would be on release by February 1934, little more than five months after the premiere of *Lady for a Day*. But despite the evidence of a working routine moving into full stride, nowhere is there a clear expression that Capra and Riskin now considered themselves a duo working in tandem and looking for stories to put on screen. Capra's recollection is that he and Riskin read a new short story in the summer of 1933 and thought it could work, though the source of the pitch to a skeptical Harry Cohn remains yet another bone of contention.

Riskin now became much more of a driving force than previously accredited in following up stories and persuading Capra and Cohn of the wisdom of going into production. McGilligan claims that Riskin received sole authorial praise for his new adaptation, just as he had from Runyon, implying that the writing was Riskin's alone.[63] It was clear, however, that from here on, there would always be some form of interaction between the two on screenplays. So it was that both Riskin and Capra adapted Samuel Hopkins Adams's short story "Night Bus" for the screen, with Capra having read the story in a barbershop in Palm Springs and then heading off to tell Riskin about it immediately. The source of the narrative was *Cosmopolitan* magazine, where they had previously picked up "Madame La Gimp." This time, rather than just making subtle changes, Riskin changed characters and the narrative trajectory of the tale considerably, a tactic that would make all the difference in the end product: *It Happened One Night*.

The hero of "Night Bus," Peter Warne, a chemist with a degree, is rather smart and a little soppy. In the final script for the film, Riskin turned him into a hard-bitten reporter who drinks, likes the company of women, and has an eye for a good story.[64] Elspeth Andrews became Ellie Andrews, a touch more streetwise but a little less sexually provocative. As the story unfolds, both of the characters gain more and more sympathy. (Capra attributed this effect to sometime collaborator and personal friend Myles Connolly, but this claim needs some qualification.[65])

From two actors who were not even clear choices or overly committed to the project—Clark Gable and Claudette Colbert—Capra and Riskin drew near-career-best performances. It was a constant feature of their collaboration that they were able to coax out the talent in the actors and actresses working on their movies.[66] Riskin's particular gift was in making actors fit comfortably into their roles. Gable came into his own as an "ironic masculine presence" in *It Happened One Night*, and Claudette Colbert revealed previously undiscovered depths in her screen persona, just as, a little later, Capra and Riskin would turn Gary Cooper "into the offbeat embodiment of small town simplicity, honesty and common sense."[67]

The casting of *It Happened One Night* tells the tale not only of studio politics in the era but of the ways in which mogul, director, and writer could offset one another's influence on casting and personality. Capra originally talked of having Myrna Loy from MGM for the role of Ellie, but when she turned it down—later pleading that the script she saw was entirely different from the one that became a movie legend—he was left with Colbert. The two had worked together on the 1927 silent movie *For the Love of Mike*, a troubling and exasperating experience for Capra, who not only fell out with the star but, soon after, left the studio, First National.

Capra also was adamant that he wanted Robert Montgomery from MGM for the role of Warne. (MGM kept appearing in these negotiations because Louis B. Mayer had promised Cohn a loan-out in exchange for Capra's work on the now-defunct *Soviet*.) Mayer didn't want Montgomery to go but came to a deal with Cohn to let Columbia have Clark Gable—who was working pro-digiously but really needed a major hit in his career—for a mere $10,000. Cohn loved the deal, while Capra and Riskin had the unenviable task of knitting two prickly stars together.[68]

Gable made Peter Warne seem effortlessly easy to pull off, and Colbert's notorious reluctance to take on the role—she vir-tually set the shooting schedule by demanding that she work no more than four weeks before her skiing vacation—is barely visible in her sassy, smart, and ultimately sexy rendition of Ellie Andrews. Considering that the word "sentimental" often arises when talking of Capra's work, it is remarkable how unsentimen-tal Riskin's characters, and especially their romances, could be. As McGilligan asserts, Riskin always strayed from the obvious, the mawkish, and the just plain slushy in favor of subtler outlets for screen romance.[69] In particular, actresses like Jean Arthur and Barbara Stanwyck brought feisty independence and a particular brand of sex appeal to the Capra-Riskin plots that never materi-alized in tales offering the most obvious of romantic finales.

Robert Sklar's interesting analysis of *It Happened One Night* attempts to distance the story from the picture's legacy as the first real screwball narrative by relating story and character to their connections to 1920s culture and society, and especially to periodicals like *Cosmopolitan* and the *Saturday Evening Post*, from which such original material came. Sklar argues that some of the rough edges of the story are taken away from Ellie and Peter in the film, and he notes that Ellie succeeds in scrambling out of her social condition, unlike the women of Capra's pre-1934 mov-ies—particularly *Ladies of Leisure*, *The Miracle Woman*, and *Forbid-den*, where only tragedy and despair await them.[70]

The argument has some merit, but even Sklar accepts that the genteel, heroic position of the male protagonist is not quite as straightforward as it might be in *It Happened One Night*'s inter-pretation of Adams's story. Riskin makes the road trip that Ellie

and Peter undertake together from Miami to New York a concoction of truth or dare, lies and secrets withheld and then revealed, wider social and sexual liaisons slowly unwrapped and
discovered on both sides. As they encounter adventures along
the way, with Ellie seeking to escape her marriage, and Warne
undertaking to escort her back to her father, romance blossoms
and the two fleeting spirits from across social divides find mutual desires. Sexual tension, the film's most resonant message, is
left smoldering once more in Riskin's trademark way. Cinematic
Warne is no longer the literary sap Warne, with only his looks
and genteel manner to bestow upon Ellie, and she is no more the
rich, provocative vamp Elspeth, with only sex and money to sell.
One might be tempted to describe this as sophisticated screwball,
but it says a lot about Riskin's sensitivity to his characters that he
can maintain the "will they, won't they" trajectory of the narrative without ever losing his players' values or ideals. They don't
have to lose their established foibles and predilections to finally
gravitate toward each other. When Peter leaves Ellie in the middle of the night, with no note explaining his absence, we might
suppose this is all a plot device. Ellie automatically assumes Peter has gone to file his sensational story of the socialite who now
wants to go AWOL from her wealthy aviator husband, when in
reality he has gone to find money so that they can be married
in better economic circumstances. But Riskin makes Warne's actions, his reluctance to reveal a moral side to his nature, and his
confusion about such a strong romantic gesture seem quite un-
derstandable and perfectly in tune with his character, rather than
just one final obstacle en route to the inevitable tryst.

One might go further in suggesting that *It Happened One Night*
was not simply the realization of a lasting 1920s cultural trope in
Riskin and Capra's work, but that their films continued to hedge
their bets between a wider, twentieth-century urban sophistication in their characters and the nineteenth-century agrarian
simplicity often identified in protagonists in future pictures. Toward the end of the film, there is a comic confrontation that sums
up this theme brilliantly for Riskin's work. Ellie's father (Walter Connolly) recognizes that his daughter has been affected by
meeting Warne. She confesses that she loves Peter but thinks he

must surely now despise her, because she ran back to King Westley (Jameson Thomas), the sop she is due to remarry in an elaborate ceremony. "He despises everything I stand for. He thinks
I'm spoiled and pampered," she says to her father of Peter. "He
doesn't think much of you either. He blames you for everything
that's wrong about me. Thinks you raised me stupidly."

"Fine man to fall in love with," says her father with a wry
smile. "Oh he's marvelous," retorts Ellie without hesitation.[71]
Ellie's father, like so many patriarchal figures in Riskin's scripts,
spots aspects of warmth and humanism in Ellie's comments and
an aching desire to break the shackles of convention. Westley acts
like royalty from the Victorian age, and Ellie's father can see how
modern and progressive his daughter has become under the influence of Warne. It was the contrast between duty and choice,
enfranchisement and passivity, that proved crucial in displaying
the enveloping control of state authority and social complicity
over people of different statuses and backgrounds, a theme first
brought to the fore in this, the biggest comedy hit of Riskin's and
Capra's careers.

Before the acclaim that would sweep over *It Happened One Night*
could engulf the partnership and transform it from the next
big thing into Hollywood's hottest property, Capra and Riskin
seemed to need to get through one more picture to show they
were capable of transferring their gifts to other stories, if not entirely different genres. The reception of *It Happened One Night*
gained momentum through the spring of 1934, but Riskin was
already working up another script for a racetrack story, a setting
he was very comfortable with.

In fact, Riskin had two scripts in preparation, the other being *Carnival*, which was to be directed by Walter Lang. He was
working at full throttle, most likely because Capra needed to get
one more picture out of the way to fulfill the obligations of his
current contract with Columbia before going back to Cohn to demand a better deal for re-signing with the studio. There may also
have been more general talk of Capra's finances that summer,
including his need to clear up anomalies on his accounts. Newspaper reports stated that the director owed back taxes to the IRS,

though the amount was small, and surely negligible for a film-maker earning Capra's salary.[72]

Nevertheless, location shooting for *Broadway Bill* began at Tanforan Racetrack near San Francisco in June 1934, even before the script was fully finished. Riskin adapted the story from an unpublished tale by New York newspaper columnist Mark Hellinger.[73] The tale was a typical against-the-odds sporting success: a no-hope horse enters a big race as a long shot and triumphs, defying everyone's expectations except its trainer's. But within the tale of a sporting David and Goliath match—a premise that had an uncanny resemblance to the future story of America's most famous racehorse of the era, Seabiscuit—Riskin provided yet another twist on the theme of love across class and social divides. Racehorse trainer Dan Brooks (Warner Baxter) is pressed by his wife, Edna (Margaret Hamilton), to pursue the family business, which is in effect swallowing up small companies and, in his case, inheriting the latest acquisition: a company that makes cardboard boxes. The sense of literally being boxed in by one's options might be a little coy, but Riskin expands this theme to encompass Dan's harsh return to the horse-racing arena. Just like Dan's training, his naturally talented horse, Broadway Bill, is naïve and rusty when it comes to such technicalities as coming to grips with starting stalls. Dan has also been away from the track too long to spot a betting scam that eventually attempts to set up the still-unknown Broadway Bill in the main race. Dan seems set to be hoisted by his own petard, but Alice (Myrna Loy), Edna's sister, who loves Dan for his commitment and passion, supports him all the way to the finish.

Riskin found the racetrack atmosphere easy to conjure, and his knowledge of the horse race game was well founded. He and his brother Everett, since arriving in California, had acquired their own racehorses—Riskin's most famous horse, Dogaway, ran often at Tanforan—and were regulars at tracks, where Riskin often invested considerable amounts of money in the outcome of races.[74] One might suggest that Colonel Pettigrew (Raymond Walburn) is something of a comic alter ego of Riskin, a man who has charm and eloquence but is somewhat loose with money. He falls for his own scam at the track, spreading a rumor about the chances of a 100-to-1 outsider, only to end up betting on the no-hoper and, predictably, losing. The lessons of Riskin's sporting fable are all crammed into the third act, which clears the way for Dan to marry Alice, having divorced Edna, but also stresses that Dan can now pursue his real love of training. In this he is joined by J. L. Higgins (Walter Connolly), who sees in Dan's passion an alternative existence beyond society's money-making clasp. Dan is no longer, in Charles Maland's words, a "social parasite" who feels himself unworthy of society because he is not following his gut instinct, and J. L. Higgins is the industrial patriarch won over to this point of view, critically questioning wealth as an inactive condition in a society craving vibrant creativity.[75]

Riskin finished the script for *Broadway Bill* and went to Europe on vacation soon after Capra began shooting. It is not clear whether he traveled with his longstanding girlfriend, Glenda Farrell, for she was in the midst of shooting four films in that year alone. Whatever happened abroad during that summer, reports by the end of the year were stating that the romance was at an end. Riskin's bachelorhood ideas seemed to have caught up with him again, though subsequent features in the gossip columns suggested that he had taken up with Carole Lombard, star of *Virtue*, and, a year later, that he intended to propose marriage to her.[76]

Capra's trouble filming *Broadway Bill* in the summer of 1934 was all about closure as well. He was just not sold on a feel-good ending that simply resulted in triumph for trainer and horse, and so he called in one of Columbia's other contracted scribes, Sidney Buchman, to fashion an ending that saw the horse of the title collapse and die after the finish line, amid the scene of its greatest victory. Buchman established a rapport with Capra that would serve him well when it came to screenwriting duties for the director's last film at Columbia, five years on. In *Mr. Smith Goes to Washington*, Buchman's more pointed political ethos would add bite to Capra's most ideologically contemplative film, a weighty political drama whose plot finale, ironically, seems contrived when compared with the bittersweet closure of *Broadway Bill*'s sporting fantasy.

Casting for *Broadway Bill* also proved to be less than smooth, though Capra was successful in bringing actress Myrna Loy on board this time, to play the romantic lead Alice. For Warner Baxter, who played the "everyday" trainer Dan Brooks, *Broadway Bill* would provide a much-needed hit after a run of flops. He was, however, neither Capra's choice nor his typical type of actor. Capra had wanted Gable again, but MGM was unhappy at lending its star out for another hit picture, which Capra's movie looked sure to be in the wake of *It Happened One Night*. As it turned out, Baxter gave a good rendition of an ordinary Joe, or "little fella"—the phrase crept into a Capra-Riskin film for the first time here—chasing his dreams.

On the face of it, the picture seems to have a simple enough premise: Brooks gets to show that his wealthy father-in-law is in business for money and little else. There is a nice running visual gag that displays everything in the small town of Higginsville, home of Baxter and his wife, one of J. L.'s daughters, as owned by J. L. Higgins. But Riskin carved out an unusual identity for Brooks as both driven by the ambition and competition of racing horses and sensitive to failure and his place within life. He is aggressive and, controversially, less than enlightened when it comes to relationships with members of other parts of society.

The film has been criticized for its racist overtones, exemplified in Dan's blunt treatment of his stable hand, Whitey (Clarence Muse). Attitudes to race and racism, however, were of little concern to Riskin in his screenplays; class and social identification were much more prominent within his writing—indeed, they were the force of most narratives. Produced in an era when Hollywood's treatment of black people matched the indifference, not to say outright hostility, of other parts of America, the film seems something of an odd target for questions of civil rights. The relationship Riskin drew out of these characters may have come from his experience within the horse-racing fraternity. It was certainly the case that stable hands were below jockeys in the pecking order of the racing game, and jockeys in this era were treated appallingly. Stable hands were also frequently young black men looking to make a little money for themselves. Riskin might have had a particular trainer–stable hand relationship in mind, but he certainly was not making a demonstrative point about race or

racism. While Whitey's name might be regarded as an invert-
ed dig at general society's condescending tone, it could just as
well be seen as an upholder of standard racist views. Despite the
character's submissive state, Riskin does throw in a few shrewd
rejoinders that hint toward future change, particularly Whitey's
question to his employer: "Boss, you mind if I have an idea?"

In retrospect the film may be seen as treading water, as being
a sideshow en route to Capra and Riskin's next big event, but
the film was popular and, even at the pace it was made, reflected
quality craftsmanship. The question of credit for *Broadway Bill*
would, however, come back to haunt the Capra-Riskin relationship at the end of the 1940s, when the situation at the heart of the
denouement's rewrite by Buchman when Riskin was not around
would affect Capra's work on remaking the movie, this time as
Riding High.

Broadway Bill was released in November 1934 and chalked up
another hit for Capra and Riskin, albeit a moderate one. But *It
Happened One Night*, released almost nine months to the day before the racetrack picture, loomed over this slight little comedy
like some much older sibling. In December, the *Los Angeles Examiner* reported on the six best film stories for 1934 and named
as the winner *It Happened One Night*.[77] Oscar talk was in the air,
and the film did indeed get nominated in virtually all categories
for the 1935 awards. It is perhaps easy to see how *Broadway Bill*
got lost in the euphoria that surrounded *It Happened One Night*
in Hollywood. But for different reasons and with different ambitions, both these pictures made Capra and Riskin the hottest
filmmaking partnership in movies in 1934.

Politics, Culture, and Riskin's Democratic Vision

Capra and Riskin made five pictures together in various states
of collaboration between late 1931 and the close of 1934. In many
people's eyes, these films more or less invented the screwball
comedy genre, as well as set the trends that defined classic Hollywood narratives, which says much for the rich vein of artistic form the pair fell into while working in tandem. And there
is no doubt that a partnership was initiated in this period, no

matter at what point both men recognized its official status. A critical and theoretical analysis of what lay behind the expressive, ideological, and commercial success of these joint ventures remains, however, a tricky pursuit. For some, this initial collection of Capra-Riskin films is defined by a matchless ingenuity for social comment and cultural recognition. Charles Maland, for one, identifies the importance of the first of these pictures in recognizing the economic climate of the time. "By celebrating the inherent virtue of middle-class informality over upper-class snobbism," he says, "*Platinum Blonde* is really the first Capra film to recognize, at least implicitly, that a depression was on."[78] The clash of social divisions also dominates the other four films in the sequence and is, by Maland's reckoning, the root of the partnership's success: a democratic vision attuned to the needs of audiences and critics alike.

Ray Carney's interpretation of these early films rests upon a meditative quality that he sees residing in the central protagonists. In comparing the pictures to the work of writers like Walt Whitman and painters such as Thomas Eakins and Winslow Homer, Carney notes the presence of an "inward-turning contemplation" within Capra's characters in the films until *Broadway Bill*. For him, their movements, their glances away from the camera, their stillness before the viewer are all the work of an artist searching for the spiritual beneath the veneer, for an inner conscience behind the simplicity.[79] It is interesting that Carney only ever refers to Capra's, not Riskin's, vision of the characters' inner workings and conscious selves; Riskin is never more than Capra's cowriter in Carney's eyes. But how does one reconcile or even add to such assessments when contemplating the films in this period? More important, how does one begin to distinguish the trajectory of Riskin's career and his contribution to the cultural and ideological tropes of each text?

Certainly, the awareness of the Depression as a backdrop to events was important. To Riskin one might ascribe the position of arbiter between traditional, individualist principles and the New Deal's collectivist mentality. As Martin Rubin states, social critics of the period such as George Soule argued for an idealized reciprocity between the self and society, a result of external (social, environmental) as well as internal (biological, psychological) compulsions.[80] Stew Smith, Peter Warne, and Dan Brooks have a Jeffersonian sentimentality for the rugged individualism of America's past, but through their observance of wealth, they also seek to remind those with money of the responsibilities of collective rebuilding in the thirties.

The concentration on urban, principally New York settings also produces a constancy of ideological framing in Riskin's scripts that offsets the rich and poor, city and rural, elite and bourgeoisie. The city is not externalized as a backdrop location in these pictures so much as it is internalized by the behavior of some of Riskin's most significant characters. Particularly with his peripheral players, Riskin brought another dimension to both the narratives and the New York setting. Bingy in *Platinum Blonde*, Happy McGuire in *Lady for a Day*, and Oscar Shapely in *It Happened One Night* all contribute what Maland calls "an urban vitality rarely present in the earlier Capra films."[81] But it is through the female protagonists that one sees a glimmer of ideological persuasion running through all of Riskin's early work, with and without Capra. It was not just that women could be independent, feisty, career-oriented characters in Riskin's pieces; it was that they were ciphers for the social and sexual revolution ignited in the previous few years. With women like Gallagher, Missouri Martin, Helen, and Alice, as well as Ann Carver, Mae, and Ida, Riskin was often able to craft truthful representations of the modern American woman. It wasn't just the outward appearance of sexual and social liberation that fueled his interest in these characters, but a dissimulative practice by which the characters were never quite fulfilling the promise of who they were or wanted to be. Ann Carver, Anne Schuyler, Ellie Andrews, and Alice Higgins all must experience transformations or confront the reality of who they are, sometimes, as in the case of Jean Harlow in *Platinum Blonde*, without the benefit of a positive outcome. This personal sense of an incipient revelatory alteration is a key consideration for the early films, because Riskin's female protagonists give contemporary, culturally embedded, and theatrical momentum to the cinematic presentation of directors like Buzzell, Cummings, and, yes, Capra.

What is further apparent in Riskin's early writing is an economy of scale and a use of dialogue, particularly with secondary characters, that is not superficial padding but is integral to the body of the picture. Women are never there to be saved, wooed, or dismissed in his stories, but are in fact invited to act as social integrators and reflexive commentators on their male counterparts' inability to emotionally relate or systematically analyze the predicaments at the heart of so many of these plots. In the Capra films particularly, Stew Smith, Tom Dickson, Dave the Dude, and Peter Warne all rely on their straight-talking, no-nonsense female companions to point out the unfolding drama. Phyllis Dickson's tantalizing comment to her husband when he cancels their anniversary plans—"I don't suppose it ever occurred to you that I might go out and find myself an attractive young man"—was a radical point of departure for a married woman in Hollywood pictures, and Riskin allows it to fester in the audience's mind until key narrative strands explode the possibility of adultery or worse. For Riskin, then, what he would later describe as an identification with, and portrayal of, contemporary cultural developments was not so much a transgression of social and ideological norms as it was a challenge to Hollywood and society to break archetypal genre, gender, and political boundaries. By the end of 1934, Riskin's writing was fully enveloping this notion and leading him toward the peak of his career.

CHAPTER THREE

THE PARTNERSHIP

All I can say is a thousand thanks for this grand script—
what a pleasure(?)!!

—Gary Cooper's comments on the front
of the shooting script for *Mr. Deeds Goes to Town*

Riskin and Capra's next movie, *Mr. Deeds Goes to Town*, premiered at Radio City Music Hall in New York on April 12, 1936.
It received much popular and critical acclaim, building on the
endorsements and favor garnered by *It Happened One Night* more
than two years before.[1] Capra had not put out a movie at all in
1935, his first concerted break from filmmaking since before his
collaboration with silent comedian Harry Langdon in 1925. But
his year away did nothing to dim the excitement and enthusiasm
for his new picture. *Mr. Deeds* was the high-water mark in the
public and press's clamor for Capra and Riskin's films, but its
making and release were also a critical juncture in Riskin's life
and another seed planted in the mythology of Capra's.

The story of what happened to the director from the release
of *Broadway Bill* in November 1934 until the appearance of *Mr.
Deeds* is now part of Hollywood legend. Capra was in the hospital when his racetrack comedy premiered, also at Radio City Music Hall, and he underwent two operations in late 1934. Capra's
appendix had burst back in 1919, but he had never had it properly treated. A first exploratory operation now found a ball of fat
that had grown inside and around the abdominal region. Cutting
out the fat unfortunately brought on peritonitis as well as other

complications, and Capra came close to death. The mythological element of the story is that the director reported being visited in the hospital by a "little man" who told him he had a responsibility to get back and make films with hope and a sense of social engagement. The story became Capra's inspiration and his own small conversion to ideological "message" films that would entertain and inform his public. Joseph McBride, however, sums up the episode in his account thus: "Most, if not all, of this fantastic story is an invention."[2]

Riskin took advantage of this hiatus to work on other projects already in the pipeline at Columbia, although he was committed to at least one of these regardless of Capra's illness. He had returned from Europe late in 1934, his romance to Glenda Farrell now over, in the full knowledge that he was once more going to write away from Capra. But while readjusting into the studio routine, at the end of the year, Riskin made a curious public declaration. In a short, droll essay for the *Hollywood Reporter* titled "The Canine Era," Riskin extolled the virtues of being in the "dog-house" for the first time in his professional career, and said how pleasant it was to be accompanied by other talents similarly confined to Hollywood's backwater. The article, while satirical in tone, comes across as slightly distressed and resentful of Hollywood's approval ladder and the arbitrary nature of success and failure, an occupational hazard Riskin was surely well aware of by this stage.[3]

Published on New Year's Eve 1934, however, it might also be explained away as a journalistic piece that Riskin wrote at a crossroads in his life. He had just publicly split from his partner while having the most successful year of his career to date, with two films from the previous twelve months having become hits, albeit on different scales. *Broadway Bill* had received enough plaudits in the press for Riskin's New Year's Eve article not to be perceived as some backlash against the critical response to that movie. The only other possibility would seem to be Riskin's disapproval of Capra and Buchman's rewriting of the ending of the racetrack comedy in favor of something more bittersweet, done while Riskin was away in Europe. Maybe "The Canine Era" was the outlet for his umbrage at having the screenplay transformed without his presence or approval. Or maybe it was simply written as a joke, designed to deflect attention from his growing reputation and to convince his fellow writers that he was just like them: he had failures, upsets, and disasters. While the writing now seems slightly contrived, it does fit the rather offbeat, satirical poise of Riskin's other essays at other points in his career. In any case, he clearly didn't dwell on the issues, because in 1935 he trod a path of success similar to that of the previous few years.

Riskin had begun assembling a script called *Carnival* midway through 1934 for director Walter Lang. Lang had been at Columbia since the 1920s but had briefly left movies and tried his hand at art in Paris. He was about to establish a name for himself at Fox, but he made this rather unassuming film for Cohn first. Starring Lee Tracy and Jimmy Durante, the film tells of the relationship between a puppet master and a pianist who end up looking after a baby when the puppeteer's wife dies. The film follows their trials as a traveling and performing duo, and the climax involves a fire that puts the baby's life in danger, only for the obligatory happy ending to follow. Shot in only twenty days and made for $170,000, *Carnival* was cheap and cheerful even by Columbia's standards, but Riskin's narrative drive and sense of engagement with his audience through character and setting were once more evident as the hallmarks of the studio's budget filmmaking.[4] Sound engineer Edward Bernds remembers the shooting of the film as troubled; he himself was pressed into service when a number of the crew got fired. He later commented that he thought Riskin's script was "bright and amusing" when he encountered it, and he knew, having worked with the writer before, that Riskin's presence was a sign of the project's quality.[5] The picture made money for the studio, and Riskin was following in Capra's shoes by enhancing the reputation of even Columbia's most meager offerings.

Riskin had also begun the preparation of a script with his friend Jo Swerling for John Ford's new film, *The Whole Town's Talking* (1935), with Lester Cowan producing. Cowan was an independent producer who pitched projects to studios like Columbia, the type of individual Harry Cohn disliked intensely. Cohn resented that Cowan represented a group of producers who wanted to exact the greatest amount of control over a picture while paying the least amount of attention to budgets and shooting schedules. Cohn also thought Cowan was not as grand a producer as he wanted to think himself. He simply wasn't on a par with Hal Wallis, David Selznick, or Sam Goldwyn, opined Columbia's chief.[6]

And the story of making *The Whole Town's Talking* was that Cowan did virtually no producing at all. Although his name appears in the credits, the film, like many others he did, was really solely directed and produced by Ford. The picture turned out to be the only one that Ford made at Columbia. By all accounts, he was happier in the calm air of Selznick's Twentieth Century–Fox, which remained his cinematic home, than in the madhouse that Columbia could be, despite Cohn's longstanding regard for his talents. The author of the original tale, W. R. Burnett, who had written *Little Caesar* only a few years before, sat in on early story conferences with Ford, and he was mystified as to why the director was at the studio at all, let alone doing a picture like this. Ford never spoke during the meetings, which was a sure sign to Burnett that he was bored by the whole venture. He later speculated that Ford was broke at the time—he had a reputation for spending money like it was going out of fashion—and so may have taken the job just for the revenue.[7]

Riskin and Swerling's double-edged double act *The Whole Town's Talking* (released in Britain as *Passport to Fame*) features Edward G. Robinson as a gangster. "Killer" Mannion takes over the identity of a soft-spoken bookkeeper, Arthur Jones, who looks exactly like him, to conceal his illicit activity. Jones has been working for the J. G. Carpenter Company for eight years and in his spare time writes anonymous verses to the woman he is in love with, his independently minded colleague Miss "Bill" Clark (Jean Arthur). This plot element is in Burnett's original story but certainly bears resemblance to the work of Riskin's early career, especially the love letter for Joe Golden to Trixie Friganza, and it probably sparked some memories for Riskin. As the narrative develops, Jones is given the opportunity to use his creative skills by writing a series of exposés about his famous look-alike for the newspapers—he is now familiar with Mannion because the police keep arresting him, and he has made a personal passport so as to distinguish himself from the crook—but in the process he brings threats of harm to himself and Miss Clark. In the end,

Mannion's gang mistake their man for Jones and shoot him, thus ending the threat against Jones and Clark, who are now free to marry and fulfill their dreams of exotic travel.

As in Burnett's other stories, the action is taut, but the two scenarists often made it lighthearted and smart too. *The Whole Town's Talking* proved to be the biggest hit of Riskin's career outside the partnership with Capra. Ironically and unfortunately, the film has become nothing more than a minor stopping-off point for scholars looking at Ford's career. There are a great deal of other features to look at in this era, of course, but Ford's dabbling in screwball comedy deserves more than Andrew Sinclair's dismissive assessment that *The Whole Town's Talking* was one of the "minor pictures of the period" (together with *The World Moves On* [1934]).[8] Tag Gallagher is one Ford scholar who has been more generous and has given the Riskin-Swerling film some further attention. He compares the picture to one from the previous year, *Judge Priest*, Ford's tale of small-town rivalries.[9] Gallagher's regard for the picture is reflected in Jean Mitry's statement: "Of all John Ford's films, *The Whole Town's Talking* is the most dynamic, brilliant and funny. . . . Not a work of genius, no, but dazzling and surprisingly virtuosic." Mitry goes on to explain, "The film's density is achieved by the greatest amount of action in the least amount of time. Rapid, alert, wonderfully cut and mounted . . . it is a work of total perfection in its genre."[10]

Riskin barely got endorsements like that for his most successful movies of the decade, let alone so-called minor ones. Reviews for Robinson's performance were equally enthusiastic. The key in Riskin's writing was to wash away the recognizable symbols of the decade's early gangster mannerisms and leave something "slightly comical" in Mannion's brutish world.[11] As Gallagher says of the film, "In treating gangster-film conventions parodically, Ford does not undermine the conventions' purposes."[12] What remains for the director in the script are genuine notions of authority and corruption exposed by Robinson's dithering, meek portrayal of Jones. With Ford's direction and Joseph August's bleak cinematography, Riskin had a very different canvas for his dialogue, a canvas replete with the tensions mired in the urban landscape of the Depression. A gangster-genre set was neatly fitted together with a screwball-genre script by Riskin and

Swerling's concentration on the dialogue and personalities of the players. Even Burnett's skepticism about Ford's attitude and the final product was tempered. He later recalled, having helped to straighten out some of the kinks in the denouement, that it was "a hell of a good picture."[13]

Andrew Sarris's comment that *The Whole Town's Talking* "reflected a tendency around the mid-thirties to burlesque the *film noir*" is a striking assessment in this context.[14] Riskin had already played around with this idea in *Lady for a Day* by creating a gang, led by Dave the Dude, who discover a soft side to their nature as they help Apple Annie. He and Swerling achieved a similar trick by getting Robinson to reassemble his performance from *Little Caesar*, but touchingly, so as to avoid making the role self-destructively parodic. Played against Jean Arthur, who is likeable, goodly, and resilient, Robinson discovers emotions and depth of character not realized in anything outside the gangster form he understood so well. The film cleverly recognized the shift that had been building in public expectations about gangster films. The first cycle was over, and a return to order was expected, in movies like *G-Men* (1935) and the later *Angels with Dirty Faces* (1938), whereby upstanding authority would triumph. Janus-like, Ford's film portrayed the authoritarian proclivity for deceit but confirmed the higher social expectations and resolve of institutions as well as individuals in mid-thirties society.

One further important feature of the picture was in the promotion of Jean Arthur through the ranks of Columbia actresses to play a leading lady for the first time. She starred, in the same year, in William Seiter's *If You Could Only Cook*, a film produced by Riskin's brother Everett and edited by Capra's longtime collaborator Gene Havlick. The film was even advertised in Britain, in 1937, as a Frank Capra production, a source of much angst for the director in his slow falling-out with Cohn. But Arthur's appearance in both films, and especially as the strong-willed Miss Jones in *The Whole Town's Talking*, must have made an impression on Capra as well as Riskin, because the role of news reporter Babe Bennett in *Mr. Deeds* would be a shoo-in for an actress with her talent and demeanor, almost as if it had been written for her.[15] In Ford's film, she is nothing short of a revelation. She nails the kind of spirited, free-thinking, individual character that Riskin had been striving for in many of his stories, and that Capra made such good cinematic use of in *Mr. Deeds* and *You Can't Take It With You*. As *Variety* said of her in Ford's film, "She's gone blonde and fresh. She's more individualistic, more typically the young American, self-reliant and rather sassy."[16]

It was not hard to picture *The Whole Town's Talking* as a Frank Capra movie, and Capra would no doubt have given the film certain unique qualities on the screen. Still, though some found it too slight and contrived, others thought the picture a delightful alternative to Ford's more traditional output. It has unfortunately been dwarfed by that output; not only the Westerns in the thirties but also the later *Young Mr. Lincoln*, *The Grapes of Wrath*, and *How Green Was My Valley* have tended to focus the attention on Ford's grander social and political oeuvre. For Richard Coombs, however, reviewing *The Whole Town's Talking* in the 1980s, there are comparisons to the brashness of Howard Hawks and the style of George Cukor, and a performance from Robinson that, as well as looking back to *Little Caesar*, anticipates his role in *Brother Orchid* (1940), where he must decide on a future as a hoodlum or a monk. Indeed, Coombs sums up the picture by suggesting that both the central performances, carried along by Riskin and Swerling's script, are what ultimately sustain the film, even though Ford invited quite divergent styles that would never, unfortunately, meet up again in his movies.[17] Riskin brought a structural and ideological style to Ford's films that was rarely apparent in the director's later career. Mixing genres and offering a subtle critique of law and order and even Hollywood presentations of the gangster aesthetic, Riskin with Swerling once more made a female protagonist the driving force of the movie. Later appreciations like Coombs's confirm a progression in Riskin's writing at the time that meant he could team up with the most unlikely of directors and, more important, give another dimension to their craft, as much as he gained new insights into his own technique.

Union Bargaining and the Road to Mandrake Falls

While Capra's sabbatical continued in 1935, the press remained fascinated both by the choice of project for the pair's next film and by Riskin's personal life. Riskin was seen out with Carole Lombard, attending premieres and Hollywood parties, and rumors of wedding bells spread rapidly around the movie community. All the while, newspaper reports focused on Columbia's ascent on the studio scale on the back of *It Happened One Night* and its assault on the Academy Awards that spring. Harry Cohn talked to the press of elevating writers to the rank of stars because what pictures were in need of most, he stated, was stories. He picked Riskin as the cream of his particular crop and described his star writer as "a modest unassuming chap" who had the talent to put stories on the screen the public wanted to see. Cohn mentioned that Riskin was currently writing a script from James Hilton's novel *Lost Horizon*, which he was due to finish at any moment.[18]

Though Capra had spoken of adapting the Maxwell Anderson play about George Washington, *Valley Forge*, on his return from convalescence, he was struck by Hilton's tale while making *It Happened One Night*. Riskin was surprised that Cohn agreed to the movie, because "every studio in town had turned [the novel] down."[19] But Capra had a vision for the film and someone in mind for the lead role of British diplomat Conway. Ronald Colman was the director's idea of the suave English gentleman abroad, but he wasn't available for at least a year. By July 1935, Capra and Riskin had therefore suspended work on *Lost Horizon* until Colman was free and were already preparing an alternative feature. As the *Hollywood Reporter* noted in its July 1 headline, the story "Opera Hat" was to replace *Lost Horizon* on Columbia's 1935–36 film program.[20] In the writing, the story quickly acquired a new title: *Mr. Deeds Goes to Town*.

Settled by now into the tradition of short-story adaptations, Riskin and Capra culled *Mr. Deeds* from the serialized magazine tale by Clarence Budington Kelland. What both writer and director took from the story by way of narrative propulsion and ideological conviction helps to illustrate the similar paths that Capra and Riskin were now treading independently of each other. Joseph McBride makes an important analogy in his biography of Capra, comparing the theme named in his subtitle, "the catastrophe of success," in which the pair fed the insecurities of their rags-to-riches story by imposing something of their own narratives on screen—how to react to fame, what to do with money—to their budding political involvement within the Hollywood system.[21] The year of the film's release saw Capra and Riskin embedding themselves ever more deeply in their respective causes, the Academy of Motion Picture Arts and Sciences and the Screen Writers Guild. The two organizations were by no means natural partners in the beginning, and it is easy to assume that Capra and Riskin would have been dragged apart by the festering politics that were infiltrating Hollywood at this time. But the real trick in understanding their relationship is not in spotting easy signs of mutual antagonism but in identifying the bonds that held Capra and Riskin together for as long as they did, through this period and beyond.

Along with their colleague Sidney Buchman, for instance, the pair had already made a prominent, though fruitless, stand against Harry Cohn's Merriam Fund in late 1934. In the California gubernatorial contest of that year, the End Poverty in California campaign of novelist, essayist, and onetime screenwriter Upton Sinclair was bitterly opposed by the studios—who thought him a left-wing maverick out to destroy them—and Cohn ordered his staff at Columbia to make contributions to elect Republican Frank Merriam, a move repeated in other studios.[22] Riskin was probably more in favor of Sinclair and his politics than Capra was, but there was certainly a principle at stake that the director well understood, even before political affiliations came into play. Capra and Riskin held out against Cohn for a short time, but the will to resist studio dictates was simply not apparent in the Columbia regime. The weak position of all the studios' employees was confirmed. The repercussions of Sinclair's Hollywood-driven propaganda defeat were still being felt eighteen months later, when *Mr. Deeds*, along with ideological developments in Hollywood that year, ratcheted up the political tension still further. But the emergence in *Mr. Deeds* of a social and ideological agenda that was shared wholeheartedly by Capra and Riskin made the creativity at the heart of their partnership that much more sustainable, at least in the short term. In fact, the success of *Mr. Deeds Goes to Town* maintained a vital ideological connection between the pair when everything around them was turning politically volatile.

Capra was elected president of the Motion Picture Academy in October 1935, just at the moment when the Academy was falling into disrepute with the directors. Capra served for three years as its president and tried in that time to revitalize its flagging fortunes, including an attempt to broker a deal for a set of working conditions for directors much like the one the Academy had tried to persuade writers to adopt only a few years before. But barely two months into Capra's presidency, he was faced with tough competition from the newly formed Screen Directors Guild, which would join the growing forces of the Screen Actors and Screen Writers guilds. Slowly but surely, the creative power was wrested away from the Academy, and labor business was directed into the hands of these separate organizations. By 1938, Capra was not only in the Screen Directors Guild but acting as its president.

Riskin had observed the infighting within the Screen Writers Guild from a safe distance for the two years since he had helped to draft a code of working rules for the guild in its earliest incarnation. In the meantime, decisions in Washington DC had provided hope and exasperation in almost equal measure for the union in its attempts to build collective bargaining power against the moguls. But when the National Recovery Administration was declared unconstitutional in May 1935, its labor-management guidelines went under as well, and the studios felt no inclination to even recognize, let alone bargain with, the guild.

The Screen Writers Guild therefore moved ever more steadfastly in 1936 toward what it hoped would be an amalgamation with the New York playwrights, those in the Authors Guild and the Dramatists Guild. Riskin, however, had allied with certain conservative voices that were less supportive of the tie-up, believing a compromise between the growing left- and right-wing factions could be negotiated. The studios as well as these more conservative forces within the screenwriting fraternity had become wary of the reactionary activists—Dorothy Parker, Dudley Nichols, and Sheridan Gibney, among others—who were looking to promote more overt political stances, particularly over issues stirred up by events like the Spanish Civil War. The rival groups struck a deal at a tension-filled meeting on May 2, 1936, when the news of competition and possible confrontation among the screenwriters brought out the Hollywood police to keep the peace.[23] The agreement, which pressed for a basic minimum wage for screenwriters, included the formation of a new fifteen-member board for the guild with the guarantee that Riskin, one of the brokers of this peace, would get one of those seats, and stipulated that a vote on amalgamation would be delayed. Riskin thought common sense had prevailed, and yet within a week of the agreement, four of the most prominent conservatives—James Kevin McGuinness, Patterson McNutt, Bert Kalmar, and John Lee Mahin—had resigned from the guild and formed their own union, the Screen Playwrights.

The left-wing Screen Writers Guild members had, in Philip Dunne's words, "been suckered" by a faction that quickly acquired the sobriquet "the four horsemen."[24] Although Dunne's description was accurate, as Nancy Lynn Schwartz points out, the studios also pressured writers to sign long-term contracts, diluting their wage demands and breaking up the power of the guild.[25] In this atmosphere, the rebel four were only the most visible proponents of a wider studio strategy that resulted in their taking more than 120 guild members with them to the new union on the pretext that the Screen Writers Guild was dangerous to writers' interests. It was estimated at one point that the guild had fewer than 40 members, and it effectively went underground for nearly two years in an attempt to rebuild confidence and credibility. But two of the members who had allied with the conservative faction to broker the deal they thought was fair stood by the guild and went on to work tirelessly for its rehabilitation; they were Sam Raphaelson and Riskin.

Typical of his principled stance, angry at what he saw as manipulation of his goodwill, Riskin stood up at a guild meeting and apologized for being associated with the people who had engineered the coup. But in his own offhand, calm, and satirical manner, he also took his revenge on the rebels in a piece for the *Hollywood Reporter* that appeared only days after the breakaway by McGuinness, McNutt, Kalmar, and Mahin. Following a tone set by the earlier "Canine Era" article that he had composed for the trade paper, this one was titled, slightly misleadingly, "I Was Going Along Minding My Own Business." In it Riskin argued that he joined the "distinguished gentlemen," as he bitingly referred to them, in order to ward off disaster for the guild, only for the "gentlemen" to claim they suddenly no longer had a constituency to represent. They had made deals; they should have a conscience concerning their actions, Riskin reasonably claimed. "Heigh-ho," he cried. "What about their OWN convictions? What about their pledge to the fifteen men on the board? What about their pledge [on] Saturday night [when the compromise had been struck between the "conservatives" and the members of the guild's executive board]? What about their pledge to me? Oh, hell, skip it!"[26] Respect for this stance, Riskin's belief in honor and standing by one's agreements, spread among guild members. The writer who had minded his own business, to a point, in the last few years now became a part of the Screen Writers Guild fraternity and began to integrate much more into Hollywood politics.[27]

In their account of this period, Larry Ceplair and Steven Englund tie Riskin's participation in the breakaway of the Screen Playwrights to his accession to the title of writer-producer at Columbia, as though the nature of the conspiratorial plot drew some reward for Riskin.[28] It did reward others, notably McGuinness, who was, according to fellow writer Ring Lardner Jr., handed a producing job at Metro for leading the breakaway.[29] Indeed, guild members regarded the Screen Playwrights suspiciously—and it failed to establish itself—precisely because they saw it as tied to the aspirations and desires of the producers. But the fact that Riskin disowned the rebel conservatives in the fashion he did mitigates the claim of his alleged traitorous reward of a producer title. In addition, after the success of *Mr. Deeds Goes to Town* in 1936, Harry Cohn knew full well he had to secure his top writer to the studio with a further incentive. By most accounts, then, Cohn prompted the announcement of Riskin's producer role himself, regardless of the battles within the guild, and had been looking to do so for some time.[30]

The experiences of Riskin and Capra might lead to the assumption that the writer and director would drift apart, at least on political grounds, as the second half of the thirties gathered pace. Capra was sympathetic to the Academy, and it was not hard to see why. The organization protected the interests of the biggest stars, and the director easily reached into that category now. Riskin had been allied with conservative forces as well, but after the coup of the right wing in the guild, he stuck with people whose political views were probably more extreme but who appreciated his conciliatory liberal stance, working-class upbringing, and, most of all, his consistent and persuasive articulation of the views of the Screen Writers Guild. And yet if this positioning of ideologies within the studio system strained the partnership, it is not discernible when or how. Indeed, Capra and Riskin actually joined forces publicly in 1938 to reestablish the guild as the leading forum for Hollywood writers—much to rebel conservative John Lee Mahin's disbelief, because he thought Capra would naturally be on the side of his Screen Playwrights. The National Labor Relations Act (commonly known as the Wagner Act) had been upheld by the Supreme Court in April 1937. Following a petition to the National Labor Relations Board that resulted in the granting of an election for union representation, which the Screen Writers Guild subsequently won 267–57, the guild was approved as the chief bargaining agent for the writers in August 1938. Urged on by Riskin, Capra attended crucial guild meetings as the newly elected president of the Screen Directors Guild with the remit to persuade certain contracted studio scribes to join the now-affiliated Screen Writers Guild.[31]

In fact, the politicization of Hollywood did not threaten Capra and Riskin's relationship at all during the mid-thirties. Rather, it promoted a creative force that would hold them in tandem over the next five years and forge a deeper and more personal social philosophy, beginning with the opening of their new movie *Mr. Deeds* and culminating in their final collaboration, immediately before America's entry into World War II, *Meet John Doe*. For while Capra and Riskin continued to play their parts in the political battles that flared up all over town between the unions and studios during late 1935 and early 1936, *Mr. Deeds Goes to Town* had already been shot and edited and was getting ready for its premiere.

The hero of Clarence Budington Kelland's short story "Opera Hat" is a tuba-playing greeting card peddler from the backwater of Mandrake Falls, Vermont, named Longfellow Deeds. Through

Deeds, perhaps more than any other character, Capra and Riskin's commonest virtues as filmmakers have been scoured and dissected. He is a man of agrarian simplicity and traditional American values; his story offsets big-city individualism against small-town communalism. Amid these oft-recognized elements, as Richard Corliss explains, the urban cynics have to be converted to simple hope, community, and zest for life by Deeds, while the mob entrusted to take sides in these disputes is nearly always right about the hero's character and the direction of his actions.[32]

There is no doubt that *Mr. Deeds* was a seminal film for both Capra and Riskin, in terms of their artistic and career development. Nothing would be quite the same in their lives after it. It is easy to see how the film fits into the canon of their following movies, both with and without each other, and how the characters, narratives, and resolutions mesh within the cinematic worlds of *You Can't Take It with You, Mr. Smith Goes to Washington, Meet John Doe, It's a Wonderful Life, Magic Town, Mister 880,* and *Here Comes the Groom.* Whether it is individual struggle, institutional examination, or visual symbolism, all of the above films date back, in one form or another, to *Mr. Deeds.* Yet one can appreciate in retrospect how recognizable the film was from what had gone before. The urban milieu had its roots in *The Whole Town's Talking, Lady for a Day, American Madness,* and even *The Miracle Woman.* Con men, shysters, and other duplicitous characters are evident not only in those four films, but also in *Platinum Blonde* and *Night Club Lady.* Lawyers and the courts emerge in *Ann Carver's Profession,* and fast-talking, smart, modern women had become a touchstone of Riskin's writing long before the scoop reporter Babe Bennett came along. So why has *Mr. Deeds* endured, and what in it was seen as original, uplifting, and definitive for the Capra-Riskin partnership? Andrew Bergman offers one understated clue. "Shrewdly," he says, "Capra added some topicality to Deeds."[33] Indeed, the "writing" partnership (which it had now become, though only after Riskin had written the initial story line and preliminary dialogue, as was always the case) had added some topicality. This growing symbiosis at the heart of the relationship, which dared to encompass current issues more confidently, was communicated by Riskin in an interview for Dudley Early while doing publicity for *Mr. Deeds* later in 1936. "The reason Frank and I get along so well is because we have the same basic story ideas," asserted Riskin. He went on to claim that they had some awful fights about scenes and dialogue but never disagreed about the constitution or direction of a story. Asked how this sense of each other's concerns and ideas came about, Riskin simply replied, "Well, we've been married a long time."[34]

Riskin expressed confidence in the interview about handling, with Capra, more delicate and progressive issues, not least because Cohn now largely left the two alone to make the film they wanted to make.[35] So Bergman's association of *Mr. Deeds* with topicality really refers to politics. Capra and Riskin had skirted the edges of political issues in a few films, notably *American Madness*, but *Mr. Deeds* is a political film, pure and simple. True, as he would later assert on occasion, Capra didn't like politics and didn't want his films to be seen as political, believing that Hollywood thought messages should be left to Western Union, and so on. But the making of the film, Riskin's adaptation, the most redoubtable scenes, and the characteristic ideas all point to only one conclusion. Asked about the underlying feeling in the film, Riskin said, "If you'll notice, the chief character is always full of something he's trying to express; [he] has just one idea he's trying to get over."[36] The thought could apply to films before *Mr. Deeds*, of course (and *American Madness* is indeed a close companion), but here the "idea" is not simply a personal statement of beliefs on behalf of a character or his immediate predicament, but an epistemological expression of the state of American society. More than that, *Mr. Deeds* is not only a film about politics in its institutional and societal forms but is intrinsically an examination of the forces of political character, and particularly the character of one politician: Franklin Delano Roosevelt.

Mr. Deeds was the first adaptation from an original source that Riskin had considerable problems with. Indeed, he ended up with a two-hundred-page script and a two-hour picture, the longest of his and Capra's careers to that point. Many, if not most, accounts of the film dwell on the extent of Riskin's changes to Kelland's story. The alterations subtly reframe the tone and style of the movie, rather than simply altering parts of the story line. In the film, Longfellow Deeds (Gary Cooper) inherits $20 million and an opera house in New York from a distant relative, Martin Semple. Accompanied by the estate's lawyer, John Cedar (Douglass Dumbrille), Longfellow relocates to New York, only to discover that city folk lack manners and traditional values like honesty and simplicity. He comes up with a plan to redistribute his fortune by giving it to needy farmers, but this pushes Cedar to try to prize the $20 million away from him by claiming Longfellow's plan is evidence of the man's instability. Ace reporter Louise "Babe" Bennett (Jean Arthur), posing as the innocent Mary Dawson, encourages Longfellow's quirky behavior in his discovery of the delights of the big city, posts the stories in the newspaper, and helps to bring on the charge of insanity to have the money placed with Cedar's firm. Longfellow faces the prospect of being detained until, in the climactic court scene, the folk of Mandrake Falls and the desperate farmers who sought his help come to his rescue.

This story line changed Kelland's tale considerably. Riskin had, for example, concentrated on the inheritance as a form of economic dislocation and a route by which to examine the marginalization of the poor. The character of Babe, whom he invented, formed the backbone of the love conquest that the narrative demanded. As Pat McGilligan observes, Riskin gave a previously unexplored emotional depth to Longfellow's rather soppy greeting card poems by having Babe read aloud a sonnet dedicated to her.[37] To add deft comic timing and lighten the corny mood, Capra thought to have Deeds trip over an ash can as that particular moment draws to a close, which Riskin acknowledged was a masterstroke. In scenes like this, cinematic framing and dialogue construction were honed to perfection. The court scene that is almost the complete third act of the film was entirely Riskin's creation. In it Deeds becomes a deeper, more laden character— mulling over the choices of his life during his prison cell vigil— than in Kelland's picture of him. But quite deliberately, Riskin left some overhanging conservative tendencies in his hero, and these not only confirm the strong political nature of the picture but also signify the Kelland touch that remains in a transformed ideological dialogue.

Kelland was an out-and-out conservative, a friend of business, and an opponent of Roosevelt. It is long forgotten that he had distinct political connections within the Republican Party.[38] He also vehemently objected to the screen treatment of his tale, and one can see how Riskin's reconstruction of the story diluted his simple, rural, go-getting entreaty for America to work its way out of the Depression as individuals, rather than as some collective herd under the auspices of a government acronym. But Kelland's protestations about his hero's ideological turnaround were only partly correct: the right-wing sentiment is not entirely lost in the movie, nor is it unsympathetically treated. Indeed, forty-five years later, actor-turned-president Ronald Reagan was prepared to use Deeds as an example of his own political philosophy. Longfellow's speech to the court near the close of the picture, for instance, describes exactly the kind of America that Reagan, who ironically was originally a Roosevelt supporter, liked to eulogize: "It's like the road out in front of my house. It's on a steep hill. Every day I watch the cars climbing up. Some go lickety-split up that hill on high—some have to shift into second—and some sputter and shake and slip back to the bottom again. Same cars—same gasoline—yet some make it and some don't. And I say the fellows who can make the hill on high should stop once in a while and help those who can't."[39]

These are the words that more often than not come back as evidence of the moderate Republican approach that Riskin and Capra endorse in the film, and of the populism that their films became associated with. And yet Riskin surreptitiously invested Deeds with transcendentalist tendencies, having him speak of Thoreau and cry "back to nature" in his drunken, naked flit through the streets of New York after his first night on the town. Adding a further dimension to this political interpretation, the scene most cited in the reviews of the time, as well as in the analyses since, is the one most conspicuously demanding the left-leaning mobilization of New Deal thought. This is the confrontation between Deeds and actor John Wray's desperate farmer, who invades the New York mansion our hero has acquired just as Deeds is planning to give it all up and return to Mandrake Falls. Turning a gun on the rich inheritor, the farmer angrily confronts Longfellow: "I just wanted to see what a man looks like that can spend thousands of dollars on a party—while people around him are hungry! The 'Cinderella Man,' huh? Did you ever stop to think how many families could have been fed on the money you pay out to get on the front pages?"[40]

Variety made no bones about a scene it thought was rich in "quasi-communistic" imagery.[41] The proletariat and the bourgeoisie would rarely clash in more profound circumstances than these in any Depression-era movie, the magazine seemed to state. But the screenwriting had more pressing claims to examine, and personal as well as social conflagrations to explore. More than simply acknowledging the extent of the Depression, and beyond expressing a Rooseveltian commitment to the downtrodden, Riskin's words also concede how much of America in the thirties was gently letting the Depression slide by because it was convenient to forget its worst excesses. The writer's great affinity with his audience is virtually tied up in the above scene, especially in the farmer's speech, a reminder of Riskin's gentle prodding about the haves and have-nots at the beginning of *Lady for a Day* nearly three years earlier. Whether you had a job or not, were penniless or just making do, there was plenty of publicity and media attention that exposed careless expressions of opulence, sensed Riskin. For almost the first time in American life, money had become shorthand for class divisions throughout the nation, and Riskin was all too well aware that his position could face the same accusation of easy acceptance, of head-in-the-sand passivity. It was as if Riskin wanted to openly confess, "Look, I know you read about me all the time, and yes, I have ridiculous amounts of money, but there is another side. The media, Hollywood, are uncaring souls and they are just interested in telling you how good we've got it and how bad it is for you. But there is another way."

If Riskin could find no easy way to square the circle of his guilt about wealth and fame other than to conceive of it on the big screen, he did so largely without condescension. In Riskin's adaptations, it didn't have to be ideals that rang true with his audiences, or preachy sentiment about their political plight, so much as the outlook and tone of his characters. Rather like Riskin's stance within the Screen Writers Guild that spring, principles were at least as important as politics: in fact, for Riskin, they were politics. It is not the farmer's threatening Longfellow with a gun that shocks the audience, but his collapse and confession that desperate poverty makes men do desperate things. When he says that he hopes he "didn't hurt nobody" by his actions, the rabid plight of the homeless and destitute, their desperate attempts to cling to principles they know to be right in the catastrophic face of misery, is brought into sharp relief in one individual. Here again, the sense of a conscious self working to articulate the psychological torment of a concerted mass is what gives Riskin's script its force and will. In this sense, Ray Carney's argument about Capra's films is absolutely right. If political philosophy in the movies from *Mr. Deeds* onward was seen by some to be "muddled," suggests Carney, it was because Capra, and much more so Riskin, was becoming obsessed with the effects that politics had on human experience and the tribulations of living, rather more than its theoretical underpinnings.[42] From life comes experience, and for experience, Riskin's scripts teach us again and again, there is no substitute for discovering moral principles and finding in them one's guidance and contentment through the bitterest of times.

This debate over the rationalization of social development is confirmed in the trial scene, when Riskin has Longfellow defend himself by denouncing the theories of Dr. Von Holler (Charles Lane), whom Cedar has engaged as the scientific proof of Longfellow's manic depression. Von Holler has charts and fancy language, but he is exposed through his "doodling" (one of Riskin's many magical words) as having equally wacky ideas. Longfellow comments, "People draw the most idiotic pictures when they're thinking. Dr. Von Holler, here, could probably think up a long name for it, because he doodles all the time."[43] Riskin manufactures a scene that doubts society's ability to scientifically construct its future if it forgets human quirks and thoughts. This is in many ways the most radical political sentiment in the picture, especially for a country coming to appreciate, in certain quarters, the emergence of psychology and sociology as doctrines of societal progression.

The infusion of ideas like these reveals that the film marks so much more than the emergence of topicality. It also signals the incipient recognition of a political debate in Hollywood, tied up in the labor relations furor of the Screen Writers and Screen Directors guilds, that precipitated questions of creative and artistic freedom for writers. *Mr. Deeds* itself was augmented in this respect by a small but significant clique of similarly ideologically grounded pictures in 1936. In particular, as Ian Hamilton singles out, the work of Nathaniel West and his scripts for the Republic Pictures features *The President's Mystery* and *It Could Happen to You* were key, as was Universal's screwball social comedy *My Man Godfrey*, directed by Gregory La Cava and starring Riskin's partner at the time, Carole Lombard.[44] West politicized what were in effect B pictures, and indeed, *It Could Happen to You*, about a possible fascist takeover in America, predated the exact sentiments of Capra and Riskin's *Meet John Doe* by five years. There were other examples of a latent social investigation, but Riskin's feat was to bring politics into the biggest commercial hit of 1936, not just into small-time pet projects. His considerably larger and more impressionable audience was led to think long and hard about the social and political effects of the Depression.

By far the most potent symbol of Capra and Riskin's push toward these overt principles in *Mr. Deeds Goes to Town* appears in the scene of Longfellow and Babe's trip to Ulysses S. Grant's tomb on Riverside Drive in New York, a trip Longfellow said he wanted to make as soon as he was informed of his inheritance and his chance to go to the big city. Riskin's writing and Capra's filming of the ensuing scene, set on a foggy, cold New York night, make it clear that they are pointedly denouncing the urban sophisticates' loss of memory and relinquishing of key historical moments. Most of the participants in the scene, including the reporter and photographers following Babe to capture Longfellow's strange behavior for the following day's edition, are not even aware of the tomb's existence, and Babe herself remarks that it is often a dreadful letdown to anyone who does visit it. In essence, they know and care little about the statue or the person fading symbolically and literally into the city's background.

Capra and Riskin remind us in this scene that it is not so much Grant's political legacy that interests Longfellow as it is his rags-to-riches upbringing and historical role as savior of the Union in the Civil War. Longfellow sees "a poor farm boy from Ohio," not a politically corrupt chief executive. The presidency as institution and symbolic artifact became a key appropriation in Capra and Riskin's work, and while many have commented on how much *Mr. Deeds* appears to be a transparent endorsement of the New Deal, its critical analysis of a transformed American society adapting to the era's political leadership is the more important critique.[45] Franklin Roosevelt was busily reshaping the institution of the presidency into one driven by the power of personality as much as the conviction of politics. When Riskin first gave minor reference to the president's innovative fireside chats at the beginning of *Lady for a Day*, little could he have realized what an enormously symbolic initiative it would be. *Mr. Deeds* transposed that small acknowledgement into a full-blown notion of a leader who, in his first term, which was drawing to a close as the film made its rounds in theaters, had transformed the nation more through sheer belief and will than through many of his policies. But what each of Riskin's major screenplays tapped into during the Roosevelt era was not just the overarching presence of the man but also the signifying of style and personality, even wealth and fame, as the arbiter of power within America.

Wealth brought influence, and influence was being increasingly engineered by a new corporate, even celebrity, elite, a realization that both Capra and Riskin were struck by and swept up in, in their making and later contemplation of the film's reception. Their work was being imbued with the responsibility of commentary and the legacy of influence concerning the values and ideas shaping American society at this time, a striking real-life contrast to their tongue-in-cheek inclusion of an Algonquin Round Table whose members pontificate on the ways of the world and taunt Longfellow in the restaurant scene of the picture. *It Happened One Night* had bought fame and prestige, and now *Mr. Deeds* provided an almost self-fulfilling prophecy for the most successful pair in Hollywood's short history. The picture exposed the wealthy hegemonic forces at work within society, satirized and remonstrated with them, but upon release found itself an artistic creation spoken of in precisely the terms of influential commentary. What it exposed, it had become.

The expectation of *Mr. Deeds* as a commercial film was considerable when it opened in April 1936, and it did not disappoint. Upon initial release—on its own, not in a package of features, as had been the Columbia custom—the film recouped more than a million dollars in box office sales.[46]

In 1936, *Mr. Deeds Goes to Town* propagandized Rooseveltian politics, highlighted agrarian demands, and reasserted faith in recovery and future prosperity. The film took on a mantle of expression that must have shocked even Capra and Riskin. Suddenly it was being talked about in the most unlikely circles and by the most influential people, and thus it took up the role of Hollywood contributor to the debates that swept the country.

Later that year, in November, Franklin Roosevelt was reelected. The movie, Roosevelt, and the politics that America had imbibed in that heady period of FDR's first term subsequently became linked in an indelible association of rebuilding, reformulation, and rededication to the spirit and sanctity of American mythology. Among the many well-known statements made about *Mr. Deeds Goes to Town* over the years, perhaps none is more famous than that uttered by then little-known BBC broadcaster and journalist Alistair Cooke. A great admirer of Capra's early films, Cooke remarked upon seeing *Mr. Deeds* for the first time that the director had "start[ed] to make movies about themes instead of people."[47] If Cooke's claim is right, then the theme at the heart of *Mr. Deeds* is a reinvention of the imaginary and an exercise in the solemnization of the past. Even this slight at the picture's supposed emphasis on closet political analysis over character helps to explain the constant reiteration of FDR, New Deal, populism, and *Mr. Deeds* as tied to each other and sharing some history.

It is hard, given the evidence, to refute the notion that there was at least some symbiosis between Riskin and Capra and their audience in this desperate craving for mythological revival during the Depression: a revival of the America of Lincoln and Washington, Franklin and Jefferson, Whitman and Emerson, and, in this case, Ulysses S. Grant and Henry Thoreau. But it should also come as no surprise to find Capra and Riskin well attuned to the ideological state of play in other cultural forms, for as Robert Sklar has suggested, in many areas of the media, as well as in politics, there was indeed a conscious attempt in the mid-thirties to "revitalize and refashion a cultural mythology."[48] In Charles Maland's assessment, this cultural embedding took the form of an aesthetically and emotionally satisfying consensus built up in the narrative of *Mr. Deeds*. Robert and Lois Self have added to this theme, claiming that *Mr. Deeds*, as well as *It Happened One Night*, contributed ideological and mythical significance through the evocation and resolution of conflict within these short-story adaptations.[49]

The film community therefore took on a role in the rebuilding process of mythic sentiment, creating, from 1936 until America's entry into World War II, what Maland describes as a definitive "American consensus" of values and attitudes.[50] The film community threw off the shackles of the early-thirties slump that had threatened to engulf it as it had so many other industries, and by the eve of Roosevelt's second term, Hollywood had recovered financially. It was now interested in making itself the alternative capital of America, of winning over its troubled masses with winsome and wholesome magic, and of becoming, in Kevin Starr's words, "the one city everyone had in common."[51] In 1936, *Mr. Deeds* found itself posing as the poster child for Hollywood's self-image as harbinger of the dreams and aspirations of a wider populace. In this environment, Robert Riskin's words echoed across the years of American history, battened, as they were, to the guide ropes of individualistic self-achievement and a spirit of human endeavor that now, in our cynical, detached age, seems cheap and fabricated, but then appeared venturesome and beatific.

Oddly enough, it was the last of these concerns that allowed the film to traverse political boundaries and that invited questions about its ideological discourse, then and later. It was in November 1981, in his inaugural year as fortieth president of the United States, that Ronald Reagan first invoked the spirit of *Mr.*

Deeds and of Riskin's ideas in the film by directly referring, in an address to business leaders, to the speech from the trial scene near the close of the movie, quoted earlier. Reagan's massive economic cuts to New Deal programs that had been the bedrock of American public policy since the Depression were explained away by Deeds's emphasis on "volunteerism" to help the "little people" out of their financial misery.[52]

The example should convince us that, more than any other film Capra and Riskin made together, *Mr. Deeds* tapped into the zeitgeist of later times as well as its own, and in doing so became more than simply cinematic entertainment or artistic endeavor. It would remain Riskin's favorite script, which is reason enough to accept its revered cultural place in the Depression era. There is no doubt that his sympathies to FDR shine through at particular moments over and above any remnant of Kelland's political position. The film emerged as a battleground between contrasting views of America and the kind of nation it was becoming in the thirties. Against the odds, this status worked to the advantage of the Capra-Riskin partnership, and it led to debates that have raged ever since in film scholarship.

The contradictory forces at play within Riskin's and Capra's professional lives in Hollywood have led to much confusion among critics over the years concerning the pair's cinematic relationship. And more often than not, those debates have been sparked by the state of their careers at this juncture. Ray Carney's theory of Capra's visual pronouncements in his films, his "American vision," is a good example of this dialectical discourse. Although the film is by no means central to his thesis, Carney uses *Mr. Deeds Goes to Town* as the initiator of Capra's series of political films, but political films that, he argues, have little concern for the New Deal, Roosevelt, financial or political institutions, and the like. They are instead, Carney suggests, a tableau in which Capra can examine his characters' "ideals and identities."[53] Carney is right in stating that Capra's critics, such as Alistair Cooke, with his backhanded compliment, thought politics was and could only be treated superficially in films from *Mr. Deeds* onward. Carney breaks the connection between politics and the political by stating that such a position might as well condemn Shakespeare's historical plays as bald support for or opposition to the Tudor dynasty. The problem, he states, is that American and European critical traditions have never allowed politics and art to mix in the way Capra wanted them to. "That is where Capra and his films court complete critical misunderstanding. In proposing to inject his characters' vaulting ideals into recognizably 'real' social institutions—in deliberately failing to maintain a clear separation between the 'pure' energies of imagination and desire and the practical forms by which such energies are expressed in the 'real' world—Capra violated an entire culture's critical assumptions about how the free imagination must be—can only be—kept from pollution by being insulated from the actualities of social life."[54]

Whether Carney truly gets away with condemning those he calls "metafictionists," who believe society, and reality, can be blocked off at the margins of their texts, is one thing, but how to explain Capra's engagement with "practical political and social events" through his art and predicament of the individual is another. At all points, persuasive though Carney's ideas appear, and important though they are for appreciations of style and framing in Capra's pictures, he never once mentions Riskin in this analysis.[55] The writer who sympathized with the political revolution in Washington, who engineered bank runs on screen, and who portrayed the hegemonic views of rich and poor surely had demonstrated ways to make politics and the political work for his visionary director. Carney rightfully emphasizes that "with his regular crew—cameraman Joseph Walker, set designer Stephen Goosson, and sound engineer Edward Bernds—Capra skillfully uses the expressive resources of cinematic space and sound as ways of registering Deeds's social and bureaucratic embeddedness."[56]

But not only was Riskin working as part of the same team, the words were his, the vernacular language was an immanent form in each text, the ideals were embedded by his realization of character and place. The topicality was not added as another ingredient but suffused into the overall concept of the narrative and pitch of the story. Even Capra acknowledged Riskin's job in keeping together what he, Capra, wanted to "say." What is funny about his account of *Mr. Deeds* is that Capra describes what he wanted to say as "nothing earth-shaking" and then goes on to list mass education, thought, production, politics, wealth, and conformity as the evils that the pitiful individual in the film is trying to fight.[57] This is the kind of description that scholars have found so infuriating over the years because it seems so contradictory. The themes cited obviously were "earth-shaking," for 1936 or indeed any other time. So why was there the desire to sometimes endorse, sometimes dismiss the messages and ideas of his films? Perhaps it is the focus upon his own standing that deflects the debate away from social or political "embeddedness," in this film and others, for Capra seems to relate Longfellow Deeds's individualism not to the cause of the New Deal, nor to any right-wing individualism, but to his own coming of age as a director and the fact that *Mr. Deeds* was the first film to be headlined "Frank Capra's." But the film did not, in fact, have his name above the title.

In 1935, the year of Capra's sabbatical, he had re-signed to Columbia for a lucrative deal that would earn him $100,000 per picture with 25 percent net profits for five films over a two-year period. The new contract, however, did not give Capra final cut on his films, which was a virtually unheard-of benefit for directors of the time, even those who had Capra's influence. Nor did it guarantee that his name would be above the title, only that each film would be announced as a Frank Capra production. The name did finally arrive above the title, but not until 1938's *You Can't Take It with You*. In Joseph McBride's analysis, the name-above-the-title pretense confirmed the belief in self-ownership that was one more notch in Capra's "one man, one film" philosophy that distanced everyone from his artistic vision, including Riskin.[58]

In fact, Capra's autobiographical account of events in *The Name above the Title*, written forty years after the film was made, set out to eulogize the mythological spirit of *Mr. Deeds* the movie as much as the technical and visionary prowess of *Mr. Deeds* the cinematic masterpiece. The film's place in 1930s culture, and the reverence since reserved for it, confirmed not only the picture's but Capra's own importance to one of America's most significant decades. Capra could dismiss the politics of the narrative, as well as the studio goings-on surrounding the film, because *Mr. Deeds* fit into grander themes. The traditions that mixed history and identity into a coming-of-age story line were certainly the ones Capra harked back to, and this was because his own past was reaffirmed in similar terms, as a life spent chasing after and upholding the historical continuity and progression of the American Dream. His career, as his autobiography explicitly conceived, was up there on the screen with the characters.

So there was certainly something more profound in Capra's telling of *Mr. Deeds*'s history than simply his will to confirm his authorial status and, later, to denounce Riskin's contribution, or anybody else's. Over the forty years that the film had been in the public domain, it had slowly accumulated a mythological legacy that, by the time of *The Name above the Title*, made it a lightning rod of opinion for Capra's career. *It's a Wonderful Life* roamed the cultural wilderness as part entertainment, part lost classic confined to television; *Mr. Smith Goes to Washington* was the near, but not quite, political masterpiece; *Lost Horizon* was the almost sweeping mystical epic; and *Meet John Doe* might have been, with a few rough edges cut off, the rakish historical warning of threats to America. All were well regarded but not revered until Capra's later rehabilitation. *Mr. Deeds Goes to Town*, on the other hand, had always risen above such doubts and was arguably the most important and resonant film he ever made. Actually, it was the best all-around film that he and Riskin ever made, and it is therefore not surprising that it preserved its status through the wilderness years. Riskin and Capra had created something complete and sustainable on screen. Capra couldn't truly lose sight of that fact. It was their film, an allegiance that, later, he should have been proud to acknowledge.

Mr. Deeds, therefore, was about small town versus big city, individualism versus collectivism, rich versus poor, and intellectualism versus popular conception of culture. But it was also the film with which Capra and Riskin clearly maintained an identity as the years passed. Riskin brought colloquial dialogue to the form of high art in *Mr. Deeds*, more so than in any other movie that he and Capra worked on. Better than that, he made it his own, and he invited moviegoers to join in and appropriate such language for themselves. In much the same way that the public had not heard of "dunkin'" their doughnuts before Peter Warne showed Ellie Andrews how to do it in *It Happened One Night*, so slightly daft, oddball characters doodled and became pixilated thanks to *Mr. Deeds*. Capra would retrospectively make even these words a testament to his authorship rather than Riskin's, but that graceless claim was happily transcended by *Mr. Deeds's* legacy as the critical and commercial peak of a great filmmaking partnership.

Writer, Producer, *and* Director

Riskin's part in the Hollywood social whirl reached a critical mass in 1936. In the days following the successful release of *Mr. Deeds*, his name was splashed all over the main pages of newspapers the length and breadth of the country. The reason for this was not entirely in his favor: Riskin had gotten involved in a fracas with fellow screenwriter Harry Ruskin in a Hollywood nightclub.

Accompanied by friends Eva Gregory and Zeppo Marx and Zeppo's wife, Riskin heard Ruskin make some unsavory comment from the next table; he went over and, with one punch, put him on the floor. The incident came to nothing, and charges were never brought. But the press proceeded to report the event in elaborate, sardonic terms. "Film Writer Kayoes Colleague in Third," screamed the *New York Daily News*; "Brawls Mark Easter Film Folk Parties," boasted an exaggerated piece in the *New York Post*; and "It Happened Again: Another Hollywood Comedy" was the play on Capra and Riskin's title that so delighted the *Los Angeles Evening News* report of the punch-up.[59] Riskin was perhaps embarrassed by this, some of the first negative publicity he had ever received as a screenwriter, but more likely resolved to present a different side of his Hollywood persona. His actions within the writers guild that summer no doubt helped. A year later, Riskin may have felt the need to defend his work a little more stridently, and thus his interviews for his and Capra's next film, *Lost Horizon*, a year after *Mr. Deeds*, were very different from the almost carefree banter of before. Riskin was, significantly, trying to create an artistic identity for himself. His comment in the Dudley Early interview during promotion for *Mr. Deeds*, that he had been married to the director for a long time, may have struck a discordant note. Of course, Capra and Riskin hadn't really been together that long at all—barely four years, in fact—and not on every picture. So Riskin's tone in his latest series of comments seemed to be laying the groundwork for moving in alternative directions while maintaining the partnership. In 1937 interviews, he sought to provide distance from any assumption that he was just Capra's "gag man," and this paved the way for what Hollywood and his fans had been expecting for some time: his first appearance behind the camera. Later in 1937, he would write and direct the Grace Moore and Cary Grant vehicle *When You're in Love*. Before that, however, he would go through the tribulations of making *Lost Horizon* with Capra.

Contentment, existence, and the spiritual center of human beings became a philosophical puzzle that engulfed Riskin in the mid-thirties. Whether it was karma, a true interest in transcendentalism, or just another of those strange sets of circumstances that invaded his career periodically is hard to fathom. But these particular concerns with the visionary limits of self-attainment, having briefly surfaced in his early screen treatments and gathered pace with the mentioning of Thoreau in *Mr. Deeds*, now became the premise of his and Capra's new film.

James Hilton had become a successful novelist in the 1930s, largely thanks to his best seller about the life of a popular and inspiring schoolteacher, *Goodbye, Mr. Chips*, from 1933.[60] But he had published eight other books to largely indifferent reaction. However, one of the novels, *Lost Horizon*, found its way onto the influential CBS radio show *The Town Crier*, and two years after its initial release, Hilton suddenly found himself with a career-defining success on his hands.

Sam Frank's account of the making of the movie of Hilton's novel is the generally accepted history: Capra picked up a copy of the book from a newsstand during a break in the production of *Mr. Deeds* in October 1935, some sixteen months before *Lost Hori-*

zon would be released as a Frank Capra production.[61] This is the account Capra himself told, and yet Pat McGilligan, in his brief synopsis of Riskin's career, has Jo Swerling getting Capra interested in the story long before *Mr. Deeds* and working as devil's advocate as he, Capra, and Riskin contemplated how to shift the novel into a screenplay.[62]

If this discrepancy over the origins of interest in *Lost Horizon* signals anything, it is that the principles that had guided Capra and Riskin so successfully thus far in their partnership were largely relinquished in this movie. Just as *It Happened One Night* became the epitome of screwball comedy and *Mr. Deeds Goes to Town* formed the conversion to classic social mythmaking, the career trajectories insist that each artist have his "troubled masterpiece." So it was for Riskin and Capra with *Lost Horizon*. In the Sam Frank and Frank Capra version of the discovery of the book, the adaptation relied upon the exploitation of themes and ideas, of a visualization of some mystical utopia that, ideologically, was utterly credible. In the McGilligan interpretation, the story already had "too much philosophic content" and really needed action and pace.[63] That the film had too much of one and not enough of the other would disrupt the trust in working practices that Capra, Riskin, and the whole Columbia team had established for themselves over the previous few years. But the less than edifying result was that a huge chunk of the movie ended up on the cutting room floor. Worse still, relations were shredded, and *Lost Horizon*, despite its decent commercial success, quite likely caused irreparable damage to the Capra-Riskin team.

The picture was the pair's first to be profoundly reshaped as it went along. Although Riskin had always altered stories like "Opera Hat" in initial adaptation and had performed rewrites and subtle alterations mid-shoot for Capra before, he had never done so against the clock and in such a dramatic fashion. Until now, the pair had confined themselves to short-story adaptations; the full-length novel brought tough choices in terms of characters' focus and motivations as well as the condensing or outright cutting of scenes from the book. The film came in at well over three hours when it was first edited, and the extraction, after previews, of a significant twenty-two minutes contributed to a further air of tension in the studio community.[64]

Lost Horizon's troubled evolution, not surprisingly, interested the newspapers and gossip columns, which now identified the release of a Capra-Riskin movie as a major Hollywood event, and any trouble surrounding the shoot as headline news. The press had gotten wind of the project in 1935, and as far as they were concerned, the production had been going for two years, despite Capra and Riskin's break to make *Mr. Deeds*. Hilton, who had been a scenarist himself, remained calm and supportive of the production. He conferred regularly with Riskin and offered fulsome praise of his colleague's efforts. "It [is] really amazing to see how Robert Riskin has kept the feeling, the spirit of the book," he enthused to Eileen Creelman in the *New York Sun*.[65] But Hilton's rather desperate defense of the changes, which he said were not important, signaled Riskin's difficulties in making sense of such a huge weight of narrative and complex arrangement of characters, all needing to be conveyed at once on screen.

Harry Cohn had authorized a budget for the film of $1.25 million, a frightening outlay for the studio and the bosses in New York, who, only a few years before, had been used to spending no more than double that figure for the entire year's roster. An elaborate set for the mythical city of Shangri-La was built in Burbank, costing $250,000 alone, and the shooting schedule was extended a number of times. Not surprisingly, perhaps, the film came in well over budget; the eventual cost, an unprecedented $4 million, sent Harry Cohn into a cold sweat.

When the shooting script was finally ready, Riskin had undertaken major alterations to Hilton's story, though the narrative progression occurred roughly similarly in Hilton's book and Riskin's screenplay: The survivors of an airplane crash in the Himalayas are led on a trek to the undiscovered city of Shangri-La, unaware that they are being lured to this mythical place as guinea pigs in an experiment to prolong human life. The leader of the party is British diplomat Robert Conway (Ronald Colman), who has helped the party escape the war-torn city of Baskul and who is the focus of the Shangri-La's elders' attention because of his humanitarianism and civic-mindedness. Conway first partakes in, then comes to doubt and, finally, resent, the false lifestyle that permits near-eternal existence, spiritual peace, and social contentment. Having come to believe that his cynical brother George is right about the place—it is simply going to entrap them—Conway leads an escape from the city with George and Maria (Margo), a woman his brother has fallen in love with and whose story about kidnapping and detainment seems to ring true. Chang (H. B. Warner), Shangri-La's erstwhile spokesperson, has warned Conway that those who leave the valley for any length of time will, if they have benefited from the city's mystical, eternal power, quickly revert to their natural age. On the treacherous journey back to civilization, this is the fate that befalls Maria, who succumbs to hypothermia and death. So distraught is George at losing his lover as well as being wrong about Shangri-La that he plunges down the snow-covered mountain to his death. Conway stumbles back to a mountain village, where British government representative Gainsford tracks him down, but Conway cannot get Shangri-La and the ideals and beliefs of its spiritual leader, the High Lama (Sam Jaffe), out of his mind. Finally, after escaping the clutches of Gainsford several times, he turns his back on the Western world's hatred and its acceleration toward another war, which he perceives as its fate, and seeks to return to Shangri-La. He spends months in the mountains trying to retrace his steps until, nearly beaten with cold and exhaustion, he recognizes the entrance to the fantastical city.

With this story line, the similarities end. The initial setting was switched from India to China. It may well have been that, as Andrew Sarris suggests, "Capra's flair for Chinoiserie," as demonstrated by *The Bitter Tea of General Yen*, had prompted a request that Riskin change the setting, even though it would give rise, as the earlier film had done, to accusations of racist intent on Capra's part.[66] Further, Riskin made the central character, Conway, a prominent diplomat rather than the minor consular figure of the book, and he transformed the "second in command" character into his brother, George (John Howard), strengthening Conway's motivation to protect his next-of-kin and escape Shangri-La in the picture's climax. Maria, George's ageless accomplice, and Sondra

(Jane Wyatt), a new character, became the central love interests for the brothers, creating the emotional dilemma for Conway in his decision to escape from the city.

Sam Frank contends that Riskin improved upon the novel in his screenplay. He cemented and enhanced the utopian feel of the book and imbued the film "with a great deal more spiritual optimism in the face of its predicted global holocaust."[67] Even though the scenes were heavily cut, Conway's meetings with the High Lama exhibit a remarkable prescience. "Look at the world today," offers Shangri-La's spiritual leader, who is in fact the Belgian priest, Father Perrault, who founded the community two hundred years before. "A scurrying mass of bewildered humanity crashing headlong against each other, propelled by an orgy of greed and brutality." Riskin's dialogue built upon the philosophic condition of society identified in *Mr. Deeds* and earlier in *American Madness*. But the setting gave him an opportunity to fulminate on a higher, transcendental plane without having to ground his beliefs in the reality of 1930s social upheaval.

Riskin therefore made the emotional turmoil of the book, initially driven by skepticism that the party has entered paradise, that much more gripping in places. But the cuts that resulted when Capra and then Cohn reedited the film removed a great deal of Riskin's spiritual contemplation, which had provided a strong criticism of the ways of the outside world. Conway's motivation for leaving Shangri-La is thus somehow lost amid the race to conclude the fable; he barely tries to convince George of the truth of his story before accepting Maria's turn of events. As Leland Poague and Charles Maland both assert, Conway is a little too serene throughout, too much in control of his rational thoughts and intellectual opinions to waver in the emotional turmoil that has him diving back and forth between the world he inhabits—and would like to shape the future of—and the utopia he ultimately suspects of lacking a soulful interior.[68]

Lost Horizon was finally released in March 1937, with Harry Cohn and Columbia effectively using its tortured production to tout it as Capra and Riskin's troubled masterpiece. Cohn had taken hold of the film, according to McBride, and sliced the running time to 132 minutes for the San Francisco premiere. He would later cut another 14 minutes before it went on general release in September.[69] This long gestation and period of exposure appeared to help the picture, though; despite mixed responses, the public produced respectable box office figures as the year progressed, although the film would not climb into profit until its reissue in 1942.[70]

Over a year after it was first shown, *Lost Horizon* also saw itself competing for Academy Awards at the 1938 ceremony. The seven nominations the film received were as many as any Capra picture garnered—a year later, *You Can't Take It with You* would receive the same total—but Capra missed out on a nomination in the director category, as did Riskin for adapted story. The two awards the film won went to Stephen Goosson for art direction and the Genes, Havlick and Milford, for film editing. In retrospect, the choices seem right. Milford had come on board at a late stage to help trim down Capra's footage with Havlick, who was wading through as much as three hours of film in one day of shooting. Forty minutes for the scenes featuring the High Lama ended up being only twelve minutes of screen time.[71] To make sense of the picture from so much narrative exposition was an incredible feat. Ironically, though, as Frank remarks, which version of the movie the Academy judges actually viewed is a subject of some contention.[72]

Goossón's award for his art direction was also a signal of the attraction the movie had for some viewers. Both *The Bitter Tea of General Yen*, four years before, and *Lost Horizon* drew (and keep drawing) fans to Capra who saw in these two pictures more thematically driven *mise-en-scène* than in his and Riskin's other, more recognizable work. Despite the plethora of cuts—to his most imaginative writing in some places—Riskin's spiritualist, transcendental yearnings still shine through and make the movie fascinating viewing, if not frustrating in almost equal measure.

In Leland Poague's analysis, the dilemma concerning *Lost Horizon* is tied up in the film's critical reception through the years. He identifies the movie as the first about which Capra became truly antagonized by the critics, many of whom voiced serious doubts about the picture. Capra, in turn, allied himself with the fans, giving rise to the practice of constantly test-screening successive films and tinkering with the final cut in response to audience reaction. Indeed, Poague compares the contemporary reviews to later, troubled assessments, by Maland and Carney, to name two, that rely on the atypical material for their doubts. By this argument, the film is so uncharacteristic of Capra's work in so many ways—setting, length, characters, narrative trajectory—that the director cannot maintain, for example, the narrative momentum and visual flair of the opening Baskul airfield scene, one of Capra's most dramatic constructions.[73]

But Poague counters this argument by suggesting that the film's problem is not that it is too distantly removed from Capra's other material but that it is too typical. The "fantastical instance of Capra's fantasy of goodwill formula" is played out in the panoramic, widescreen landscape of the Valley of the Blue Moon, he reasons, as if it were the ultimate realization of a utopia sought by his other heroes, only here manifest in a "lamaocracy," to use Elliot Stein's phrase.[74] Of course, the film was also similar to *The Bitter Tea of General Yen* in its Asian backdrop and to Capra's early action-adventures, the daring "seat of the pants" thrillers like *Submarine* and *Dirigible*.

Lost Horizon's unevenness in tone and setting, mentioned as only Capra's issue for many years, in fact has less to do with its visual splendor and pacing than it does with the dilemma of Riskin's script. The first major issue is that pairing the two principals as brothers has only limited effect in the film. George is impetuous, desperate, and hopeless in places, while Robert, the man of destiny about to become Britain's foreign secretary, is analytical, masterful, and even impervious. But the problem, as already mentioned, is that he is at times too laid back and unconcerned. George urges his brother to give the party some account of the plane's hijacking from takeoff at Baskul and landing on a remote plateau only to be refueled by local tribespeople. All Robert can impart as an explanation is "I give it up. But this not knowing where you're going is exciting anyway." Riskin's problem with Conway is balancing the characteristics of what today we would call an action hero with the meditative contemplation of what he believes in and what he finds in Shangri-La. The Baskul scene establishes Conway's credentials as a courageous risk taker. In fact, viewed from a comparative historical perspective, the first thirty minutes of *Lost Horizon* uncannily resemble the opening forty-five minutes of Steven Spielberg's *Indiana Jones and the Temple of Doom* (1984). Just as Spielberg's roller coaster ride of escape establishes the intrepid archaeological hero of the title as a devil-may-care adventurer escaping 1930s Shanghai in a plane that then crashes into a mountain as the pilot bails out, so Conway initially assumes a heroic pose as he helps his four companions escape the clutches of, presumably, Chinese revolutionary forces taking over the airfield as they board the last plane out. But the difficulty with this opening scene is that Riskin cannot make his hero live up to this level of action in the rest of the story, and he thus compensates by making Conway's brother George a weak-willed, excitable, and, at his death, manically hysterical individual.

The second matter related to Riskin's contribution is that, in the original version of the film, the female protagonists were integral to the plot and its ideological musings. Gloria Stone, in particular, is another of Riskin's finely drawn, complex figures. Gloria's illness at the start of the film, which turns out to be tuberculosis, has been contracted through her engagement with men over a period of time, although this is never directly referred to. She seems oddly subdued in these early scenes, until she suffers hysterics on the plane—an emotional correlation with George, possibly echoing an earlier meeting between the two—but she also abrasively spits out her contempt for the opposite sex, looking forward to seeing them squirm under the threat of death, a threat she has lived under for a year, according to her doctor. In fact, Gloria had lines in the scene at the airfield, but they were cut from the final print; abridging the unfolding of her resourceful and revengeful personality is a loss for the audience and a frustration of Riskin's writing. While Hilton's novel contemplated patriarchal power struggles, the film's Gloria, Sondra, and Maria are tacit reminders that Riskin engaged the battle between the sexes. The reliance, approval, and strength that lie at the heart of these characters are antidotes to Conway's world of political machismo and Shangri-La's implied conventionalism.

Riskin's doubt about his script was exposed, in a way, through these three female characters. With no conventional setting in which to parade the social and cultural tropes he had gotten used to, Riskin searched with only limited success to find a way for their characters to express themselves in the environment they inhabited. At times he was successful; many of the scenes that did not appear in the film were politically and idealistically strident, hopeful, and redemptive. But he felt constrained by the established structures and narrative conventions of the book, a position he would be no stranger to in future years. Riskin spent as long on the script for *Lost Horizon* as he did on any project in his career. That he remained troubled by it only served to remind him of the writing principles by which he had established himself in Hollywood. Indeed, so brutally honest was Riskin about the final result that he felt able to commit the following to print, even prior to the release of the picture: "*Lost Horizon* was a tremendously exciting subject and completely different from everything else I have written. The story fluctuates up and down emotionally instead of continuing upwards until reaching one big climax. If it is a success, you can cancel everything I've said on how to write a scenario."[75] The test of his judgment concerning the film's success is demonstrated by the fact that, within a year, he was redirecting his attention to the basics of writing for the screen; for the rest of his career, he would stay firmly entrenched within the three-act structure and American settings.

If the elongated process that was *Lost Horizon* hadn't already been shown up for the time and money that it was costing Columbia Pictures, then the fact that Capra's crew shot a whole other picture between breaks on the movie—Richard Boleslawski's *Theodora Goes Wild* with Irene Dunne and Melvyn Douglas, a film produced by Riskin's brother Everett, written by Sidney Buchman, and frequently compared to *Mr. Deeds*—and that Riskin made his own picture while *Lost Horizon* was being edited ought to be proof enough that the story of Shangri-La had become an obsessive trial.

Riskin's acceptance of his first directing job for *When You're in Love*, an offer that predated *Lost Horizon*, is cloaked in some confusion. Harry Cohn had spoken of Riskin as a natural director for some time, and both McBride and McGilligan seem to feel that niggling disputes with Capra on the set of *Lost Horizon* made up Riskin's mind for him.[76] And yet when things finally did fall into place, the writer appeared to get cold feet. A February 1937 report on the making of the picture, headlined "$750,000 Panic for Riskin," said that Columbia's star writer claimed he had never anticipated directing *When You're in Love*, an obviously evasive comment, since nobody else had ever been talked about as director. He was now locked into what was, by the studio's standards, a pretty big budget and an equal amount of anticipation.[77] The "panic" almost certainly came from Riskin's realization both that he was overworked, conducting the dual role of writing and directing, and that he had gone somewhat lukewarm about the story that had come from the back of the Columbia files. The outline of the plot had shades of *Lady for a Day*'s reinvention of character—a European opera star needs to maintain appearances by acquiring a husband to accompany her on a tour of America— and had thus initially proved attractive to Riskin. The story had been put together originally by Ethel Hill, whose work Riskin knew and had adapted before, in 1932 for the film *Virtue*, and the musical interludes were coming from the likes of Jerome Kern and Cab Calloway.

Although Riskin was happy to be teamed up with his brother Everett as producer, other aspects of the film troubled him. Grace Moore, who would play opera singer Louise Fuller, had been a big star for the studio in the early thirties with her selection of operatic musical comedies such as *One Night of Love* (1934), for which she had been nominated for an Academy Award, and *Love Me Forever* (1935). But the format was becoming tired, and Miss Moore's performances a little repetitive. Riskin was not used to story lines that had musical numbers interrupting the plot, only little skits that accompanied the characters' actions, such as Longfellow and Babe's spontaneous renditions of "The Swanee River" and "Humoresque" on a park bench in *Mr. Deeds*.

Cary Grant brought comic timing and some impeccable style and taste to the piece as Jimmy Hudson, but Riskin's writing only sporadically worked its light-touch magic: it brought spontaneity, originality, and sparkling dialogue to the fore merely in patches. Riskin's copy of the shooting script is heavily annotated with alterations to dialogue and scenes on almost every one of the 158 pages. He himself claimed, with his director's hat on, that the picture needed a decent writer. "Every scene I wrote seemed unsatisfactory," he said, openly admitting that he missed the quality control and editorship that Capra brought to cinematic mounting.[78] The demands of *When You're in Love* may well have been what put Riskin off directing for good.

Despite Riskin's misgivings, the reviews of the film were pretty good in the end, and almost all spoke of this outing behind the camera as being the first of many for Columbia's leading writer.[79] Moore was still a star, even if a temperamental one, and Riskin managed to get her and Grant to establish some degree of chemistry.

And yet over the next two years, Riskin would not attain acclaimed directorial status. By the summer of 1938, reports were circulating that Riskin, a month away from the end of his Columbia contract, was in talks with Samuel Goldwyn about a move to his production company. The details of such a move were not discussed, however, and speculation suggested that Riskin would in the end thrash out a new deal with Columbia. A part of the appeal of this new contract with the studio would be the opportunity to direct Claudette Colbert in *Our Wife*, from a script already in preparation at Columbia, though one apparently not associated with Riskin.[80] The offer to helm another picture was not enough to sway Riskin, though; he did not sign on with Columbia again, and the chance of becoming a major Hollywood director passed him by.

Riskin's career dilemma was made quite apparent by his experience with *When You're in Love* in 1937, which had thrust him center stage as the outright auteur. Riskin's ascent to the Hollywood major league collided with his reluctance to be the lead figure or take the limelight at the studio. He was used to attention, of course, and rather liked aspects of the celebrity lifestyle and publicity routine, but he was uncomfortable having overall responsibility for projects.

Riskin's reticence about his background and history apparently contributed to an array of misinformation. The *Richmond (VA)*

News-Leader, for example, providing encouragement for his first solo film in February 1937, heralded this shift to behind the camera with a feature on *When You're in Love* wrapped around a biographical profile of Columbia's latest directorial talent. Among a number of "soft" facts given about him in the article, several were less than accurate: Riskin's birthplace as Baltimore, his teaming up with Capra for *The Miracle Woman*, his studying at Columbia after World War I, and his marriage to and divorce from Edith Fitzgerald. It is not clear whether Riskin himself offered this information to journalists or they culled the "facts" from clippings. Whatever the answer, Riskin's life story remained more or less private. His wider influence on the screenwriting profession, his true vocation, was another issue entirely. The *News-Leader* article mentioned that the scripts for *American Madness* and *Lady for a Day* had been adopted by Columbia University in New York for its fledgling courses on screenwriting, a clear sign of the high level of regard in which Riskin's composition and structure were now held.[81]

The growing academic reputation that his scripts engendered, together with a rise in interest in studying film at some of America's most prestigious universities, motivated Riskin to share his screenwriting experience and talk about his influences much more than he had when he arrived in Hollywood. Prior to 1937, Riskin, like so many other Hollywood scenarists, had seemed reluctant to offer the press many details of his working routine and craft, partly because the journalists themselves had little interest in or regard for the work of screenwriters. Riskin's reluctance was, however, also born of a diffident and self-deprecating regard for his work, in marked contrast to some of the self-publicists working in Hollywood. But in the late thirties, he finally offered a crash course in the art of screenwriting in an unsigned piece. The timing does not seem coincidental. Riskin was getting more offers to share his screenwriting experience, and up-and-coming talent, the next generation of writers, was already starting to appear at the studios. By 1938, in addition to being on the curriculum for students at Columbia University, Riskin was contributing to the screenwriting art by reading work and giving advice to classes that had been set up at the film school at the University of Southern California. The president of the university wrote him a thank-you note in August of that year for his involvement in the students' Motion Picture Story and Continuity class, part of the burgeoning focus on movies that was to make USC's film school the most prestigious in the country.[82]

Riskin's essay "The Theme's the Thing" begins with an explanation of the intent of *Lost Horizon*. His first aim was to write an adventure story, but within that story to approach themes of hope, tolerance, "do unto others etc" to persuade the audience to consider questions of the hero's dilemma. Having established his motivation and ambitions for *Lost Horizon*, Riskin then broadens his argument to talk of construction and organization within his screenplays. His comments confirm his preference for the three-act structure he utilized virtually his whole career. He asserts that he is much more convinced of the use of the script and weight of the dialogue for pacing than the conscious use of the camera. "I have had scenes run for minutes at a time—and remained on a 'two shot' until its conclusion—having found that it was more impressive this way," he comments. "To disturb [the scene] with 'close-ups' and 'different angles' would rob the scene of its intended purpose." In other words, he reveals a preference for standard shots that do not distract from the dialogue or coach the audience away from narrative and character development. "It is wise to know what your scene is—and then tell it in the smoothest—quickest—and most effective way," he contends, almost as if admonishing himself that he somehow did not follow this maxim steadfastly enough in *Lost Horizon* or *When You're in Love*. He concludes with the most significant lesson of all: "THERE ARE NO RULES." Riskin counts "dramatic instinct" as the prevailing and most vital attribute of the filmmaker. Only by following your instincts, he explains, do you get original and unusual storytelling and cinematic presentation: "The screen is too pregnant a medium to stagnate it with a set of rules."[83]

Riskin's article had to accommodate the wealth of interest in his work and satisfy the need for public pronouncements and publicity on the films, but there was also a good deal of self-interest in his exposure to the press. This was a conscious effort on Riskin's part to establish a serious profile for his work that took in more than the odd punch-up in a nightclub with a fellow scribe or the latest beautiful Hollywood actress on his arm.

Thus the essay was important in two crucial respects. It established his credentials as a serious Hollywood player, but it was also a rededication to his own instincts as a writer, to his abilities of forming character and narrative, and a promise of the direction of his future work. The article contended that he was foremost a writer and that themes were the heart and soul of his writing. Hollywood, Riskin believed, could accept social and political commentary within the confines of his screenwriting methodology.

Riskin's title was near enough a call to arms for fellow writers with social and political concerns, and it was certainly his most telling foray into the definitions of screenwriting. The article placed great emphasis on a writer's knowing his or her theme and how that theme can and should work, whether the genre is comedy, melodrama, or message film. This rule clearly influenced Riskin all through his adaptation of the George Kaufman and Moss Hart stage play *You Can't Take It with You*, which was to be his and Capra's next film. *Lost Horizon* had been a troubling experience for Riskin, and he seemed determined to avoid ever again having concerns in the script that required a postmortem explanation.

He took his own advice to heart. Nearly a year later, as *You Can't Take It with You* was heading for the screens, reports of the film's production placed Riskin's value of themes at the heart of the movie's design. The *Los Angeles Evening News* quoted him as saying that the play could be placed on the screen virtually intact, but "if played for wild comedy . . . its theme might be submerged."[84] Riskin had reestablished his writing credentials with "The Theme's the Thing," but *You Can't Take It with You* was about to intensify the speculation about his next career move.

CHAPTER FOUR

THE IDEALIST

"Everybody gets so worked up about it. Everybody takes it hard."[1] If Riskin's words appear perplexing, it is because he felt perplexed about what he had gotten himself into following the release of *Lost Horizon*. The April 1937 interview in *Variety* suggested that Riskin needed to achieve some measure of closure and desired to break the bonds of the debate over the movie that was raging around him and Capra. The article did not specify how critics and audiences felt about certain aspects of a picture that had engendered more critical and analytical discussion of the pair's cinematic capabilities, as opposed to their social or political concerns, than virtually any movie they had made to this point. But the tone of Riskin's interview was unmistakably philosophic and, to a degree, contrite. As legend has it, Capra just about saved the picture after disastrous previews when he threw away the first two reels and started the film with the Baskul airfield scene and the escape of Conway and his party.[2] Although this and further reworking by Harry Cohn helped to make *Lost Horizon* a moderate success, it sparked a row between Capra and Columbia's chief over royalties for the picture. Capra's lawyers eventually used the case of *If You Could Only Cook*, the Jean Arthur vehicle released in the UK as a Capra picture in 1937, as leverage to sue Columbia, to prompt Cohn to back down and to accelerate the production schedule for the next picture.[3]

Amid the rankling, Riskin felt doubly unhappy about his screen treatment of Hilton's novel and the finished product of his first directorial effort, *When You're in Love*. The *Variety* interview found him confessing that he had to relearn things, but he also wondered about his abilities to take on certain subjects. In response to a question about *When You're in Love,* Riskin declared that he would not write and direct together again. His escape to Europe in 1937 signaled a desire to find some solace and heal some wounds, but also to contemplate his plans for the future.

The *New York Evening Post* stated in April that Capra and Riskin were heading for Britain. Along with Gloria Swanson, Marlene Dietrich, Douglas Fairbanks, and, interestingly, Riskin's ex-partner, Glenda Farrell, they were accompanied by Charles Laughton to the coronation of George VI.[4] They also fulfilled publicity duties and attended the British premiere of *Lost Horizon.* From London, Capra and Riskin then traveled to the Soviet Union to be received by filmmakers there. Capra took up a long-standing invitation from Sergei Eisenstein to visit Moscow and to talk about his work, a body of films that had become much admired in Russian filmmaking circles. Accounts of Capra's meeting with Eisenstein and his impressions of Stalinist Russia are contradictory, and there is no way to take stock of Capra's comment in his autobiography that Riskin was disappointed at "socialism's much-vaunted Utopia."[5] Riskin at least acted as the gracious guest and heaped praise upon the Soviet cinema. A report in *Izvestia* paid tribute to Capra's work and quoted Riskin as saying, "You, Soviet cinema workers, are the millionaires of dramaturgy." The conversation was further directed toward film techniques and the use of film stock, no great surprise for a pair who had always paid attention to the visual properties of their movies and had reshaped Hollywood's cinematography and use of montage, a Soviet-honed technical development.[6]

The trip seemed to allow both Capra and Riskin time for reflection. *Lost Horizon* was still being recut in Hollywood, and Capra was falling into the dispute with Cohn over *If You Could Only Cook.* At some point during the year, if not during the trip itself, Riskin had consciously redirected his attention toward the technical and artistic endeavors that went into screenwriting and had settled down to write his article "The Theme's the Thing." As Capra and Cohn slowly resolved their differences through the year, and Columbia agreed to the purchase of Kaufman and Hart's play *You Can't Take It with You,* Riskin set about recapturing past glories once the European sojourn had concluded.

There seemed to have been a concerted consolidation of everyone's position on the Columbia lot at the beginning of 1938. Any lasting troubles among Cohn, Capra, and Riskin appeared to have been ironed out in the course of the previous few months, and the studio put its full weight behind *You Can't Take It with You*. Thomas Schatz argues that Cohn's willingness to pay $200,000 to secure the rights to the play was a sign of his determination, if not desperation, to keep Capra at Columbia after the dispute over *Lost Horizon*.[7] Familiar characters came into view in the adaptation to relocate the Capra-Riskin concerns of contemporary urban sophisticates and quirky oddballs, rich and poor mismatches, and ever more strident ideas and opinions about American society. It was this last element that, for a short time, threatened to scupper the success of the movie. Just as Clarence Kelland had held court on the problems of Capra and Riskin's adaptation of "Opera Hat" in 1936, so Moss Hart went public in 1938 to decry his and Kaufman's screwball comedy as having been hijacked by "social significance" messages. Riskin met with Hart to listen to the writer's complaints, told him that his comments had helped to clarify the story, and then happily stated that his adjustments would make the film even more socially significant.[8] Riskin's mischievousness was not only the product of a writer who himself knew that letting go of one's writing, once completed, was the only way to work in Hollywood, but was also indicative of a desire to distance his screenplay from the stage drama. Riskin's fascination had long been with social structure and progression rather than any definite political position. He knew from the start that Hart's objections to the screenplay for *You Can't Take It with You* were not based on his and Capra's insertion of social and political ideas: they were about the exclusion of Hart's and Kaufman's political values. As it turned out, the play's nods to anticommunist rhetoric were largely discarded, if not reversed, by Riskin on the page and by Capra on the set.

From the beginning of Riskin's career in Hollywood, almost all of his screenplays had additionally dealt with patterns of generational and historical change. America was leaving behind its rural past and, to an extent, its federalist philosophy in favor of more corporatist national structures. *American Madness, Ann*

Carver's Profession, and *Mr. Deeds* had examined these ideas and their impact more or less explicitly, but they had cropped up in many of the writer's other scripts as well. *You Can't Take It with You* carried this line of thematic development further than many of his other screenplays had ever attempted. The film did not simply highlight the age-old coming together of David and Goliath, big business versus the "little fella," but actually contemplated the meaning and value of progress and modernism. It was possibly the insertion of these notions into Kaufman and Hart's play that troubled the playwrights most.

You Can't Take It with You is the story of an offbeat family living in the path of a New York City urban development. The family's patriarch, Martin Vanderhoff (Lionel Barrymore), is adamant that they will never sell to the developers. Arguing that the community of friends the family has built around itself is the kind of social grouping that needs to be preserved and cherished, the family members vow to never give in to the mighty corporation that wants to push them out of their neighborhood. Older daughter Alice (Jean Arthur) is the one member of the family content to live within society's regulatory confines; that is, she works for a living, or at least brings home a regular paycheck. She also is in love with Tony Kirby (James Stewart), son of Anthony P. Kirby (Edward Arnold), whose firm, where Alice works, is the one that wishes to build on the site of the Vanderhoffs' home.

Romance therefore gets entangled with business and family loyalty. Alice runs away after the family's disastrous stab at entertaining the upper-class Kirbys one evening. Martin resolves to keep the family together and therefore to sell to stay with Alice, but Kirby senior provides a satisfactory resolution to this familial splintering. *You Can't Take It with You* appears at first glance to follow a path toward social conjunction similar to that in *Broadway Bill*, in which wealthy patriarch J. L. Higgins rejects his fortune to tag along with Dan Brooks and train racehorses. Anthony Kirby turns up at the home of the Vanderhoffs, joins Grandpa in a harmonica duet, and puts his industrial wealth to one side, preferring to enjoy the simple pleasures of life's rich tapestry with this odd but engaging family. Kirby's demonstration of material rejection is one thing, but setting it within the place whose existence scuppers the aspirations of his company—without the

Vanderhoffs' house and land, the company cannot build its offices—gives the act revolutionary proportions. In *Broadway Bill*, Higgins's flit from his wealth and family is a personal statement of comic pretense that fails to affect social and economic structures. Kirby, on the other hand, lines up against that which only a few moments before he had owned, controlled, and stood for, proceeding now to reject those structures outright.

If the film does not quite achieve the force of such symbolic pronouncements, it is probably in part because of Riskin's portrayal of the family's guardian. To be fair to Hart's criticisms, Riskin's not-so-subtle attempts to politicize Martin Vanderhoff by painting him in bright liberal colors, particularly in his early confrontation with the IRS man, create, as Robert Sklar points out, confusing and disquieting moments.[9] Unlike the colonel in *Meet John Doe* a few years hence, who wishes to be cut loose from society's controlling grasp, Vanderhoff quickly becomes, in Riskin's hands, a mad, rather disgruntled figure raging at society, at least in the first part of the film. The initial scene in Kirby's office, when Vanderhoff sparks a minor revolt among the staff and whisks away the timid Poppins (Donald Meek) with the promise that he can create more things like his mechanical rabbit coming out of a hat, is fine. When he remarks at home to his daughter-in-law, a budding playwright—a nice Riskin touch—that she should write about "isms" because, he claims, everyone today goes out and gets an "ism," one can see the recoil from the state of ideological play in the world. But when the IRS man arrives, insisting that Vanderhoff pay his taxes—else who would pay for the courts, Congress, and the president?—the old man states bluntly that *they* are not getting one penny of his money. And yet just moments before, Vanderhoff was extolling the likes of Lincoln, Jefferson, Washington, and Grant. It is they whom he admires for not needing "isms" but who were, nonetheless, beneficiaries of taxpayers' money who went on to make the nation great.

Making Martin Vanderhoff too tetchy and irascible a character, while other residents of the house, like Ed (Dub Taylor), seem to enjoy nothing more than setting off fireworks to celebrate the Russian Revolution, combined with the rather meek construction of Stewart's Tony Kirby, went a long way toward making the family a rather abstruse bunch that seem neglectful and naïve rather than pleasantly quirky and quixotic. This was a problem of adaptation that would come back to haunt Riskin a few years later, when his brother Everett asked him to work on *The Thin Man* movie series. Short-story adaptations gave Riskin plenty of room to manipulate the motivations and designs of his protagonists. But he felt constrained when characters had already been brought to life in other realms, be they on the stage or already existing on film, especially in these two productions. Alice, the female protagonist, unsurprisingly sits most comfortably with Riskin's notion of character and outlook. But one senses the nagging tension in the script that she could do better than Tony Kirby. Her fiancé does not suddenly reveal a reserve of resilience and confidence, as Alice might desire; rather, the plot requires that Tony's father ultimately grab the bull by the horns to save the day, and the house, for the Vanderhoff family. Capra and Riskin attempt to solve any lingering doubts about Alice and Tony's union by repeating familiar patterns of romantic engagement, as Ray Carney explains: by literally revisiting *Mr. Deeds*'s "Swanee River" improvisation on a park bench, but now playing it out between Stewart and Arthur rather than Cooper and Arthur.[10]

In McBride's analysis, the Vanderhoff family composition was the type of crazy, rather dysfunctional structure that Capra could recognize from his past rather more than Riskin could from his. It was Capra, according to McBride, who wrote into the script Grandpa Vanderhoff's lines about Kirby senior's being a "failure as a man, failure as a human being, even a failure as a father," as though these were biographical indictments of Capra's own father, Salvatore.[11] But if the film may be seen retrospectively as out of sync with the layers of thematic concerns, familial relations, or ideologies that Riskin understood so well and had worked into previous screenplays, it didn't weigh too heavily on the minds of the critics and fans at the time. Ironically, Riskin's reputation was so strong, the backing of the film so great, and the Academy so taken with the picture that he ultimately received an Oscar nomination for the adapted screenplay of *You Can't Take It with You*.

Perhaps most tellingly, when the film opened to universally rave reviews, Hart decided that retraction was the better part of valor and so went public again, on this occasion to acclaim the film. It could not have done any harm, because *You Can't Take*

It with You found itself nominated for seven Oscars, including those for best picture and director, as well as screen adaptation. At the awards, held at the Biltmore Hotel on February 23, 1939, the film won the first two of these awards. Riskin, however, failed to carry away the award for his category and was eclipsed once more by Capra, who had become the first filmmaker ever to win three Academy Awards for best director.

On the third draft of the script for *You Can't Take It with You*, dated March 17, 1938, Capra wrote on the front page, "The best one you ever wrote," and Jimmy Stewart added, "It's a great ride and a pleasure to be saying the words in this script."[12] Although it was not Riskin's best work, the script had an unshakable quality that echoed his belief in structure and composition. A belated endorsement from one of the play's writers, good box office returns, and an Oscar nomination to boot: Riskin could, it seemed, put to rest the trials of *Lost Horizon* and *When You're in Love* in the wake of this latest success. He did indeed put the problems of the previous year behind him, but he did so by abandoning Capra and Cohn after the movie, to the surprise of many who thought *You Can't Take It with You* had worked the old magic.

Rumors surrounding Capra's and Riskin's positions at Columbia had in fact continued throughout 1938, on the back of Capra's legal battle with Cohn and Riskin's unsuccessful directing stint. Thus, long before *You Can't Take It with You* was released, a weight of expectancy had fallen on the pair's next move. A report in the *Motion Picture Daily* in June claimed on good authority that Capra and Riskin as a duo were nearly certain to join United Artists after Capra's final contracted picture for Columbia. Capra famously made the cover of *Time* magazine on August 8 with a glowing tribute to his career that heralded the release of *You Can't Take It with You* and pondered the direction of his future career in Hollywood.[13]

Other issues that complicated matters at this juncture need to be understood when looking at the relationship of Columbia's most successful filmmaking duo. In the summer of 1938, Capra finally joined the Screen Directors Guild and forged a close allegiance with Sam Goldwyn, who encouraged him to think about coming to work with his independent production company. Devastatingly, on the day Capra screened the postproduction cut of *You Can't Take It with You* on the lot, his three-year-old son, John, died after a routine tonsillectomy. Capra was shocked to his core by his son's death, and accounts from friends confirm that Capra was never quite the same cheery individual he had been. After this tragedy, he seemed most dissatisfied, even angry, about many parts of his life. The event made him less preoccupied with the state of his career and more devoted than ever to his family.[14]

Perhaps wishing to remove himself from the bidding war for his services, Capra let certain career moves pass him by at this time. Although, by virtue of political dealings in Hollywood, Sam Goldwyn appeared to be the main negotiator for Capra's future projects, David Selznick had been trying for a year to get the director to join Selznick International Pictures. Capra had rejected the services of agents looking after his business, and his whole career was, by this time, being represented by Selznick's brother Myron, who wanted a contract set at $200,000 a picture for the director. Selznick finally decided not to go for the deal, and subsequent attempts to lure Capra with an arrangement that would include Riskin as writer also failed.[15] Capra's failure to jump at any of the offers coming his way was understandable though inopportune.

In Bernard Dick's assessment of Columbia and Cohn, the wrenching from the studio of some of its most talented personnel had a double edge. Cohn wasn't keen to lose Capra, Riskin, Swerling, or any of his other top people who had made Columbia a real player in the Hollywood stakes. But neither did he think any one person was truly bigger than the studio, even Capra. Additionally, Dick reveals interesting financial considerations for Columbia's head. Cohn had invested heavily in Capra, in terms of screen rights and budget, to bring *Lost Horizon* and *You Can't Take It with You* to theaters—and he was about to do it one more time, buying Lewis R. Foster's novel *The Gentleman from Montana* for Capra to turn into *Mr. Smith Goes to Washington*—but these two films almost single-handedly decimated Columbia's net profits in 1938 and '39, reducing them from a high of $1,318,000 in 1937 to $184,000 the following year and a measly $2,000 twelve months from then. The films acquired rich praise in some quarters, won awards, and had considerable box office returns, but

Capra's net value to Columbia by these financial terms, asserts Dick, was questionable.[16] As one studio insider observed, Cohn had lived with Capra's threats to leave the studio year after year, listening to his plan to go it alone and run his own production company responsible to no one. Finally, whether or not he was influenced by finances, Cohn just let him.[17]

Sam Goldwyn, meanwhile, though unable to lure Capra to his company, had been successful in persuading Riskin to move across town. Columbia's star writer signed on with Goldwyn Pictures for a reported $500,000, almost five times what he had earned under Cohn. Goldwyn offered an alternative path for the most successful Hollywood writer of his generation: not as a director, writer, or both, but as a producer and executive assistant to the studio head himself. Riskin had acquired the producer title at Columbia two years previously but had not put it into effect. Whether Riskin thought executive control was a real prospect at a studio run by Harry Cohn is unknown, but Goldwyn was a big admirer. He enticed Riskin with more money and, potentially, more freedom, working for an independent company (which then sought distribution deals with the majors), than he had experienced even on Columbia's lot. Goldwyn's admiration for Riskin was evident from his continuing to smooth the writer's path into the company by getting Riskin's closest companions from Columbia to accompany him. Less than two months after Riskin had joined in August, his great friend Jo Swerling also signed on with Goldwyn, in October 1938.

Successive analyses of Capra's and Riskin's careers during this period have always maintained that they were partners, and that when they left Columbia Pictures, they naturally went together. What is implied is that Riskin had no thoughts about working with anyone else at this point. That the two would be together in their own independent company barely fourteen months after the premiere of You Can't Take It with You only serves to illustrate their ties and working relationship, it would seem. However, to what extent did Riskin actually want to move away from Columbia and, indeed, away from Capra? Certainly, even if Riskin did desire a clean break at this time, there is no suggestion that it was engendered by any dissatisfaction or antagonism between the two, and Riskin's move was clearly not predicated upon any claim for recognition or authorial praise. But the events of the previous year had certainly shaken him up. Not only had *When You're in Love* questioned his directorial talents, but Capra's "saving" of *Lost Horizon* by dropping many of what Riskin thought were his best scenes in the picture had damaged his confidence and credibility. He began to ponder his future direction and place in the industry, and he was tempted by the thought of alternative work. Riskin, now forty, was an integral part of the Hollywood establishment, a position that few writers could lay claim to. He was almost certainly tired of Cohn's antics and his dominance within Columbia's confines, but he never had felt entirely frustrated with or beholden to Cohn's moods of approval and reproach. It had been more than three years since he had worked on a project with anyone other than Capra, except for *When You're in Love*, and he now wondered what might be next for him if he broke the bonds.

The other aspect of the move away from Columbia, and the separation between Riskin and Capra, came from the director himself. Capra followed up *You Can't Take It with You* with *Mr. Smith Goes to Washington* some fourteen months later, by which time he had already jumped Columbia's ship and was beginning to incorporate his own production company with Riskin back in harness. All of this seems a convenient progression in their story, but it wasn't guaranteed at the time to be that way. Other accounts suggest that Capra began another picture for Columbia, with Sidney Buchman, who wrote *Mr. Smith*, preparing a script based on the life of the composer Frederic Chopin. Capra wanted to film the story in color and Harry Cohn agreed, but Jack Cohn and the moneymen back East balked at this. They were very uneasy about a lavish costume drama and the audience it would or could attract. The New York office won out, the Chopin project was shelved, and Capra left Columbia for good.[18] But the account shows that a reuniting of the partners was anything but a given; it took another series of coincidental developments for their paths to return to the same track.

While Capra's future was still unresolved in the first half of 1939, Riskin had settled in at Goldwyn Pictures. He produced two movies for the studio that were distributed through United Artists, both in that year, both of which managed to achieve moderate returns at the box office. *The Real Glory*, directed by Henry Hathaway, concerned an army medical officer in the Philippines during the era of the Spanish-American War. With a cast including David Niven, Broderick Crawford, and Kay Johnson, Gary Cooper played a U.S. Army lieutenant serving on the islands in 1906. As American expeditionary troops evacuate, the indigenous peoples slowly establish control, and Cooper's medical officer gets into all manner of scrapes and romantic entanglements. Riskin knew it would be a picture with zest and quality because Jo Swerling contributed to the script, adapting Charles L. Clifford's novel. While *Variety* described the movie as "an innocuous melodramatic yarn" and a "vehicle for Cooper to perform some unusual feats of gallantry," it did well enough at the box office and went on to become a popular, if controversial, feature of Hollywood's World War II output.[19] Riskin's second producing effort, however, did not provide the same comfort.

They Shall Have Music was an ill-fated attempt to make heartthrob Jascha Heifetz a movie star. Heifetz played himself as a talented violinist who helps a music school for poor children. He was aided by Joel McCrea and by Walter Brennan, who would later star in *Meet John Doe*. With Archie Mayo (who had helmed *Illicit*, the screen version of Riskin and Edith Fitzgerald's play *Many a Slip*) directing, the picture was filmed by Gregg Toland, who was about to collaborate with Orson Welles on *Citizen Kane*. There was no lack of talent on the project, but the story (by Charles Clifford, again) and script (by John Howard Lawson and Irma Von Cube) simply didn't work. Riskin found producing was getting to be as troubling and frustrating as directing. In the course of making *They Shall Have Music*, he discovered that working for Goldwyn was actually a far more exacting experience than working for Cohn had ever been, partly because he couldn't pass himself off as merely the writer anymore but had to deal with problems and personalities on set. The trials of responsibility cropped up again. When Capra resolved not to sign on with Columbia, as *Mr. Smith Goes to Washington* was about to hit theaters, Riskin saw a chance to escape the mistake of his Goldwyn deal. McBride suggests that Capra approached Buchman first when starting up his independent company, but that appears doubt-ful; Capra and Buchman's relationship was, as McBride himself points out, somewhat strained by the writer's strong left-wing politics.[20] It didn't take long, in any case, for Capra and Riskin to come up with a plan for independence and, they hoped, a chance to direct their own futures.

In the summer of 1939, Riskin left Hollywood and traveled extensively in Europe. Once more steeling himself for his next career move, he sought sanctuary and new horizons in foreign lands. In Scandinavia especially, the press gave a high profile to Riskin's visits to Stockholm and Copenhagen, mentioning his many triumphs almost as though he were a great auteur rather than script man at one of Hollywood's less well-regarded stu-dios. This recognition of Riskin's talent as a writer contrasted significantly with the attention the press paid to writers at home, where many of his colleagues remained anonymous among the Hollywood cavalcade. Riskin was no longer unrecognizable, but neither was his life well known. While he was away on this tour, a report by Nelson Bell in the *Washington Post* served up anoth-er slice of Riskin mythology. Bell commented that "Mrs. Robert Riskin" had slipped quietly into the capital and was occupying an apartment in Wardman Park.[21] This was the kind of odd refer-ence to his personal life that had crept into Riskin's biography since his days with Edith Fitzgerald. The mystery woman was never identified, although it could have been Loretta Young, with whom Riskin was beginning to be seen at this time. Riskin most probably lapped up with amusement and interest the sug-gestions of the mysterious movements of his "wife." But the con-trast between his gossip-subject status in the United States and the serious adulation he received abroad drew him even more to the European attitude toward cinema and filmmakers. Riskin's specifically anglophile tendencies would direct him back to Eu-rope, and Britain in particular, during the long years of struggle in World War II.

By October 1939, Riskin had returned to Hollywood, and he and Capra made their play for freedom. They joined with lead-ing Hollywood attorney Loyd Wright in filing articles of incor-poration with the secretary of state for California for $1 million.[22]

The title of the new company was Frank Capra Productions; it fixed its capital at one hundred thousand shares of stock without par value, and one hundred thousand shares at $10 each.[23] The company moved into the offices that had been vacated by William Randolph Hearst's company, Cosmopolitan Pictures, on the Warner Brothers lot, and leased stage room and storage while at the same time financing operating costs.[24] Capra and Riskin now had their own company and were free, in theory at least, to make their own decisions. The company's letterhead made the equity of the relationship very clear. In the top left-hand corner was Capra's name; in the top right-hand corner, Riskin's. Symbolically, at least, this was a joint venture, although the financial distribution of stock within the company told another story: 65 percent of the company was to be owned by Capra; Riskin took the other 35 percent.[25] All they needed now was a first story and a deal for distribution of the movies they wanted to make.

The Life and Death of Frank Capra Productions

The new partnership seemed to have a very bright future in late 1939, but eighteen months later, the plan had backfired for both Capra and Riskin. By the middle of 1941, after only one film, *Meet John Doe*, they were looking to dissolve their company. Thanks to an elongated writing and production schedule, *Meet John Doe* had come in over the $1.25 million budget that Warner Brothers insisted on for a movie of its scale.[26] Yet the omens had looked so good.

Sometime late in 1939, Riskin was "handed" the material for a screen treatment called *The Life and Death of John Doe*, by Richard Connell and Robert Presnell. On November 28, 1939, the new company bought the rights to the short story on which the screen treatment was based, Richard Connell's "A Reputation," written in the 1920s.[27] Frank Capra Productions also gained access, through Riskin's friendship, to Jo Swerling's incomplete script *The World Is an Eight Ball*, which was an early attempt to dramatize Connell and Presnell's treatment for the screen. Most reports suggest that Riskin showed the story to Capra, probably when the director was doing publicity for *Mr. Smith* in the autumn of 1939. But how was the story "handed" to Riskin? The answer may well be personal contact with one of the writers. In addition to Swerling, Robert Presnell had been one of the contributors to *The Real Glory*, and it seems highly likely that he pushed the screen treatment Riskin's way, with some help from Swerling, during the making of that picture.[28]

The three pieces—"A Reputation," *The World Is an Eight Ball*, and *The Life and Death of John Doe*—combined to form the inspiration for the screenplay that Riskin constructed. The job of sifting through these fragments of work produced the most significant, elongated gestation period of any writing in his career. Connell and Presnell's title remained as the working heading for the film until the summer of 1940, when it acquired the shortened version *The Life of John Doe*, having finally been assigned a production number in the Warner Brothers shooting schedule.

In early 1940, Capra and Riskin tied in Warner Brothers, Vitagraph, and the Bank of America to a finance deal that was considered quite advantageous to the pair. They got control over virtually all aspects of shooting, as well as final cut. In fact, some within Warner Brothers felt the deal was too good; a renegotiated contract in early 1941 for distribution of the picture under the Warner Brothers banner gave the studio 25 percent of the net revenue once the picture grossed $2 million.[29] The deal became something of an albatross to the partners, and there turned out to be little profit in the venture for such a small company, despite the film's going on to make money at the box office. Congress had pushed through an excess-profits tax that drastically reduced profit margins for independent ventures like Capra and Riskin's.[30] Although Capra and Riskin didn't know it at the time, *Meet John Doe* would be their last full-scale collaboration. The film, though made in difficult circumstances, and with all manner of alterations, rewrites, and concessions in theme and narrative, is arguably one of the best they ever made. Riskin put the vicissitudes of *Lost Horizon*, *When You're in Love*, and even *You Can't Take It with You* behind him, and *Meet John Doe* reasserted the jocose, eloquent disquisitions on American society and politics that had so successfully infused his early features. The story returned the pair to the familiar ground of short-narrative adaptation. Connell's "A Reputation" was written in 1922 for *Century Magazine*. In the story, office worker Saunders Rook invades a posh Park Avenue party to declare that he intends to commit suicide, in protest of the unenlightened state of the world and its many injustices, by jumping into a Central Park reservoir on the Fourth of July. It was a story that Jo Swerling had been fascinated with but could not develop further in his rough draft of a theatrical version of the story, *The World Is an Eight Ball*. Swerling had the idea to infuse contemporary social commentary into the satirical persona of a rehashed lead character, Ferdinand Katzmellenbogen.[31] He wrote the character as a loud, drunken exhibitionist who cannot remember any of his proclamations when sober. Swerling liked the characters and the sense of social engagement but couldn't develop a third act. Connell came back to the story in 1939 and, together with Hollywood writer Robert Presnell, attempted a screen treatment now called *The Life and Death of John Doe*. Capra was immediately gripped by the treatment and spent his time reading and making notes on the train journey back from the East Coast. He and Riskin agreed that the story should be slated as the first movie in the life of Frank Capra Productions.

The new company made a great stir in the Hollywood community during the early months of 1940. In many respects, Capra and Riskin's leap into the independent void foretold the breakup of the studio system some twenty years later; at the time, it was thought that both names were big enough to effectively break studio control over the major stars of the day. Unlike United Artists, which had been linked with the pair in 1938, Capra and Riskin were not looking for a studio to challenge the majors, but were simply seeking creative autonomy.[32]

The publicity machine that marked the breakaway of Hollywood's most successful writer-director partnership kicked into gear in February 1940, when both *Variety* and the *Hollywood Reporter* ran major advertisements from Warner Brothers stating, "The mighty magnet of showmanship now adds the magic names of Capra and Riskin." The banner headline proclaimed that the pair's first production, still at this point titled *The Life and Death of John Doe*, would begin shooting on April 15. It was reported that Capra and Riskin had sunk as much as a million dollars of their own money into the venture. Failure, by these accounts, was already not an option.

It just so happened that Riskin set to work on writing a screen treatment for *The Life and Death of John Doe* at exactly the same time that his personal and professional life was changing dramatically. In 1940, as he and Capra were getting their independent company off the ground and Riskin set to writing again, he was reported to be dating the actress Loretta Young, the woman who might or might not have sneaked into a Washington hotel masquerading as Riskin's wife the year before. The two showed up at the premiere of Lewis Milestone's production of Steinbeck's novel *Of Mice and Men* in April. Riskin's past also unexpectedly resurfaced at this time. Briefly and without explanation, Edith Fitzgerald came back into his life. Riskin may have spotted her current misfortunes in the newspapers: reports during May 1940 claimed that Fitzgerald, once more the "ex-wife" of Robert Riskin, had been involved in a car crash and had landed in jail, the implication being for drunk driving.[33] There is no indication of contact between them or, indeed, of what happened to Fitzgerald beyond the initial arrest. It is not even clear that they had any dealings with each other at all in the late thirties, but the story added to the publicity building around the newly independent venture with Capra and to the confusions at the heart of Riskin's personal affairs. In any case, Riskin's current flirtation with Young would be brief; within a year, it would give way to a much more serious courtship with another actress, Fay Wray. Within two years, the pair would be married, and Hollywood would lose, according to prime gossip columnist Louella Parsons, its most eligible bachelor.[34]

Meanwhile, the production of *The Life of John Doe* was beginning to be time consuming and tortuous. The shooting schedule had been set at fifty-seven days, starting on August 7, 1940, and concluding on December 9, but Capra and Riskin spent the summer months grappling with the script and, especially, the final reel of the movie.[35] Both of them felt hamstrung by an ending that seemed to have no redemption. In Connell and Presnell's story, John Doe is slated to commit suicide, but writer and director put off this closure as unpalatable for as long as possible. The title of the film, even without the mention of death, remained untouched almost until postproduction. Further, Capra had originally wanted to be reunited for the film with James Stewart and Jean Arthur, the pair whose chemistry had made *Mr. Smith* such a success. Warner Brothers, though, with money and time invested in the project, pressed for an even bigger star than Stewart. In the end, both sides settled on Gary Cooper, and the female role went to Capra's previous leading lady and romantic fixation, Barbara Stanwyck, who was cast only a month before shooting began.[36] In fact, both Cooper and Stanwyck signed on without ever seeing their lines; working with Capra and Riskin was deemed good enough for them. This faith in the team's working partnership, however, masked the dilemma at the heart of the production: the absence of a completed script until well into production. Even characters' names were subject to alteration. Early drafts of the script had the publishing tycoon as D. B. Wells and the female journalist as an unlikely heroine called Dot Brush.[37]

Finally, Riskin concocted an ending in which the main character, Long John Willoughby, would survive, but this reconstructed climax lacked bite and resonance. Capra had already fallen into the habit of test-screening and readjusting finales, as well as middles and beginnings, from the nervous process of *Lost Horizon* onward. While the essence of the story remained intact, the same tinkering with plot emphasis and situations continued to afflict *Meet John Doe*.

In the story that Riskin settled on prior to the commencement of shooting, Long John Willoughby (Cooper) is a minor league baseball pitcher seeking money to fix his "busted wing," as he puts it, so he can get back into the game. He accepts an offer from the *New Bulletin* newspaper to pose as a stooge, the anonymous John Doe of the title, who has supposedly written a letter to the paper protesting the ills of the world with the promise to jump off the City Hall roof on Christmas Eve. The letter is a fake, however, a final hurrah from columnist Ann Mitchell (Stanwyck), who was sacked in a purge by new editor Henry Connell (James Gleason) at the behest of the *Bulletin*'s latest owner, D. B. Norton (Edward Arnold).

Sensing glory and financial reward, Mitchell and Connell help to shape a huge story around John Doe, printing details of his life in the paper and having him broadcast an engaging, homespun philosophy over the airwaves of Norton's radio station, with words conjured from the diaries of Ann's dead father. John Doe clubs spring up all over the country, the circulation of the *Bulletin* expands, and Connell and, especially, Ann benefit from Norton's patronage. Norton, however, has had an ulterior motive from the outset: the clubs will help to perpetuate a political movement that will propel him into the White House and allow him to instigate totalitarian control using his storm trooper–like security force. Ann and an enlightened Connell find out about the plan, but seemingly too late to stop the momentum of Norton's support. At a giant rally for the John Does on one of Capra's trademark rain-swept evenings, Willoughby is exposed as a fraud, and he retreats, even leaving behind his constant companion, the colonel (Walter Brennan), to ponder his future. Sickened by what he thinks is Ann's betrayal of the John Doe philosophy and by the political manipulation wielded by Norton, Long John decides that the only way to make the public see the error of supporting the fascist tycoon is to print a real suicide note in the newspapers, revealing the massive plot that has been constructed around him. He heads for the City Hall roof on Christmas Eve, intending to go through with the fictional John Doe's plan of jumping as the bells ring and the clocks chime out for Christmas Day. But, as he perches on the ledge of City Hall's bell tower as the moment arrives, Norton and his cronies, sensing that Long John might attempt such a plan, intervene to stop him. Unbeknownst to Long John and Norton, Ann, the colonel, and John Doe supporters from the small town of Millville who met Willoughby earlier are also thinking the same thing, and together they race to the roof to save Long John.

Riskin had all the right ingredients for this cocktail of emotional turmoil, political intrigue, and comedic observation, but the amount of each, as well as the troublesome ending, plagued him and Capra as the production developed. What should happen to Willoughby in this last scene, and how might this develop in the story? The shooting script for the film indicates several elements that were hard for Capra and Riskin to resolve. First, initial shooting made the case for Norton's fascist instincts far more clear cut and hence suggested that Long John's determination to stop him must be that much more desperate, even suicidal. An initial scene that was meant to introduce Norton's character has him sitting before a roaring fire reading Hitler's *Mein Kampf*. An interesting interoffice memo from the time refers to Capra and Riskin's wish to procure copies of *Mein Kampf* and Marx's *Das Kapital*. The front office presumed, as explained in the communication, that the script would use the books "in a manner intended to discredit the works and their publishers." However, the note also claims that the scene was something that "has grown up on set," almost as though Capra and Riskin were looking to sidestep any insinuation that they were making some radical political statement or to obscure the fact that the scene had been in the draft script from early on.[38] Either included in or adjacent to that scene, the original shooting script for the film also had Norton being confronted in his home by an elderly man who tells the tycoon to stop robbing people. Even in its briefest form, this is a moment that looks uncannily like the scene between the farmer and Longfellow Deeds from five years earlier. At some point in the shooting of the picture, the overtly radical persuasion of the scenes with Edward Arnold's character, given the political climate, came home to the pair: both these elements were later cut from the final edit and what is now the recognized version of the film.

Second, it was not clear to writer or director the extent to which Ann should be duped by Norton's ambitions, while also captivated by his power and charm. Norton's sexual allure to Ann remains an undercurrent of their relationship that is quite important but rarely remarked upon. Ann is charmed by his presents, which make her seem at once feminine and important, such as the fur coat she receives for writing Long John's speech at the rally, an oratory that ultimately is not delivered. Norton, in making Ann "report directly to him," assumes a paternalistic control that suggests he may be grooming Miss Mitchell for a role by his side in the White House. But Riskin's shooting script questions the extent to which this relationship should be allowed to develop before crumbling in the face of Long John's decisive actions in the picture's climax. In the key scene in which Norton makes his pitch to business leaders before the huge John Doe rally, for instance, his inclination to bring about a fascist coup in the United States with the support of industrial and labor leaders becomes clear, but Riskin's notes suggest that Ann claps enthusiastically at the power and clarity of Norton's speech. In the final version, this endorsement, however naïve it may have been, is transformed into Ann's merely shuffling in her seat and uncomfortably asking whether she can speak with Norton in private.

Ann is, in essence, Riskin's great final female protagonist for the Capra films. Over the course of a decade, Stanwyck, like her character, had evolved; she had grown as an actress since appearing in Capra and Riskin's early stories. Here, she is ambitious, determined, resolute, and loyal. She contradicts male authority perpetually, and like so many Riskin heroines, she also has a mission: to uphold the dignity and ideals of the one great man in her life, her father, Doc Mitchell. It was only the ending of the film that diluted her strength and resolve, just as it did for Capra and Riskin. In Ann, therefore, an ironic puzzle was played out that Hollywood's most successful team couldn't resolve: how to close the movie.

But Capra and Riskin did have to resolve John Doe's death, one way or another. In the first previewed version of the film, Willoughby looks down from the top of City Hall on a snowy evening, but he accepts the invitation of the John Doe Club members and Ann to return to the fray and oppose Norton. Connell speaks the final words in the picture, but they merely address Willoughby's sidekick, the angst-ridden colonel who has hated the plan, materialism, and the state of the modern world from the beginning. "Come on, Colonel," urges Connell as John carries the emotionally exhausted Ann down the stairs. It was reported at the time, and has since passed into movie folklore, that Capra and Riskin did film a suicide ending in which a contrite Norton, seeing what he has done, orders that the suicide note be published and the truth about the John Doe clubs revealed. But, as Charles Wolfe's detailed assessment of the picture has documented, no footage or evidence in the production notes of a suicide ending has ever been discovered.[39]

The suicide that plagued the ending of the film is wrapped up, it is clear now, in a battle throughout the narrative between what Glenn Phelps calls the forces of "secular materialism" and the demands for "Christian communalism." The ideological pre-determinations that dominated the Capra-Riskin films of the previous decade are here confronted head-on in a clash that Phelps identifies as raging between the anti-Christ figure of D. B. Norton and the God-like spiritual presence of Doc Mitchell, Ann's father.[40] In Phelps's reading, the Capra heroes from *Mr. Deeds* onward are not static political participants but, in fact, characters whose views and philosophy unfold before our very eyes. That philosophy, he asserts, is moving toward a communal belief that needs to recognize the transitory nature of political systems and dominant elites. Phelps adds to this oppositional fragmentation by asserting that the colonel occupies a third role, that of "asocial individualism," a position that rejects societal conformity in any guise, be it individual or communal. "Society and social responsibility inevitably destroy a person's independence. The Colonel singles out relationships with women, working for wages, and money as especially ruinous to a man," claims Phelps. "You're stuck on a girl," suggests the colonel to Willoughby, realizing almost wearily what this means. Phelps makes the comparison between self and shared interest inherent in his observations about *Mr. Deeds*, *Mr. Smith*, and *It's a Wonderful Life*. The Capra characters, his argument concludes, are in the process of "becoming," of learning about the world and realizing that while they can shape it, they can't alone change it.[41] And Longfellow Deeds, Jefferson Smith, and George Bailey do all seem to reaffirm that condition: a condition of action but also hopeless resignation to the state of society and their place in it.

Other analyses by the likes of Maland and Donald Willis similarly presume the Capra hero to be the default ideological creation of the director.[42] In fact, successive analyses of Capra's films have constantly worked toward this position with the protagonists. They are always the "Capra heroes," and they appear to take on subtle and like-minded traits that coalesce into the personalities that infiltrate the famous later films, from *Mr. Deeds* onward.

In fact, however, the characters are as much, if not far more, resonant of the narrative and ideological trajectory of Riskin's scripts, including those written away from Capra. From *Ann Carver's Profession* through *Carnival* and, especially, *The Whole Town's Talking*, heroic transformation and the political dichotomy of individual attainment and communal sacrifice lie at the heart of Riskin's scripts. His ability to initiate a profound ideological revelation within his characters is nowhere better demonstrated than in his dialectical positioning of Connell late in *Meet John Doe*. The hard-bitten world of Riskin's editorial functionary is utterly changed by one confessional moment, a scene that advances a powerful argument for Riskin's ideological agenda in the Capra movies. In the best speech in the film, one of Riskin's best scenes in any of his scripts, a drunken Connell confronts Long John in a bar just before John's Wrigley Field address. Riskin constructs a marvelous allegorical reference for Connell: America's great leaders of the past were "the lighthouses of the world." His entreaty to Willoughby not to let Norton turn out those lighthouses is a significant spur to Long John's later moral contemplation. But more important still is Connell's reference to his father, who died beside his son in the same regiment in the Great War. It is a touchingly eloquent gesture for a character whose career and life, it now becomes clear, have been cloaked in sacrifice and regret. Connell is not gruff and unfeeling simply for effect but lives with the reality of lost innocence and idealism. He urges Long John to consider the practical lesson of this loss, but he also wants Long John to preserve his idealism if he can. Political endeavors and spiritual guidance were facets of *Meet John Doe* that Riskin had written about in *Lost Horizon* and *Mr. Deeds*. Now, amid an unfolding global conflict, he brought those ideological strands together and demonstrated the extent of his ownership of all the characters. The Capra heroes, it turns out, also belong to Riskin.

On a visit to New York to negotiate a further distribution package for the picture in January 1941, Riskin told reporters quite

candidly that his and Capra's new film would have to be subjected to more test-screenings, a confession that parts of the picture, and certainly the ending, were not yet right. On March 12,
1941, *Meet John Doe* was released in seven theaters in four major
cities, but it was pulled two days later. On March 23, Capra returned with cast members to reshoot some of the final scenes and
to incorporate the now-recognizable final line from Connell on
the City Hall roof: "There you are, Norton! The People! Try and
lick that!"[43] In addition, Capra cut a few scenes to shorten running time but also weaken some of the inferences. For example,
the penultimate scene in the mansion sees Long John confront
Norton, Ann, and the assembled great and good who are there to
plot Norton's ascent to the White House on the back of the John
Doe movement. Capra cut Riskin's line for Willoughby in which
he says that he now understands why people take up arms and
give their lives to protect decent people. The line may have been
regarded as inflammatory by the studio or by Capra himself, or
possibly was removed after generating reaction at the preview
screenings. Whatever the reason, one of the most incendiary
comments in the movie disappeared in this editing.[44]

Meet John Doe went on general release in April, backed up
by an elaborate marketing campaign from Warner Brothers. The
studio touted it as the "glorious peak of all the achievements
that won them more awards than any director-writer team." By
any modern standards, Warner Brothers pulled no punches in
its ingenious selling of the movie, making newspaper mock-ups
with John Doe gossip and even challenging people to set up
John Doe clubs.[45] Warner Brothers' files, however, reveal how
far removed this full-scale exploitation of the movie's narrative
precepts was from executives' nervous expressions during the
making of the picture, and how suspect they were of its contemporary reflection of events. There is, for example, among the
collection of documents held about the picture, a file devoted
to *Meet John Doe*'s likeness to the moral rearmament movement
that had been prominent in Southern California in the previous
couple of years. The movie's convention scene, filmed at Los Angeles' Wrigley Field, supposedly bore a striking resemblance to
the movement's meeting at the Hollywood Bowl in July 1939, a

gathering that Capra and Riskin might have attended, although there is no proof.[46]

The problems concerning the ending, release, and rerelease of *Meet John Doe* weren't the only ones that plagued the movie. An April 1941 letter from attorney Peter J. McCoy stated that authors Robert Shurr and Pat A. Leonard were claiming an infringement of copyright for scenes and story closely related to their play *The Stuffed Shirt*.[47] In November, a Warner Brothers interoffice memo hinted at more problems to come. A stage play, *Washington Jitters*, by Dalton Trumbo, had appeared; it was derived from a novel with a character named Chester Willoughby, *Monkey on a Stick* by Henry Clune, which had appeared at almost exactly the same time as the film. The insinuation was that Riskin had somehow adopted the character as his own for *Meet John Doe*, but further communications from within Warner Brothers accused Clune and Trumbo of copying aspects of Capra's earlier *Mr. Smith*.[48] Still later correspondence on behalf of Trumbo suggested that Riskin had seen *Washington Jitters* on stage, implying that he had taken influence or characters directly from the production for his own adaptation.[49]

It was ironic that so many problems should afflict *Meet John Doe* and that Capra and Riskin should tinker with the movie for as long as they did, for it had defenders and plaudits from early on. John T. McManus's article in the March 2, 1941, *PM's Weekly* outlined the development of the film and mentioned that Capra and Riskin's investment in the project amounted to as much as $1 million. He was writing in response to one of the sneak previews of the longer version of the film (two hours, nineteen minutes) shown to some critics in mid-February. McManus reported that the audience cheered, cried, and filled out reaction cards. He scored the screening as a triumph and indicated that that version of the film was sure to be a success for 1941.[50] The *Hollywood Reporter*, on March 13, rapturously endorsed the picture. It described the narrative, setting, and theme as timely and noted that Capra and Riskin were now acting almost as one. "The reviewer who pretends to say where writing ends and directing begins is deluding only himself," the paper asserted. Almost everybody associated with the film received praise in the article, and Gary

Cooper was described as unforgettable. "It is a brave thing Capra and Riskin do in allowing a character to have his full say, almost without interruption," the review concluded.[51] The affirmation of the movie at this point prompts only one question: why did the pair make further changes to the end if the film was well received by some and was set to be a hit?

The answer seems to lie in the reviews Charles Wolfe considers in his excellent critical analysis of the movie. Assessments by the influential Bosley Crowther in the *New York Times* and Edwin Schallert in the *Los Angeles Times* followed patterns similar to those by McManus and the *Hollywood Reporter*. Both marveled at the performances of Gary Cooper, Barbara Stanwyck, and, in particular, James Gleason as the cantankerous editor Connell. Both also heaped praise on Capra and Riskin, whose work Crowther described as "superlative." But both also homed in on the close of the movie and, specifically, Norton's conversion to the John Doe cause. Crowther called it an "obvious sop" of an ending, while Schallert thought the finish "makes it difficult to believe that the fine principles [Willoughby] espouses . . . would or could be revived anew. He has been dubbed a fake and the John Doe idea has been shattered."[52] *Meet John Doe*'s rewritten denouement made concessions to these comments, but it did not swallow whole the implications of their objections. In Schallert's words, Willoughby should have paid the "fatal price" and been killed off. As Capra famously said, however, you can't just kill Gary Cooper. Long John remained alive in the revised closure. *Meet John Doe* stuck with resolution and redemption at the end. Capra and Riskin's finale was not to conclude with glorious tragedy.

The legal, contractual, and artistic disputes concerning the movie were either settled or simply faded away during the course of the next year, along with Capra and Riskin's company. *Meet John Doe* did make money, but not enough to satisfy the studio, the financial backers, or the two principals of Frank Capra Productions. As Warner Brothers' financial statements attest, by October 31, 1942, the film's gross receipts amounted to $2,098,182.82, only a small amount beyond the $2 million figure Jack Warner had set as the level at which his studio would begin to recoup straight profits from the venture.[53] For Riskin, the debate over the ending of *Meet John Doe* provided a form of closure in itself. *Lost Horizon, You Can't Take It With You*, and the spell of producing for Goldwyn had all, in one way or another, and despite continued successes, been frustrating experiences. They had been saved from the threat of outright disaster by good judgment, the quality and ambition of the scripts, calm heads (not least Capra's), and a store of artistic and commercial credibility that made the films hits whatever the difficulties reported in the press or actually occurring in the productions themselves. At the February 26, 1942, Academy Awards, held at the Biltmore Hotel in Los Angeles, Riskin found himself in an odd position after years of nominations, tributes, and some successes at the event. His brother's film *Here Comes Mr. Jordan* was up for all the main awards, and so he was happy and keen to support the family. But the only Oscar that *Meet John Doe* won that night went to Connell and Presnell for best original story. It seemed the ultimate irony: Riskin and Capra had put in so much work over the previous two years, more for this picture than for any other they made, and what had it been for?

Tellingly, more than a year before, when journalist Theodore Strauss asked Riskin why he and Capra had made the leap for independence, Riskin didn't have a concrete answer. He thought it had something to do with creative fulfillment and the "feeling" of freedom. This same intangible force would drive Riskin toward his own company after the war, but the disappointing result for Capra and Riskin's most committed project to date probably led him to believe that something else was going on. He had received rich acclaim again for his script, even from those who doubted the movie's closure, but Riskin's instinct told him that something was not quite right.

The films of the last few years had all been ambitious, creative, challenging, and often sweeping articulations of Riskin and Capra's vision together, and sometimes apart. But the movies had also become huge, floating, insoluble masses upon which financial dependency, audience expectation, and critical examination lingered and festered. Riskin and Capra's movies were important to Harry Cohn, and to his conception of Columbia as a major studio, but they had also become important to Hollywood. Riskin and Capra had become an industry, a trademark, a signpost of how successful the studio system could be. They had traded upon their names and now had to feel the weight of expectation every time a new project was announced. And slowly but surely, consciously or unconsciously, they had tried to delay or sidestep that weight of expectation a little more each time.

Between 1931 and 1936, the pair made six movies together, Capra made three alone, and Riskin contributed to at least six further screenplays. Between 1937 and 1941, Riskin produced two movies, Capra made one—*Mr. Smith*—without Riskin, and the pair worked on just three pictures. Was the creative well drying up, as must happen to artistic talent at some point? Not exactly: it was just that the ambitions, the projects, and the vision were changing. Both Capra and Riskin were more ambitious; they both wanted to produce more demanding, adventurous films, and these took more time. Riskin had already stated, and after the war would restate, that quality films took time to make; artists could not simply turn the creative flow on and off like a faucet. What of course had happened was that success had bought both Riskin and Capra time, and time to think was the enemy of the studio system. Almost nobody else at Columbia, and few other people within the industry at the end of the 1930s, had the sort of creative freedom Riskin and Capra did. They had churned out films without even thinking in the first half of the decade, like so many of their contemporaries; the only difference was that they had had enormous success. But they had subsequently become discerning of material. Spontaneity and the willingness to make things work were thus replaced with doubt, with too many occasions to alter films to please their audiences. After the *Meet John Doe* experience, Riskin grew wary of writing to please and, what was worse still, writing for some preconceived audience expectation. He was not averse to test-screenings, but he felt the result was always a diminution of his artistic vision rather than Capra's—that is, of the writing rather than the visual composition. Despite the two forming a true partnership and consulting on all aspects of *Meet John Doe*, this division of labor between the visual and the written word was still the mainstay of their collaboration: Riskin's talent was the dialogue, Capra's, the cinematic aesthetic.

Not only did Riskin have nagging doubts about the postproduction routine, but he also simply did not have the commitment to sustain a working company, where he and Capra had all the headaches of financing and producing even before the writing and directing of the picture. Paradoxically, Riskin was perceived as being good at management negotiation despite his professed ignorance and hatred of it. Gradwell Sears, the president of Vitagraph and part of Warner Brothers' sales organization, put Riskin's business acumen into perspective: "He's one of the best businessmen I ran into." Sears, who observed the writer's ability to conduct negotiations while concluding deals for *Meet John Doe*, added, "He has a perfect mind for analysis. He's as good figuring out sales angles as he is figuring out plot. He takes nothing for granted, which is why every detail in the deals he makes is as clear as the details in his stories."[54]

But shaping his destiny in the boardroom, brokering deals and getting contracts, wasn't the career move Riskin had in mind. In the summer of 1941, he and Capra were still being referred to as partners, but Riskin was busy making his break. He had told Theodore Strauss at the beginning of the year that there were no plans at that time for another film. Riskin's intuition may have been telling him that he and Capra had nowhere else to go artistically, that the partnership had run its course. Riskin had more idealistic pursuits in mind, a chance to work toward something again. The war in Europe offered meaning, something tangible and worthwhile: a cause. He accepted an invitation to go to London on assignment for *Liberty* magazine, but while there, he offered his services to the British Ministry of Information, which was well into the production of propaganda material for the home front as the war intensified.[55] A deal was struck for Frank Capra Productions to produce one more picture for Warner Brothers, and the studio's office in Hollywood even gave Riskin an advance to aid with expenses during his stay in Europe, but Capra went ahead and negotiated this contract as a director only.[56] That film was *Arsenic and Old Lace*, a movie Capra made in late 1941 and finished in early '42—with Cary Grant in the lead role—just before he headed off to make propaganda films for the military.[57] The film was, in essence, made without Riskin's input at all. It is remembered as one of Capra's quirky little gems, but it, too, proved a troubling and unsatisfying assignment. The pair would never work in tandem again. The critical and commercial peak of Robert Riskin's Hollywood career had been reached. But the most intriguing phase of his life and career had just begun.

CHAPTER FIVE

THE LIBERATOR

For Robert Riskin, the Second World War began well before the United States' entry into the conflict in December 1941. Indeed, it is somewhat ironic that Riskin's role in America's propaganda efforts during the war should have been obscured for so long, considering his singular commitment to the cause from early on. Having taken leave of Capra and their production company, Riskin accepted an assignment with *Liberty* magazine late in 1941 that sent him to Britain to report on wartime film activity there. Riskin did more than simply report on the state of British movie production, however; he actually offered his services to the Ministry of Information and acted as a liaison on initial propaganda features that were to become a staple of the early British wartime morale effort. These films later informed his ideas for a propaganda series initiated for the Office of War Information (OWI) back home. Pat McGilligan suggests that Riskin's solid Democratic Party outlook and his Jewish heritage are good reasons to suppose that he wanted rid of German and Italian fascism as quickly as possible and flew to Europe to assist the cause quite willingly.[1] Only after the attack on Pearl Harbor did Riskin return to America, to spend a restless few months waiting for his chance to become involved in his own government's organizational effort through the OWI.

Riskin was by now in a relationship with actress Fay Wray, and they met again in the spring of 1942 in California. Wray was preparing for a picture at Columbia called *Not a Ladies' Man*, with Lew Landers directing, and Riskin was thinking over his next move following his return from London. He had in fact already

161

accepted an invitation to write a *Thin Man* script for his brother at MGM. The two had not worked together since their unhappy experience writing, directing, and producing *When You're in Love* five years earlier. The successful series of detective stories seemed like a perfect point at which to reunite. It would be Riskin's first scriptwriting stint since his final tinkering with *Meet John Doe* nearly eighteen months before. The *Thin Man* films were what might be described today as a franchise, though with nothing like the commercial instincts that drive modern sequel/prequel stories like *Star Wars*, *X-Men*, and *The Matrix*. The original 1934 film *The Thin Man*, featuring William Powell and Myrna Loy as the husband and wife detective team Nick and Nora Charles, was based on the characters created by Dashiell Hammett. Powell and Loy had a fizzing chemistry on screen that, as David Shipman remarks, was enhanced by their characters' interest in alcohol, sex, and money.[2] It was a winning combination, and they went on to reprise their roles in *After the Thin Man* (1936), *Another Thin Man* (1939), and *Shadow of the Thin Man* (1941) before the Riskin brothers came on board. The first three films did conform to modern-day franchise rules in one respect, by having the same director-writer team at the helm. W. S. "Woody" Van Dyke, aided by scriptwriting couple Albert Hackett and Frances Goodrich (who would later help to write *It's a Wonderful Life* for Capra), created smart, modern detective thrillers with just enough light touches and "red herrings" in the plot to keep the audience both amused and concerned.

Fay Wray asserts in her memoirs that the job of continuing the series was not one that Riskin relished, because his mind was now firmly set on putting his talents toward the war effort.[3] He took on the script as a job and as a favor to his brother.[4] Riskin, however, could not achieve any affinity with the characters; he felt that there was little room to develop personalities that had already been so well established in the earlier films. The story for the latest installment would eventually be credited to Riskin and Harry Kurnitz—who had cowritten the previous *Shadow of the Thin Man*—and, despite Kurnitz's reservations, Riskin pushed him to alter the protagonists, Myrna Loy's Nora in particular. Working with director Richard Thorpe (Van Dyke having died), and with the help of fellow writer Dwight Taylor, Riskin looked to create more melodrama and less tough detective narrative in his first screen treatment of the story—originally to be called *The Thin Man's Rival*—but he wrote Nick (Powell) as a bowdlerized version of his earlier incarnation.[5]

By the late spring of 1942, Riskin and Wray were apart again, she working on a theater production in Cambridge, Massachusetts, while he labored with the script in Hollywood. Riskin wrote to Fay complaining of that "dreadfully dull *Thin Man*" film and confessing that he wasn't even sure "what the scenes are about." He predicted in his correspondence that the screenplay would take about a month to get into shape, though the subtext of his letter suggested that he would have been far happier to deal with it for a week and then forget about the whole thing.[6] Riskin's commitment was virtually as low as it would get on any production in his career. Not only was his mind firmly set on getting into the government and working toward victory in the war, but he had also quickly spotted how unsuited his writing was to the nature and style of the *Thin Man* series. The stories were a little bawdy for his taste, and he found it difficult to fashion the detective couple into subtler and more vulnerable characters.

Riskin's attempt to find nuances within the pair included a plot whereby Nick and Nora return to the small town of Sycamore Springs, where the Charles family lived. The introduction of this picture-postcard community where nothing ever happens is, predictably, the cue for shifty characters to spring up and a complex plot to unfold, involving the murder of a local boy, Peter Burton, on the steps of the Charles house. A collection of social misfits and comic caricatures, especially Donald Meek's art shop owner, keep the audience guessing until art forgeries and the discovery of confidential plans for a technologically advanced airplane propeller shaft reveal Peter's killer to be the local pathologist. The story required intricate knitting to allow the drama to resonate with the comedy. Through the summer of 1942, Riskin labored under the weight of this heavy-handed construction.

Finally, before the summer was out, Riskin did manage to untangle himself from the script, as his letter to Fay had predicted, but the production staggered on. A second incomplete script was authored by Dwight Taylor and submitted October 12, 1943, a third produced on January 7, 1944, and a fourth filed on April 20 of the same year.[7] In fact, Riskin and Kurnitz would both return to tinker with the script one more time before putting their name on a final version submitted on August 22, 1944. Ultimately, it would take more than two years for *The Thin Man Goes Home* to be produced and reach theaters, and it still had many of the flaws that had worried Riskin from the start. A review of the film in *Variety* claims that the problem resided, as he well knew, in the dialogue.[8] Nick's father (Harry Davenport), the town doctor whose dreams of a new hospital are threatened by a conspiracy involving Sycamore Springs' village elders, veers rather disconcertingly between wise and principled authority figure and bumbling, confused old man. His reaction to threats is too often to call people names for comic effect and little else. Nora, though, does have some rather saucy rejoinders. When Nick remarks that attending his birthday dinner, hosted by his parents, makes him feel as though he is again a young boy in short pants, Nora coyly suggests that she would like to see that. The sight gags, too, work pretty well, and Asta the dog, the Charleses' constant companion, remains the canine star of the show. All in all, *The Thin Man Goes Home* was a serviceable, if unspectacular, addition to the series, relying heavily on Powell and Loy's relationship while trying to convince the audience, with limited success, that Sycamore Springs had a dark underbelly.

While he labored over the *Thin Man* screenplay during the early summer of 1942, Riskin, through Wray, did find a route into institutional circles and the offer of a government job in wartime propaganda. Wray received encouragement about her companion's prospects from General William Donovan, whom she had met a few years previously and who had helped her in his capacity as an attorney during a separation from her then husband, John Monk Saunders. Donovan was a veteran of World War I, had run for governor of New York, and was just now beginning a lengthy engagement with the government, first as director of the Office of Coordinator of Information, then as a founder of the Office of Strategic Services, and later with the Central Intelligence Agency. Wray had met Donovan again just prior to Pearl Harbor, while she was trying out for a play in Washington and he was recruiting John Ford into his special unit.[9] She claims no memory of writing to Donovan on Riskin's behalf, but a telegram from the general did arrive informing Riskin that playwright Robert Sherwood, who was heading up a recruitment drive for the OWI, would be in touch.[10]

The OWI had only recently been formed, by executive order, in the chaotic summer of 1942 following the Japanese attack in Hawaii. The agency's creation resulted from a complex series of political maneuvers initiated in Washington at least a year beforehand. President Roosevelt's establishing the Office of Civilian Defense in May 1941 was meant to clear the way for domestic propaganda as the war in Europe intensified and American participation became a distinct prospect. Instead, the man Roosevelt put in charge of the Office of Civilian Defense, larger-than-life New York mayor Fiorello La Guardia, found his loyalties divided between this government assignment and his role as leader of America's largest city. He therefore commuted his Office of Civilian Defense duty to that of protecting the civilian population, not Roosevelt's intention for him at all. As a result, the office quickly came in for sharp criticism. Meanwhile, Donovan's Office of Coordinator of Information, created in July 1941, had a much different charge: to engage in black propaganda and disinformation as Donovan himself envisioned and directed.[11] The Office of Coordinator of Information's lineage and relationship to the Office of Strategic Services and, later, the CIA was thus set in train very early by a director whose clear idea of the agency included, in his own words, "a flavor of subversion."[12]

In the late summer of 1941, Robert Sherwood, one of FDR's closest friends, was brought on board the Office of Coordinator of Information to come up with ideas to counter the anti-American propaganda of the Axis powers. The Foreign Information Service that Sherwood headed up under the aegis of the Office of Coordinator of Information would in time become better known as Voice of America. As Clayton Koppes and Gregory Black point out in their study of Hollywood and World War II, Sherwood's attitude toward propaganda summed up the confusion that was raging in a Washington still holding to neutrality and trying to extol higher moral virtues as the war developed in Europe. The Foreign Information Service head wanted to highlight the won-

derful accomplishments of democracy but "did not want to move
into the agitational propaganda that Donovan favored."[13] Roosevelt attempted to find a temporary solution to this ideological
impasse between agencies by establishing the Office of Facts and
Figures, which effectively took up the functions of the Office of
Civilian Defense. Its spokespeople—La Guardia again, as well as
librarian of Congress and poet Archibald MacLeish—went about
the task of trying to disabuse the public of the notion that the new
agency's role was the dissemination of propaganda.[14] The implicit
protest that the United States would never engage in anything as
underhanded as disseminating duplicitous information or visual
manipulation was curious to some New Dealers in Washington,
whose actions over the previous eight years—especially in areas
like the Federal Art Project—might have been regarded as particularly suited to the task now at hand. But La Guardia and even
Sherwood naïvely believed that telling the truth and providing
accurate information would convince the American people of the
righteousness of their cause, which in turn would bring victory
soon enough, they argued. Not surprisingly, William Donovan
thought that this was nonsense and that the United States ought
to engage in the same battle for hearts and minds that the Axis
powers were undertaking. The various agencies and subgroups
therefore found themselves at loggerheads, and it took the events
at Pearl Harbor to begin to resolve the issue.

Roosevelt initiated an executive order on December 17, 1941,
that effectively joined Washington and Hollywood at the hip for
the remainder of the war and, indeed, long after it had concluded. The Office of Government Reports was to have a Hollywood
liaison officer charged with making sure that the motion picture
community held firm to its pledge of aiding the war effort and
providing not only appropriate full-length features but documentary shorts as well. The man Roosevelt appointed for this
role was former journalist Lowell Mellett.

Mellett took up the task of being the government's point man
for what Koppes and Black describe as an uneasy alliance between Hollywood, which was keen to keep its independence and
to secure profits, and the government, some quarters of which favored the kind of wholesale takeover of wartime production that
had been the fate of steel companies and auto manufacturers.[15]

The Hollywood office that would deal directly with the studios was set up in April 1942, and Mellett put a young publisher with no movie experience, Nelson Poynter, in charge of it. Just a few months later, the movie liaison office, having assumed the name Bureau of Motion Pictures, would find itself a part of the Domestic Branch of the OWI, the all-powerful body that President Roosevelt eventually saw as the answer to the propaganda agency confusion that had been building in Washington for a year. The overseas branch of the agency was built out of Sherwood's Foreign Information Service, cut off from Donovan's charge toward covert operations in what was about to become the Office of Strategic Services. It was through Sherwood, therefore, that Riskin came aboard to head up the distribution of films in foreign theaters. But it was the growing independence of the agency and of Riskin's role within it that would provide the means for him to articulate the ideals of, and then produce, arguably the most significant propaganda of the entire war carried by the United States to its allies worldwide.

The two branches of the OWI were for, on the one hand, home front entertainment and propaganda shown only to American audiences, and, on the other, foreign propaganda efforts not intended for Americans to see. Riskin's influence in the overseas bureau would change all that and, indeed, lead to a very ambitious proposal to permanently unite Hollywood and Washington, a proposal that he would campaign hard for as the war came to a close.

The director of the OWI was onetime radio commentator Elmer Davis. Though Davis often reiterated the mantra that the OWI was interested only in telling the truth to its audiences, the way to that truth could be highly convoluted and open to interpretation within the agency's approved cultural output. The projected ethical stance was contradicted many times, not least by Davis himself, who, later in his tenure, commented, "The easiest way to inject a propaganda idea into most people's minds is to let it go in through the medium of an entertainment picture when they do not realize that they are being propagandized."[16]

Throughout its existence, the OWI not only maintained that commercial films could have a strong ideological bias but continued to be a bastion of New Deal thinking. Riskin had to wait nearly two years for confirmation from the Civil Service Commission of his suitability for a role in the OWI, and it is possible that testimony concerning his liberal, pro-administration stance within Hollywood was sought before he was accepted into the fray. The Bureau of Motion Pictures (BMP), in particular, as the Hollywood arm of the OWI, wielded an important Rooseveltian influence over the sophisticated treatment of wartime aims within fictional movies, led by its chief, Mellett, and by Poynter in the Hollywood office.[17]

The BMP, until funding was virtually cut off by Congress in 1943, maintained an uneasy relationship with Hollywood. "The OWI has entrusted the full sweep of war power to gentlemen with no previous film experience," exclaimed producer Walter Wanger, reflecting the movie community's perception that the BMP's purpose was to tell the studios what to make and how to make it.[18] Both Mellett and Poynter went to great lengths to emphasize that this was not what they wanted to do, though they still produced many guidelines and informational booklets that suggested certain topics and themes.[19] It was in fact these themes that hinted at the New Deal philosophy in practice, although in many respects Mellett and Poynter were as keen to counter accusations from anti-interventionists in Washington, and from the notorious Nye-Wheeler investigations of 1941 in particular, that the movie industry harbored pro-Allied (that is, pro-intervention) sentiment before Pearl Harbor.[20] The spirit of this delicate coming together led Thomas Doherty, among others, to assert that the wartime relationship being built between Washington and Hollywood was not stated; it was "in the air, not on paper."[21]

Nevertheless, there was a clamor to provide positive views of ideologically questionable allies like China and Russia, support of workers aiding the war effort, and rejection of war-themed adventures like *The Real Glory* for foreign audiences. The rejection of that film, which Riskin had produced at MGM in 1939, was based on the suspicion that the picture—set in the Philippines during the Spanish-American War of 1898—suggested American colonial intent. All of this created a sense that liberal, New Deal ideas pervaded the work of the BMP.[22] It was a perception that, even after Nye-Wheeler, was not lost on Congress. By the summer of 1943, it would identify the BMP as doing a far better propaganda job for the president than for the country's war effort and would duly cut the agency's budget.

Personal Commitments and Agency Responsibility

In the summer months of 1942, Fay Wray relocated to New York to do a radio series called *Rosemary* at NBC, and Riskin began negotiations with Sherwood about joining the OWI. Riskin and Wray had by now become an official couple in Hollywood circles, confirmed by Fay's delivery of a birthday cake to Riskin's party that year, held at Rosalind Russell's house. Convinced by her psychiatrist that it was the right thing to do (though her letter to him at home in Hollywood stated that she had consulted their mutual and dear friends, Flo and Jo Swerling), Wray took the plunge and asked Riskin to marry her.[23] Her relaying of the story suggests Riskin had serious reservations about embarking on a partnership for life, though his letters to Fay continued to hint that this was what he desired. Two months later, when Riskin arrived in New York, they talked for hours about each other's past, their beliefs, and Riskin's Jewish faith, and he asked directly whether Fay had any financial worries. She did, a striking reminder to Riskin of his early years struggling with money and debt. Indeed, Riskin's commitment was summed up by his overwhelming desire to protect Fay from any money problems. As she herself wrote, what signaled his acceptance of marriage and his very sincere wish to take care of her was a letter from him, now back in Washington, insisting that he wouldn't have her "stewing about money" and enclosing a check.[24]

William Donovan may also have played a hand in the match. It appears he spoke to Riskin in Washington about organizing a celebration for the happy couple in New York, after having talked with Fay and having been impressed by Riskin's style, manner, and regard for Fay, his client and friend. The colonel set up a ceremony to be conducted by an associate of his. And so, on August 23, 1942, Riskin and Wray were married by Donovan's "friend," Judge Ferdinand Pecora, in Donovan's suite at the St. Regis Hotel in New York with, among others, Ellin and Irving

Berlin and David Selznick in attendance. One of Riskin's friends, Kay Chacqeneau, confided to Fay, "With Bob, you will never know a dull day."[25]

Before the end of the year, Sherwood had invited Riskin to join the OWI to head up the overseas film unit of the organization. Riskin's appointment came in the midst of a major shakeup within the agency. By the close of 1942, the overseas unit had acquired the title of Bureau of Overseas Motion Pictures and thus ceased to be strictly a division of the OWI. Indeed, it now had the same status as the BMP in Hollywood, and Riskin, as overseas chief, held a rank equal to that of Lowell Mellett. His job was approving but also, increasingly, producing films that would be shown in Europe and other theaters of operation as liberation spread. Eventually the overseas bureau would have twenty-six outpost offices around the world, from London, Dublin, and Madrid to Tehran, Bombay, and Chungking, and on through to Canberra and Anchorage. It became a huge operation that eventually did not rely on the BMP's direction and authority. It is not clear that the ascent of the Bureau of Overseas Motion Pictures had anything to do with any tension between Riskin and Mellett, but the reshuffle across the rank and file of the OWI's operations did give Riskin far more leverage to act on his own initiative, since he needed to report only to Sherwood and then Davis himself, the OWI head.

It is also interesting to speculate, in the midst of this political maneuvering, how much advice Riskin took from his friend Donovan and to what extent he was encouraged to proactively make the overseas bureau a true propaganda unit. As Doherty argues, while the BMP was seen as a domestic controlling force, the overseas unit of the OWI was perceived in Hollywood as an agency similar and related to the Office of Censorship.[26] And it was certainly true that Riskin's initial function was to choose the films that received export licenses to be shown in Europe and farther afield. He had been in the job only a short time when he found himself at the center of a controversy involving his rejection of Warner Brothers' *Casablanca* for viewing in North Africa. The film appeared to have all the right anti-fascist rhetoric while managing to avoid painting all the German characters as evil, but

Riskin remained troubled. He took the brave step of writing to the Hollywood office in January 1943 to inform them that he was rejecting the film on two bases: Riskin thought that Humphrey Bogart's character Rick was just too cynical—and hence suggestive of a rather detached American attitude—in too many long stretches of the picture. Also, astutely, he thought that the image of the French in the film might disturb the delicate relations that the American government had at the time with both the Vichy government and de Gaulle's Free French.[27] The decision was an early indication of Riskin's sixth sense of understanding the hidden values and messages that could be conveyed by even supposedly supportive features, but while this role was a dominant part of his job, it did not remain Riskin's or the overseas bureau's sole function for the duration of the conflict.

Following his appointment, Riskin's base of operation was not in Hollywood but back in his hometown of New York. The OWI rented office space on West Fifty-seventh Street, and Riskin was given authority to pick his own people as writers, directors, and producers for OWI features. He knew the kind of assistance he wanted: individuals with experience in documentary making, those who knew how to put things together cheaply but with rigor, discipline, and imagination. Riskin had, in fact, a vision of fusing Donovan's hardened propaganda ethic with Sherwood's democratic aesthetic. What he was interested in showing to the rest of the world was not simply an idealized, mythic America—though some productions did encompass such a vision—but films that emphasized a spiritual and cultural vibrancy within the United States. In letters home to Fay from Europe, Riskin often remarked how much people looked to religion in times of crisis. "You see, people need goodness to lean on in times of wickedness and evil," he said.[28]

Riskin made charity, faith, and generosity of spirit his propaganda tools. While the OWI's output and, indeed, Riskin's admiration for other documentary films of more conventional wartime footage and enemy denunciation remained constant, the selection of some twenty-six short films that he personally commissioned and authored, some of which he produced and wrote, and all of which he oversaw in their entirety, were the most visually stylish, culturally influential, and politically potent of the entire war. They were also the most ideologically contemplative. In asserting a "history from below" examination of American society in a majority of the features, Riskin and his writers and directors brought to life a primary mode of documentary filmmaking that would be more clearly appreciated in, and later associated with, the 1960s and '70s. Riskin's recruitment philosophy was equally astute. He hired for the Bureau of Overseas Motion Pictures reliable Hollywood figures like writer Joseph Krumgold; Irving Lerner, who had worked on documentaries for Columbia in the thirties and had recently been cinematographer on Robert Flaherty's acclaimed Department of Agriculture film *The Land*; and, in particular, his old friend Philip Dunne, who had just finished the script to John Ford's Oscar-winning film *How Green Was My Valley*, and whom Riskin put in charge of production. His greatest achievement, however, was recruiting a stellar cast of Hollywood talent who worked for next to nothing to make this series of profoundly influential short features.

In addition to the responsibilities of his desk job in New York, Riskin readily took on the role of roving salesman and general booster for the war effort in particular, and Hollywood relations in general, throughout much of Allied Europe. In 1943 and '44, Riskin traveled extensively in Britain and on the European mainland that had so far been liberated from the Nazis. His role overseas was perhaps prompted by his familiarity with places he had been before. His 1937 travels around Europe with Capra and their status as invited guests in Russia no doubt provided him with knowledge of European cultures and values. Riskin had also visited Scandinavia in the summer of 1939, just as war was about to break out. But even more important than his geographical awareness was the help Riskin provided in establishing a method of operation for the overseas bureau: filmmakers and OWI representatives worked at the center of military operations and moved in to act as liaisons between Allied units and civilian populations as the Axis powers were driven back. Riskin knew time was of the essence and wanted to convey to liberated peoples at the very moment their freedom was being handed back to them the sorts of ideals and the kind of lifestyle they could aspire to in a postwar world. His confiscation of enemy propaganda and unauthorized material before supplying theaters with OWI films was another critical facet of the bureau's operation under his leadership.

At the beginning of 1943, Riskin was ready to declare the overseas bureau's intentions for the coming months. Having benefited from the OWI shakeup of the previous autumn, Riskin helped to propel the agency into the spotlight with a series of reports on Hollywood features and news conferences about OWI productions to be undertaken in the following year. In January 1943, the *Hollywood Reporter* identified the principal films that the overseas bureau saw as fundamental to its propaganda exercise in North Africa, a key theater of operations at the time. Among a lengthy list of pictures being shown, the most successful titles were Alfred Hitchcock's 1940 espionage thriller *Foreign Correspondent*, set at the opening of the war; William Wyler's story of middle-class values in wartime England, *Mrs. Miniver*; and Walt Disney's *Dumbo*.[29] But even these amazingly popular features were not beyond the need for subtle and diplomatic maneuvering. *Mrs. Miniver* found itself banned in certain theaters in Britain, whose audiences felt the characters too clichéd and anachronistic. In Norway, filmgoers took a dislike to the action-adventure *Commandoes Strike at Dawn* (made at Columbia, with Paul Muni in the lead role), which they felt portrayed Norwegians' fight against Nazi tyranny in tired historical costumes with exaggerated manners.[30] Riskin approached such matters delicately; he always set a tone for OWI policy that was above reproach, thus increasing the confidence felt in his judgment by both the BMP and Davis, head of the OWI. He had to retain good relations with the studios, which didn't wish to hear that their films were being criticized, as well as support material he thought crucial to Allied morale overall, even if disapproved of by small minorities. He laid down a marker for OWI policy, for example, by aiming to be impartial about the suitability of his own work. The same report that stated problems for *Mrs. Miniver* and *Commandoes Strike at Dawn* also pointedly remarked that Riskin had banned his own film, *Meet John Doe*, because of possible misinterpretations of the movie's fascistic tone wrapped up in D. B. Norton's evil publishing tycoon.[31]

On the whole, however, a steadily growing list of features contributed to the studio output of propaganda and the OWI's increasingly sophisticated distribution of features and shorts.[32] By March 1943, the *Motion Picture Herald* reported that Riskin's bureau had approved sixty-four full-length films and fifty-two shorts for distribution in North Africa alone.[33] In a related report, the *Herald* confirmed that the OWI's overseas arm was ready to implement the next plan—making its own features—and already had release dates for its new *Projections of America* series. The films were to be distributed around the world, both in commercial packages that would accompany standard Hollywood features and through the channels of a special government system for the organization of distinctly American propaganda material. The *New York Times* described the bureau as having the aim of "a production program through which [the OWI] hopes to counteract in foreign lands the impression that the United States is a country of gangsters and cattle rustling cowboys." The OWI's mandate was to tell the truth and "dispel fanciful conceptions" about America.[34]

The seriousness of the OWI's intent to communicate American ideals and make high-quality, far-reaching propaganda was confirmed in its establishment of what amounted to a propaganda school. At the same time that Riskin was establishing the overseas bureau's documentary program in the spring of 1943, the agency was renting the two-thousand-acre estate of Marshall Field on Long Island in New York to recruit trainees to undertake classes on many aspects of filmmaking, as well as radio operation, decoding, and preparing news information and publications in foreign countries. The graduates would then be dispersed to OWI outpost offices around the globe.

In addition to arranging for the distribution of the overseas bureau's own productions, one of the first deals that Riskin negotiated for the bureau, also in March 1943, was one that brought distribution of the Capra series *Why We Fight* through the auspices of the OWI.[35] Capra had taken a different route into military service, only a few days after Pearl Harbor in 1941. Given exemption while he finished some of the shooting for the ending to his final "prewar" film, *Arsenic and Old Lace*—Capra rushed to finish the movie, but it did not get a release until 1944—Capra joined the Signal Corps in January 1942. During that year, he negotiated himself into the position of producing the famous *Why We Fight* series of films for the military under the approval of Army Chief of Staff George Marshall and the man Marshall charged with working alongside Capra on the venture, Brigadier General Frederick Osborn. Riskin concluded a deal with Osborn, the director of the Information and Education Division of the Army, to distribute what were at that time seven films from the propaganda series that Capra was producing as a part of the War Department orientation program.

At the same time, Riskin was keen to distance his operation from the kind of material that Capra and other directors, like John Ford and John Huston, were producing for different agencies during the conflict. The fifty-two shorts that the OWI had worked on and approved up to that point were for distribution in the United States alone and were split equally between the *America Speaks* series and the *Victory* films, which were a collection of combat shorts tied to the OWI's magazine of the same name. They included scenes of enemy demonization and flag-waving patriotism, much in the vein of documentaries being prepared within the State Department and other bodies. Among an extensive series of documentaries from various military and civilian outlets, the celebrated *Why We Fight* series went on to assume the status of definitive propaganda collection. Riskin was the first to acknowledge the films' and Capra's right to that claim within the propaganda genre. It was typical of their careers that Capra quickly garnered the plaudits and Riskin was left in the shadows. Riskin's series never had quite the same impact or recognition, either at the time or since, and it certainly has never been subjected to anything like the same concerted analysis. And yet his was a far subtler collection of features, in comparison not just to *Why We Fight* but to the other OWI series as well, that attempted to encapsulate the essence of American identity and ideology for its foreign allies. As a result, Riskin's films have a more abstract legacy; their reputation among critics during the war was not sustained afterward, and yet they found generous and receptive audiences at the time and may have served as a stepping stone toward postwar ideological reconstruction.[36]

When the *Projections of America* series was announced, only one of the films had been completed. However, right away, it both demonstrated the ideological conception of the series that Riskin, as the overall executive producer, had in mind and reflected the talent and expertise he could pull in by virtue of his reputation in Hollywood. The combination, he realized, was crucial. Each element defined the propaganda ethos Riskin was searching for, and the weight of the personalities involved strengthened the portrayal. It wasn't unusual for celebrities to endorse the war effort in other propaganda films, but none were used as distinctively or uniquely as in the *Projections* series.

The first completed film, *Sweden [or Swedes] in America*, was to be distributed, naturally enough, through the Stockholm outpost office. The star and narrator of the film was Ingrid Bergman. Her role in stressing the enormous contributions to industrial and cultural growth that had been made by Swedish immigrants in America was as important and powerful as the content itself, argued Riskin. As Bill Nichols has explained in his analysis of the genre, the voice in documentary is often the "voice of oratory," and this voice embraces not simply narrative and reason but a sense of evocation and poetry and, even more crucially, the instilling of conviction.[37] Riskin understood this notion from the start and made his star a part of the story, having Bergman visit the offices of Swedish organizations in the United States and undertake a pilgrimage to the American Swedish Historical Museum in Philadelphia. The uplifting, almost spiritual contemplation of the successful immigrant tale incorporated into the narration helped the film achieve exactly what we might suppose Riskin wanted: it superseded cultural boundaries. It became more than just a story about Scandinavian immigrants; it took on the series' thematic concerns about the determination of liberty and freedom in America. So taken was the British Ministry of Information with the film, which had nothing to do with Britain, that it requested, in October 1943, four hundred prints—to show cinema audiences in the UK, the *New York Times* reported gleefully, how the United States treated minorities.[38]

Riskin's follow-up was a one-reel documentary that set out to reveal Chicago as a city of churches, museums, art galleries, and some of the most important industrial activity in the nation, not a "bullet-riddled warren of gangsters and hi-jackers."[39] The text of the documentary was written by screenwriters Vera Caspary—a Chicago native and author of the best-selling novel *Laura*—and, famously, Ben Hecht, the man who in 1927 had written perhaps the first true gangster narrative for the screen, *Underworld*. And whom did Riskin engage to disentangle the roots of Hollywood imagery that had latched onto the history of that city since the gangster genre had become so popular? The narrator of the documentary was Edward G. Robinson, the Hollywood gangster's gangster and the man Riskin wrote for in *The Whole Town's Talking*. With such choices, Riskin achieved what no other documentary series was looking to do or, indeed, was capable of during the war: he transcended the resonant Hollywood mythology of the age and paid homage to a documentary tradition dating back to the beginning of the century. The Chicago documentary and the later pictorial assessment of New York that complemented it, written by Harry Kurnitz and Arthur Kober, incorporated references to the cycle of "city symphony" films from the late 1920s— *The Man with a Movie Camera* (1929), made by legendary Russian filmmaker Dziga Vertov, and *À propos de Nice* (1929)—as well as the work of American artists like Paul Strand and even the challenging consumptive polemics of Willard Van Dyke's recent film *The City* (1939).

A fan of the genre since arriving in Hollywood in the early thirties, Riskin had already soaked up the structures and stylistic nuances of the documentary. Some of the early British propaganda efforts of the war were themselves city symphonies in the spirit, if not the form, of the earlier influential pieces, as Richard Barsam's history of nonfiction film establishes, but Riskin's viewing of these was just one demonstration of his inculcation into the form.[40] Riskin turned to his advantage the twin legacies of documentary film and Hollywood movie-star creation. Not only did he conceive of a series that incorporated observational, poetic, expository, participatory, reflexive, and performative modes of documentary style, sometimes all at once, but he also utilized such interdisciplinary forms to show the world the vitality of American film culture as a responsible agent of social progress. In this fashion, he helped to accentuate the notion of film as a communal entity and a spark for postwar nation building.

Other titles followed quickly as the year progressed. Arthur Arent, a graduate of the Works Progress Administration Federal Theatre Project of the thirties, put his name to Riskin's documentary of the West, *Cowboy*. In the short, narrated by actor Ralph Bellamy with his wonderfully resonant voice, Arent demonstrates, through the eyes of an expatriate Englishman, that cowboys and ranchers were modern, hard-working individuals, dedicated to their lifestyle and tradition, and existing in an environment a million miles from the Hollywood conception of the West as overrun by gunslingers, shanty towns, and saloons. The young outsider is disappointed when he arrives because there is no Wild West atmosphere, but he slowly comes to respect the work of the cattlemen. *Cowboy* too had its antecedents. Its look could be attributed at least in part to John Ford Westerns; its themes and its exploration of working people tapped into Arent's background at the WPA; and both elements certainly alluded to previous statements on western life, notably Pare Lorentz's famous, sweeping documentaries of 1930s dustbowl life, *The Plow That Broke the Plains* (1936) and *The River* (1937). The influence of Lorentz in particular was clear in the values and tone of each *Projections* series film. Further, as Paul Arthur argues, the persuasive articulation of the power of industrial technology that Lorentz espouses in *The River*, for instance—which is about the benefits of hydroelectric power—has its roots in the work of Soviet documentary makers like Vertov.[41]

The organic development of the genre in such ideologically contrasting venues as capitalist America and Communist Soviet Union was far from conflictual for Riskin. He saw in both traditions linear progressions of montage, crowd scenes, and other stylistic signifiers that he had admired and used as part of his work with Capra in the thirties. Hence technology and rationalization became enduring and critical themes within the series. But with *Cowboy*, what Riskin and his team were intent on achieving was not a repudiation of the Hollywood legends that had established these mythical entities but an updated statement of the values and beliefs upon which these legends had been founded. Riskin chose a feature of the West that was recognizable, the cowboy figure, and pledged to put that symbol into a modern context that overseas audiences could still look upon with awe and wonder. The Ministry of Information in London, with much enthusiasm for the topic and its British connection, distributed the film throughout UK theaters as *The Cowboy on the American Scene* beginning in late 1943.

Yet *Cowboy* also pointed the way to a propaganda initiative that was an integral part of the bureau's responsibility. The film, in showing how beef was transported to soldiers fighting overseas, touched on the popular theme within propaganda of the collaborative war effort. But what it really suggested was that, lend-lease or not, the United States had burgeoning markets ready to be claimed in the postwar world. Farming and food production on a large commercial scale stood at the vanguard of a merchandising and marketing boom for American farmers in the aftermath of the war, and *Cowboy* did its bit to promote the American consumerism about to be unleashed on an unassuming world. Riskin would become uneasy with these overt economic efforts, but he nevertheless realized the value of the sacrifice for the sake of energizing a foreign populace that needed to trust America's postwar mission.

While Riskin's Bureau of Overseas Motion Pictures was busy expanding its horizons in mid-1943, the OWI's Domestic Branch was getting into hot water with a newly emboldened conservative faction in Congress that did not like its Rooseveltian tendencies. Almost as significant was the fact that, as *Cowboy* hinted, the OWI was being taken over by consumer-driven advertising and marketing executives. Allying capitalist marketing and cultural regeneration to FDR's personal agenda, argued Republicans as well as southern Democrats, was too partisan a political platform to stomach. In the summer of 1943, Congress began hearings on the Domestic Branch's spending and ideological outlook.

Interestingly, the hearings effectively cornered the OWI as a collective, requesting the attendance, for example, of Robert Sherwood, the overseas director, and mentioning Riskin by name. One member of the Appropriations Subcommittee cited Riskin as an example of the OWI's profligate use of money. How come, he asked, Riskin was now earning $4,000 a year at the government's expense, when he had been paid only $2,000 in Hollywood? Sherwood pointed out, to little effect, that Riskin had been paid $2,000 a *week* in Hollywood, and therefore the government was getting quite a good deal. No defense worked, however, and when Representative Joe Starnes of Alabama suggested to the House that the OWI had "a distinct state socialist tinge," the writing was on the wall for the Domestic Branch. Its funding was cut to $2,125,000, barely a quarter of what it had been a year before: not quite so little as to kill it, but sufficient to stifle its activity.

More significant within this overall budget contraction, the BMP (the OWI's Hollywood liaison office) had its appropriation cut from $1,300,000 down to only $50,000, and this did effectively cause the operation to fold.[42] Oddly enough, then, the Domestic Branch's mauling on Capitol Hill largely benefited the overseas bureau, as Koppes and Black observe.[43] Riskin's bureau got extra staff and much of the money remaining from the congressional slashing, but the amount of authority and influence that was passed specifically to Riskin has not been clearly understood. The BMP had served to coordinate the production of Hollywood product and propaganda shorts such as those that the overseas bureau was now making. After the demise of the BMP, Riskin had comparative free reign to decide the type of collective program to be shown in overseas theaters, without interference from the Hollywood office.

The overseas bureau would have to defend its actions one more time, later in the year, before plunging further into its bold program of films. Just as Riskin was about to announce another selection of documentary shorts, the OWI faced a new series of investigations in Washington. *Variety* reported in October 1943 that, despite the successful reception of American films in the

Italian theater that had just begun to be liberated, Congress was balking at an appropriations supplement of $5 million to the agency.[44] In a closed-door session, OWI head Elmer Davis was met with a frosty reception as some congressmen came to realize that they hadn't killed off the OWI in their summer purge of the budget. Davis and the overseas bureau survived the investigation, however, with its budgetary plans intact, thanks in no small part to Riskin's convincing summary of its North African and Italian operations. The way was now clear for arguably the most ambitious collection of propaganda shorts that any government agency produced at any time during the war. Less than a month after Davis's grilling before Congress, Riskin set in train the bureau's grand plan.

If the overseas bureau was worried that its outward show of support for the president and his political ideals had vexed the right wing in Washington in 1943, the next crop of *Projections of America* films didn't show it. *Pipeline* was the story of the construction of the longest oil pipeline in the world up to that point, from Texas to New Jersey; *People to People* was an experiment in inviting foreign workers—four British trade unionists—to observe American industrial relations in operation, on shop floors like the Chrysler Tank Arsenal in Detroit and the Lockheed plant in Los Angeles, and was narrated again by Ralph Bellamy; and *The Town* was a wry, often sentimental look at how the small Indiana town of Madison was dealing with the war and its own community melting pot. *The Town* was perhaps the most cinematically accomplished film of the whole series. From the social engagement of meeting at the bar, shooting pool, and watching movies, to the institutional interplay of the library, newspaper office, and courtroom, Madison participated in a discourse of freedom and hope. Produced by Joseph Krumgold, the film was directed and cut by Josef von Sternberg. Helen Grayson and Larry Madison's film *The Cummington Story* took an alternative look at the absorption-of-foreign-influence tale by following just one family and their assimilation into a community; Aaron Copland composed the musical score for the film. Irving Lerner contributed yet another element to this theme with *The Place to Live*, a short film underscoring America's welcoming, communal spirit, striking a chord with the huddled masses everywhere striving to get to the United States. The witty *Autobiography of a Jeep* gave the workhorse vehicle almost human characteristics, with its technologically grounded practicality, and paraded it as the military's friend and companion, shepherding troops around the world, admired by the likes of Churchill, Roosevelt, and even King George VI.

With its documentaries on lend-lease, especially *Valley of the Tennessee* (also called *The Story of the TVA*), the overseas bureau could never be described as equivocating in its support of the New Deal. In addition to featuring President Roosevelt eulogizing the Tennessee Valley Authority's (TVA) achievements, the film focused on its most important patrons, Senators James Polk and George Norris, TVA director David Lillenthal, and University of Tennessee president Harcourt Morgan. The TVA story was a triumphant tale of America's bringing back to life one of its discarded and most rurally backward regions and its subsequent transformation into a vibrant, industrial powerhouse of the New South. Yet the film was more than an endorsement by these patrons of southern renewal and progressive thinking. Once again, the film was shaped by the earlier documentary tradition that Riskin insisted be woven into each new film; it identified communal harmony and organizational logic within the grass roots of American society.

Valley of the Tennessee was also one more example of the documentary talent Riskin brought on board for the series: he commissioned the influential Austrian-born filmmaker Alexander Hammid to direct. Hammid, who with his wife Maya Deren made the landmark experimental film *Meshes of the Afternoon* (1943), worked not only on the TVA film for the *Projections* series but also on shorts about the Library of Congress and *A Better Tomorrow* (1945), a film that looked at the New York high school system. The most famous and influential figure working with Riskin on these films, other than Hammid, was Willard Van Dyke. Van Dyke had been a cameraman for Lorentz on *The River* and had directed Lorentz's screen treatment of *The City*. For Riskin he made *Oswego* and *Steeltown* (both 1943), as well as *Pacific Northwest* (1944), which extolled the virtues of Oregon and Washington State and their contributions to the war effort. But his most important ideological statement for the series came with *San Francisco*, one of two films that were instrumental in addressing the ideological proponents of postwar settlement through the eyes of the overseas bureau.

Each of the new films was set to be translated into at least twelve languages over the course of the following few months and distributed around Europe and the wider world. A number of other documentaries were also announced in November 1943, but one stood out as squaring the circle that Riskin had established within the series over the previous year. America's economic and industrial might had been well served by the films, as had its meritocratic and assimilationist social ambitions, but culture, art, and music in their purest, undiluted sense had not been tackled as yet. Music was, of course, an important propaganda tool during the war, important indeed to many documentary features produced by the OWI, which backed popular patriotic pieces like Irving Berlin's musical *This Is the Army* and Glenn Miller's famous swing album, *American Patrol*. But Riskin had one further aim with the *Projections* series: to unite the stirring emotions of music with the cultural dynamism of American art, and to wrap it around one figure, a recent immigrant to the United States who, the film would argue, had brought his genius to bear on mankind's greatest battle. The film was to be titled *Toscanini*.

So convinced was the OWI of the worth of such a film that not only did Riskin, together with Philip Dunne and Lerner, supervise the making of the documentary, but Robert Sherwood came on board to woo the maestro. It was well known that Arturo Toscanini was a delicate artist who guarded his privacy. Only three years before, he had refused an offer of a film biography, reputedly turning his back on $250,000. In December 1943, he accepted the overseas bureau's invitation to do it for nothing.[45] As Riskin, Sherwood, and Dunne knew full well, the chance to use Toscanini's fame and history was too good to miss, though the film would offer merely a glimpse into the conductor's work, not a full-fledged life story, which would be impossible to produce in the short running time. This was the man who had derided

World War I and had fled his beloved native Italy rather than play the fascist anthem, even before Mussolini's ascent to power. And where had he sought refuge? Where so many others looked to find freedom of expression: in America.

Riskin and his colleagues constructed a feature that would give the music prominence but would also display the freedom and comfort that even the world's great artists sought. Informal footage was shot at the conductor's estate in Riverdale, New York, together with brief conversation, although in the final cut the maestro spoke not at all. The highlight remained Toscanini conducting his own, personally assembled NBC Symphony Orchestra with Metropolitan Opera soloist Jan Peerce, recorded (behind locked doors) at the NBC studios in Manhattan. The film opens with Verdi's *La forza del destino*, uses "The Garibaldi Hymn" for the tour of his estate and a voiceover description of other famous Italians working in America, and concludes with the piece that became the documentary's informal subtitle, "Hymn of the Nations." Riskin had established the nominal length of the films in the series at eight thousand feet, or around twenty minutes' running time. *Toscanini* measured twelve thousand feet and ran for a half hour, such were the conviction of the piece in his mind and the power of the performance in actuality. Filming took place over two days, December 8 and 20, 1943, and the documentary was ready for distribution by January. Its first port of call was in Italy, but it would eventually be translated into twenty-three languages. For many, it remains the definitive recording of Verdi's piece, and the continuing availability of the audio recording on CD is testament to Riskin's belief in the film's subject and the quality of his work.

Peace, Propaganda, and the Future Hope of the World

Riskin was well aware of the aims of the propaganda exercise he engaged in during the war, but he also knew that the film industry was on a wider mission to expand and consolidate its worldwide markets. Thanks to his charm and his lucidity concerning the place of American film in the wider cultural environment,

Riskin was able to handle the business concerns underpinning his role without raising suspicion about the OWI's engagement in a campaign that, after the war, would result in the widespread dominance of American cinema in Europe. Indeed, he was not altogether convinced that Hollywood, through the Bureau of Overseas Motion Pictures, should be solely concerned with the bottom line or the popularity of American movies once fighting ceased. In an interview with the *London Evening Standard* in November 1943, while staying at Claridges Hotel in the heart of the British capital, Riskin attempted to sidestep any insinuation that he represented a Hollywood invasion of European film markets designed to direct people's attention to American movies. He stated that he could not foresee what pictures the public would want to watch after the war was over. "You cannot forecast public taste . . . and anyway I never think of the market. I work on impulse," he claimed.[46]

It was a calculated reaction that served Riskin well. While he intimated the prospect for a free market in film distribution once the conflict had ceased, the groundwork was already being laid—by his agency as well as others—for a saturation of liberated Europe with Hollywood features and propaganda films that directly articulated American ideals, values, and beliefs. Riskin was unable to deny his part in such a plot, operating all the while with this distinct purpose.

In early 1944, Riskin, as head of the Overseas Bureau of Motion Pictures, met with several representatives of soon-to-be-liberated European countries. The reactions, problems, and demands of each were instructive in determining the way the bureau directed and distributed its material and managed revenues. In the Netherlands, Dutch representatives of the national film industry outlined the extent to which the occupying Nazis had effectively destroyed their country's film community. Jewish people constituted about 11 percent of the top personnel before the war—exhibitors, distributors, and producers—but had, they reported, been liquidated, and more than five hundred thousand able-bodied Dutchmen, who could have helped in the distribution of material in the liberated country, had been deported to

German labor camps, many never to return. Riskin agreed that the overseas bureau would act as trustee for the missing, dead, liquidated, or deposed owners of various sections of the community until such time as monies from the revenue of Allied shows could be distributed.[47]

In Norway, the situation was very different. Film officers of the Government Information Branch expressed the view that German occupation had not, for the most part, disrupted the Norwegian film industry. Indeed, they noted that a public boycott of German films compelled the authorities to show some Vichy, Swedish, and old French pictures.[48] French authorities, meanwhile, were concerned to determine their own film policies and operations from the moment France began to be liberated, despite Riskin's reservations. He thought it quite apparent that his Free French colleagues, Lieutenant des Jardins and Monsieur de la Rocque, had no knowledge of the film industry's practices.[49]

The various representatives also laid out, some more explicitly than others, one remaining issue: how the overseas bureau would move in with liberating forces to take over cinemas, storage, and film stock in each of the countries. Paul Levy and Louis Boogaraets of the Belgian Ministry of Information stated categorically what was to happen at this point. The record of their meeting with Riskin and other BMP representatives on March 11, 1944, describes their position: "Both Mr. Levy and Mr. Boogaraets reported that complete lists of Belgian collaborationists were being compiled and kept up to date and would be available to our (OWI) film representatives at the proper time, to make sure that none of the Belgian quislings participate in the distribution of Anglo-American films after liberation takes place. They indicated that most of the collaborationists would be very quickly eliminated or liquidated by the proper Belgian authorities."[50]

Levy, who was a popular radio broadcaster in Belgium before the war, had spent fourteen months in a German concentration camp before his escape to England, where all the meetings took place. The Belgian Ministry of Information's plan was quickly reproduced in other countries. This was the stark reality of war for Riskin; it put into focus film's place in the events. The battle for propaganda had itself become a literal campaign that could end only in triumph or in death. Amid this realization, Riskin was heartened that while the various authorities all requested footage of their country's liberation or their soldiers in battle to heighten the fervor for the Nazis' imminent defeat—Norwegians, for example, wished for the films to give credit to their cameramen—many were particularly keen to have Riskin's *Projections of America* ideology thrust upon their people. Again, from the report of the Boogaerets and Levy meeting: "They felt that British and American feature films, shorts and documentaries, would be very welcome, but expressed the opinion that there would be very keen interest in the United States, in our war effort and in our civilization. They urged that balanced programs, therefore, be provided which would not only entertain but would underline the unique characteristics and values of American civilization."[51]

Riskin remained based in London until the end of March 1944 to make sure such films could be regularly distributed to benefit the liberated peoples. He looked to make agreements on behalf of the OWI and did indeed set up negotiations, in early 1944, with J. Arthur Rank's British film company for a deal that would help distribute material in mainland Europe.[52] By April 1944, after Riskin had returned to Los Angeles, the *Hollywood Reporter* was more than happy to quote his contention that the OWI, with its mixture of documentary and feature films, had contributed to a 100 percent increase in cinema attendance in Italy. Not without significance, the article's headline referred to a "film invasion of Europe" as the war reached its climax.[53]

The Italian campaign also showed how closely the overseas bureau units worked with military operations at the front to promote OWI's product. Riskin had visited the film crews in early 1944 and personally supervised the work of seven mobile units that both traveled with the army and organized civilian shows in forward theaters of operation almost at the point of liberation. The conversion to the Allied cause and the inculcation of American views was swift and efficient. By April 15, 1944, Riskin reported to the *Motion Picture Herald*, three hundred movie houses in Italy were playing OWI programs and were holding the revenues from ticket sales until after the war's conclusion, according to the OWI agreement, in special trust accounts for studios associated with the production.[54] Riskin commented that the studios' cooperation was miraculous now that they saw unprecedented profits from this arrangement that would result in a windfall for them at the war's end. But he remained rather circumspect about Hollywood's and OWI's motivations, and he wished to distance his agency from the financial celebrations that were going on elsewhere. "An unsavory opinion seems to prevail within OWI that the Motion Picture Bureau is unduly concerned with considerations for commercial reasons," he wrote in August 1944.[55]

One might argue that "*solely* for commercial reasons" would have better represented Riskin's own position. He was, after all, a part of the commercial juggernaut he identified rolling around Europe and other parts of the world. But his vision for postwar Hollywood was a little more detached from the studios' and the BMP's outlook than has previously been acknowledged. Indeed, there is some evidence to suggest that, having put together a varied and much-applauded documentary series in the course of the previous year, Riskin was not entirely happy with the OWI setup and the direction it was taking in 1944.

In February of that year, a number of OWI executives were reported to have resigned, among them James Warburg, the director of propaganda policy; Joseph Barnes, the deputy in charge of Atlantic operations; and Ed Johnson, the chief of the editorial board. In truth, they had been pushed out by a dispute dating back to the previous summer. Through the Voice of America, on July 25, the OWI had broadcast a miscalculated attack on Italy's new leaders, King Victor Emmanuel III and his premier, Marshal Pietro Badoglio, Mussolini's replacements but still themselves fascists. The uproar resulted in public statements by both Roosevelt and Winston Churchill trying to soothe any ill feelings in a country on the verge of ousting Il Duce. After such high-level diplomacy had to be employed, both Warburg and Barnes were compelled to accept responsibility for the broadcast.

Elmer Davis took personal charge of a delicate reordering of the overseas bureau in the aftermath of the episode, but in early 1944, with the mainland invasion of Europe imminent and the War and State departments pushing for a wholesale shift in

OWI policy and competency, orders were given to publicly oust Warburg, Barnes, and Johnson. Robert Sherwood refused, and a spat ensued between him and Davis, who thought the axing of the three the prudent thing to do. Sherwood resigned amid the uproar over the Voice of America broadcast, and Riskin was now senior figure in the overseas bureau's operation.

It is not hard to conclude that the pressure brought to bear on the overseas bureau disillusioned Riskin further. Not only was the bureau's work being given a lukewarm reception in Washington, but Roosevelt himself thought that the agency was superfluous, despite Riskin's testimony about its films' reception outside the United States. By April, reports were circulating that Riskin was on the verge of quitting the agency, ostensibly to go back to filmmaking, according to the *Hollywood Reporter*.[56]

Only a month after these rumors surfaced, however, Riskin initiated a major publicity drive in Hollywood and in the media to highlight the bureau's work and, pointedly, to head off further government criticism. Riskin returned to Hollywood to recruit technical talent to work on future projects. He also reported on the success of certain Hollywood features—among them *The Great Dictator*, *Sergeant York*, and the musicals of Deanna Durbin—and lined up special screenings of some of the *Projections of America* series for studio heads and the press at the Motion Picture Academy. Both *The Town* and *Toscanini* received enthusiastic endorsement from the Academy and journalists.[57] The influential *New York Times* film critic Bosley Crowther wrote a glowing tribute to the series in his column, and Virginia Wright, drama editor of the *Los Angeles Daily News*, wrote that it was a great pity that American audiences were not seeing these films at the moment, "for we as well as the liberated peoples, could stand a little propagandizing about ourselves," she reflected.[58] Crowther reserved a special mention for *Toscanini*, which he described as a "magnificent piece of work." He went on, "This brilliant display of glorious spiritual freedom, so exquisitely devoted by one man and, with him, by a musical company to the entertainment and inspiration of all, is a tribute to American democracy and to the opportunity which Toscanini has found here." Crowther's appreciation was a further testament to the series' status as a vital component in the educating of America's allies on its ideals. Crowther was even more effusive in his appreciation of Riskin's work when contrasting the *Projections* series with Hollywood's fictional attempts at propagandizing the war effort, pointedly in the Irene Dunne vehicle *The White Cliffs of Dover*. Crowther worried what the English reception would be of this "muddle of clumsy insults" about America's principal allies.⁵⁹ He needn't have troubled himself. Riskin's OWI was as concerned about the film's one-dimensional, simplistic politics as Crowther, and by December 1944, it had been granted a license to play only in France and Italy, not Britain.⁶⁰ Crowther's comparative review highlighted the complex ideological projection that was to be found in Riskin's films but rarely elsewhere in documentary or Hollywood features.

In May 1944, the overseas bureau was so taken by the reception it had received that it looked to expand its horizons and promote material nearly simultaneously in Europe and the United States. Riskin announced that the bureau was going to widen its operations and begin showing films that were suitable for domestic audiences as well as liberated peoples abroad.⁶¹ The OWI thus began to distribute a limited collection of its films to American cinemagoers in select theaters across the country. Riskin's program had come home and fulfilled Virginia Wright's desire that America be promoted to itself.

During that defining summer of the Allied invasion, Riskin's influence spread far beyond the bounds that any other propaganda maker achieved during the war. In June, the *New York Times* reported on the cheering, almost ecstatic reception of a stage version of *It Happened One Night* in Moscow, renamed *On the Road to New York*. Audiences applauded and laughed out loud at a live presentation of Capra and Riskin's classic screwball comedy, shown for the first time in Russia, ten years after the film was released.⁶² For the remainder of the summer, as liberation progressed, the OWI's documentary *Salute to France*, narrated by Fredric March, triumphantly followed the Allied invaders around Europe.

Riskin spent much of the remainder of 1944 in London and Europe. Despite continuing rumors, he pledged to serve as overseas motion picture bureau chief until the war ended. The agency could simply not afford to dispense with Riskin's knowledge and experience. Liberation across Europe, far from smoothing the path of propaganda, actually made some matters worse. The OWI production chief in London, William Montague, was turning out as many as six newsreels a week, but his office was forced to work in overdrive because the production situation across the English Channel was so bad. In April 1944, Riskin had welcomed Major Arthur Loew, with his vast experience in film distribution around the world, to work as associate bureau chief in London with William Patterson.[63] Even with this additional expertise, however, Riskin became aware during late 1944 and early '45 that the situation with printing and distribution of films in France was grave. OWI staff there could not easily find accommodations to sit and work, and raw film stock was becoming increasingly difficult to find. Black market peddling pushed existing stock costs to astronomical amounts, and Riskin eventually stepped in personally to negotiate a deal to supply coal for the Kodak factory outside Paris to provide stock to the rest of France, as well as Britain.[64] Just distributing the films was a tough enough job for the bureau. With liberation well under way by December 1944, it came as no surprise when the OWI announced it would remove itself from the direct production of propaganda features by the following June. The emphasis was already shifting to the Far East theater of operations, and no new productions had been scheduled for Europe.[65]

As the Allies swept into Europe, French liberation provided a different kind of problem for Riskin and the overseas bureau. In early 1945, the French banned *Toscanini*; the newspaper *Le Franc-Tireur* claimed, in explanation of their refusal to celebrate one of the world's greatest conductors, "There are Italians and Italians."[66] The rejection was a sobering jolt for Riskin, who became ever more aware, working directly with his British and French counterparts, that the American film industry required a permanent liaison in Europe to promote Hollywood products overseas.[67] In the March 1945 *Hollywood Reporter*, Riskin first laid out his idea for a new company that would act as a successor to the OWI.[68] The plan was prompted by a couple of developments: Philip Dunne had screened three more *Projections* series films at the Motion Picture Academy in January, including *Valley of the Tennessee*, to very favorable reaction. Dunne had also made a report on Riskin's behalf concerning his friend's tour of France and the Netherlands and describing the overwhelmingly positive reception such features had received. Spurred on by this, Riskin returned home to Hollywood to discuss plans for a new postwar office with both the State Department and Hollywood studio heads.

Whatever it was that Riskin had seen in Europe, the company he proposed certainly encapsulated a mood of foreboding that was not apparent in America, where the successful liberation of Europe prompted feelings that the end of the war was not too far away and that the status quo would quickly be restored. For Riskin, though, the need to show America's goodwill, its desire to contribute to a new world order, and its determination to spread the ethic of cultural and artistic freedom was a priority that Americans had not yet grasped. The company he proposed was not to be a profit-making organization. It would make documentary shorts, twenty-four to begin, in much the same vein as the *Projections* series, and the films would initially be shown only to influential audiences in private screenings. Riskin emphasized that the screenings would begin to create a "mountain of goodwill" among America's allies and its most recent enemies.

The extent to which Riskin's plans predicted the onset of political breakdown, bipolar global relations, and ultimately the cold war might be overstated. No doubt he believed that any new organization would play the fullest part in the rehabilitation of Germany, as much as it might prevent any schism between East and West at the war's conclusion. As late as the end of April 1945, the *Motion Picture Daily* reported that Riskin's film project was on track, though the reality was that he had received positive feedback and commitment only from smaller independents, not from the major studios or the government. But if Riskin's foresight about American relations in Europe counts for anything, then his declaration of "ongoing concern" that OWI films had been replaced in the Soviet Union by Russian-only propaganda shorts should be seen as significant.[69] Only the previous month, the political stance that the overseas bureau was adopting at the crucial juncture of the war had been made blatantly apparent by Riskin's announcement of its intention to make a film based on the United Nations conference in San Francisco later that year. Two films emerged, in fact: One was *San Francisco*, the short directed by Willard Van Dyke, which used the basis of the meetings as a call to future generations to work for peace and cooperation. The second film, entitled *Watchtower over Tomorrow*, was a dramatized omen, recalling how fascism had unfolded during the 1930s and considering what the Security Council and General Assembly might do if confronted by an aggressor nation. The film made plain the bureau's support for global reorganization, interlocking government mechanisms, and bureaucratic structures that would prevent new arms races and keep new totalitarian figures from rising up through economic and political degeneration. To Riskin, the American experience—its history, democratic impulses, and cultural liberation—seemed a natural component of future freedom and security pledges. The fate of OWI films in the Soviet Union was a small but prophetic signal, and Riskin was one of the few to see how the extension of wartime filmmaking could influence American ideology in the world. But he lacked the political sensibilities to carry the fight to Washington or his own film community, and thus the new agency project was abandoned in most circles even as Riskin was promising a future for it.

Riskin had proposed that which Washington and Hollywood were both uneasy about: a permanent arrangement for their mutual dependence, at least abroad. In the film studios, producer Lester Cowan led the way in thoroughly denouncing Riskin's plan. He pointed out, with some validity, that any organization dedicated to producing documentaries to send around the world, however good they might be, would taint Hollywood with the stigma of being a propaganda machine for the government, the same accusation it was laying at the door of the fascist-sponsored film industries in Germany and Italy. The government, meanwhile, seemed reluctant to provide the funding of up to $1 million that Riskin estimated the new organization's operations would cost. In addition, the government representative on the proposed board of trustees would need to represent Republican and Democratic aims, but it was not clear how to achieve this. What favorable aspects of American life could be agreed upon without generating partisan influence abroad?

The proposal never got a serious hearing, and Riskin didn't wait around to promote a lost cause. Despite his pledge to continue as head of the overseas bureau until fighting ceased, at least in Europe, Riskin resigned from the OWI on May 1, 1945, only days before the German surrender. Riskin's deputy Louis Lober took up the role of bureau chief, but the agency had little to contribute in the final days of the war effort, and the OWI's operations were quickly disbanded in August. Ironically, the organization was soon after reconfigured as a set of agencies approximate to, if not exactly in, the image Riskin had had in mind. President Harry Truman, keen to pursue a cultural program of liaison, handed over OWI work to the State Department's new Office of International Information and Cultural Affairs. In 1953 this would become the United States Information Agency, but in the meantime, the Marshall Plan, instigated amid the rubble of war-torn Europe, commissioned a series of documentaries, including *Village without Water*, *Project for Tomorrow*, and *Rice and Bulls*, which were related to the work of the overseas bureau and similar to the kind of propaganda effort that Riskin had pushed for.[70] Within the terms of the Fulbright Act of 1946 (which established an international educational and cultural exchange) and the Smith-Mundt Act of 1948 (which provided for the production of official U.S. materials for audiences abroad) lay the foundations of what Riskin had been proposing at the close of the war, but none of the agencies involved had the Hollywood connections or influence that he deemed so important.[71]

Riskin had supervised twenty-six documentaries in the *Projections* series and had them translated into twenty-seven different languages, with many distributed from every OWI outpost office around the world. He had also approved hundreds of Hollywood and War Department shorts, as well as standard Hollywood features. In just less than three years, Riskin had made some of the most vital and pertinent films of his entire career. Within six months, it was all practically forgotten, and Riskin was back in Hollywood, with a new studio and his own production company.

A Legacy of the American Documentary Tradition

In the conclusion to their influential study, Koppes and Black suggest that the problem for the fusion of entertainment and propaganda during World War II was that "neither Hollywood nor the OWI was prepared to go beyond a vaguely felt appeal for internationalism and collective security as an antidote to the mistake[s] made after World War One." They continue, "The propagandists and the movie makers did little to give Americans a basis for judgment and discrimination in their new world of internationalism."[72] In his analysis of propaganda broadcast during the war, Gerd Horten asserts that one of the longest-lasting effects of wartime radio propaganda was "the reaffirmation of corporate dominance over the civic sphere," "the powerful reinforcement of a master narrative of corporate hegemony, which was consolidated during the war and spilled over into the postwar period."[73]

Both views are persuasive, and never more so than when applied to an analysis of the work of the OWI, Riskin, and the Bureau of Overseas Motion Pictures. The *Projections of America* series did offer a flavor of collective security in its endorsement of the United Nations and its idealized scripture for the hope of the world in appropriately named titles like *A Better Tomorrow*. Meanwhile, features like *Cowboy* and *Pipeline* more than hinted at the new dawn of America's corporate behemoth. The bureau felt compelled to endorse these messages, but Riskin always had some awareness of their profound implications. No sooner had he persuaded the studios of the rightness of their cause, distributing the propaganda films with Hollywood features around Europe, than they busily started calculating the profits, rather than simply recognizing the service they were providing to their country and free peoples around the world. There were more advertising and marketing executives than filmmakers in the OWI by the end of the war, such was the race to convert wartime economic possibilities into peacetime market actualities. And yet Riskin's series of documentary shorts went further than what Koppes and Black and Horten allude to. The films did educate and sustain the world community. They crossed cultural and philosophical boundaries, and Riskin correctly adjudged Hollywood postwar influence a key staging ground for attitudes toward the United States as the buildup to the cold war intensified.

Indeed, the sober appropriation of distinctly American attitudes in the *Projections* series stood in contrast to the tone of other propaganda materials produced during World War II. Riskin called his an "eavesdropping method of propaganda"; Bosley Crowther, on seeing *Swedes in America* and the other early documentaries for the first time, was moved to write, "Noticeable in all these films is a lack of passion and punch. They narrate their stories simply and in a straight reportorial style. Nobody harangues or lectures; there are no fifes or kettle-drums—and this, according to Mr. Riskin, is by very careful design." He concluded that the "pictures are being studiously applied to the uses of peace and understanding."[74]

Throughout the whole operation, Riskin worked most closely with screenwriter friends Philip Dunne and Joseph Krumgold. Together they supervised a peerless collection of documentary shorts whose quality, substance, and relevance transcended their immediate purpose as wartime propaganda. As McGilligan asserts, it was typical of Riskin that his short documentaries—informational, ideological, and simply entertaining in places—should lack any ostentation and should be crisp and well observed and boast the best talent. The films oozed style and technical accomplishment, mixed with a sophisticated nostalgia borne not of any light-minded idealism but of a call to reclaim the principles of humanity. A later assessment judged some of the films to have an "oversimplified patriotic vision" but concluded, "Nonetheless they are films of simple beauty and deep feeling, emphasizing the values for which Americans were fighting."[75] In a "melting pot" documentary like *The Town*, for instance, von Sternberg was moved to show Madison, Indiana, as a town neither disengaged from world events nor naïvely idyllic, but one where a simplicity of existence reflected tolerance, hope, and community. The series seemed to instill humanitarian characteristics into each film of its own accord, as though as a matter of course. As Arthur Mayer commented at the time, "In OWI Overseas are to be found many of the best known pre-war documentarians . . . [and] these men . . . have gathered copious material for an unforgettable story of America on film."[76] With this approach, Riskin hoped that his documentary work had breached an ideological divide between the Allied nations as they came to terms with their victory, and that Hollywood had found a role for itself in contributing to the future direction of the world.

CHAPTER SIX

THE PRODUCER

Riskin returned to California permanently in 1945 and settled back into the Hollywood existence, with one major alteration: the bachelor scenarist, who had been away from the movie capital periodically for three years, now had a family to look after. Together with Fay Wray, Fay's daughter Susan (from her marriage to John Monk Saunders), and two recent additions—Bobby, who was already two by July of that year, and Victoria, who was born that summer—Riskin moved into a big, two-story English Tudor home on Stone Canyon Road in Bel Air. Situated below the famed Bel Air Hotel, it was a neighborhood where many of the film community already resided: Charles Brackett, Billy Wilder's writing partner, lived next door, and Greer Garson, Lee J. Cobb, and Cary Grant all owned houses close by. Vicki Riskin remembers it as a wonderful place to grow up.[1] Her father now had commitments of an entirely different standing from his prewar bachelor days, and the family became ensconced in a close-knit, happy routine. They observed the end of the Pacific war from their home and were given a taste of the consequences of the previous years' home-front actions in California: the gardener whom the couple engaged after the war, George, had recently been released from one of the state's Japanese-American internment camps. Riskin's new postwar existence was a mature reinvention of the Hollywood lifestyle he had enjoyed for much of the previous decade. No longer could he engage in the bachelor pursuits of horse racing and attending the smartest parties. Little did Riskin know that Hollywood, too, had matured, and in the aftermath of the war was facing tough questions about the kind of industry moviemaking was becoming and the types of films it could and would produce.

Riskin had left the OWI under a cloud in the spring of 1945. His idea to extend the wartime production of documentaries on American topics and themes had been met by an extremely cool reception, though aspects of his plans were subsequently put in motion by the Truman administration. But at this juncture, the disappointment of rejection was tied up in a "short-termism" that Riskin identified among his colleagues in government as well as those in movies. He saw beyond the physical rebuilding program in Europe that would be required in the coming months and years; he foresaw the need to rehabilitate Europe psychologically and philosophically, particularly Germany and, for different reasons, the Soviet Union. Importantly, he identified the need to condition these nations as well as others for an inevitable development: the rise of American cultural influence on a global scale. The way to do that, thought Riskin, was to extend the goodwill of wartime cooperation and to continue to extol the virtues of the American way. The *Projections* series for the OWI had been hugely successful in this respect, and thus abandoning its mission now, he sensed, would be a mistake.

So convinced was Riskin of the importance of communicating this message that he continued, for a time, to make his case for postwar documentary films. In an interview at the end of May 1945, less than a month after he had effectively resigned from the Bureau of Overseas Motion Pictures, he was quoted as saying that only a long-term diet of both entertainment and documentary features would smooth the path of Germany's rehabilitation. Riskin supported the presentation of Nazi atrocities to German audiences, especially films of the concentration camps. But he also felt that, "after the initial period of occupation, when some semblance of normal living returns to Germany, the occupying governments will be confronted with the necessity of getting people into theaters by attracting them, because the German people are no different from other audiences when they are free to shop for their entertainment. Then we must furnish German theaters with films of entertainment in order to get them in to see the newsreels, documentaries, and educational films." Warming to his theme, Riskin went on to point out that it had been thirteen years since the Germans had been permitted to watch American movies, and in that time, they had been fed a diet of lies about America. So, at this juncture in their history, it was even more crucial that a carefully selected balance of programs be provided for a people both weary and shocked by the events of the past few years.[2]

Riskin's willingness to express opinions like these, along with others' growing appreciation of the role he had played by the end of the war, prompted invitations for him to expound these views further. In September 1945, he was invited onto two panels discussing the relative merits of Hollywood films and their propaganda role. The first widely publicized event was Riskin's participation in one of ABC radio's *Town Meeting of the Air* programs, broadcast on September 6 from the Philharmonic Auditorium in Los Angeles. The transcript of each program was also published weekly in the popular *Reader's Digest*. The subject of this edition was "Should Hollywood Make Movies Designed to Influence Public Opinion?" Moderator George Denny Jr. made it clear in his opening remarks that the discussion was not concerned with documentary films, but the impetus for the debate was certainly Hollywood's recent liaison with Washington and the change in public perception of Hollywood features that offices like the Bureau of Motion Pictures might have effected. Riskin appeared with three other guests: Constance Bennett, onetime star of screen and radio and now a producer; actor Donald Crisp; and MGM executive, former writer, and adversary of Riskin in the conservative revolt within the writers guild a decade before, James K. McGuinness.

The debate that unfolded was, from a historical perspective, more than illuminating. Riskin's and Bennett's arguments combined to oppose the views that Crisp and McGuinness expressed, leaving no doubt as to why anti-Communist purges and attacks upon certain "left-wing" ideals were about to invade Hollywood and haunt it until the mid-1950s. Riskin, who spoke first, uttered a line that went on to be much quoted by his supporters as well as his detractors: "When you blow your nose, you are influencing public opinion." His argument was simple: No film ever made did not start out with an idea, and ideas influence people. Movies are for entertainment, of course, but at their best they provoke debate, thought, and dialogue. Drawing on his recent experiences, Riskin argued that American films had been vitally important to building goodwill, spreading hope and enlightenment, and teaching foreign audiences about the United States during the war, and Hollywood must both be aware of this influence and continue to exercise it responsibly. Constance Bennett said she was "heartily in accord with Mr. Riskin," but Donald Crisp argued vociferously for Hollywood movies as entertainment, illusion, and nothing more. James McGuinness, while agreeing that movies had to influence people, thought the political element that had been added to some films of recent years was wrong; politics was not the business of filmmakers.[3]

The program went on to invite questions from the audience of celebrities and entertainers. While freedom of expression and creativity clearly remained the watchwords, it was also apparent that worries and prejudices about extremism were already beginning to rear their heads in the postwar atmosphere. Riskin was asked directly whether it was okay to make a film that promoted Communism, to which he replied, "I don't think Hollywood should make a picture promoting Communism, or fascism, or one about the love life of a bedbug. The only point I make is that the screen should be free as other media of communication are free." Both Crisp and McGuinness, who was already highly influential in the soon-to-be-notorious Motion Picture Alliance for the Preservation of American Ideals, intimated that Hollywood really wanted to peddle socialist values, had ideas of controlling studio output, and was looking to twist people's minds toward the pursuit of causes.[4]

The program, and the arguments lined up against him, must have had some impact on Riskin, because a little more than two weeks later, on the similarly marketed *The Reviewing Stand*, produced by Northwestern University on the Air, Riskin pursued his theory even more stridently. He argued that propaganda should reflect reality, a position very much in line with the OWI's wartime philosophy and espoused by the agency's leading figures. Riskin additionally claimed that it would be good to have more "idea films" in Hollywood. Once again he was asked about a possible Communist cabal operating within the studios, this time through the lens of propaganda, as set out in a film like Michael Curtiz's *Mission to Moscow* (1943) for Warner Brothers. Riskin's response probably did not set the matter to rest as much as it could have. He claimed that Warner Brothers, which had just borrowed $37 million from various financial institutions, didn't sound like a company going out of its way to make Communist propaganda. His point was to emphasize that Hollywood was so tied up in capitalist market philosophy and practice that logic dictated that it would not adopt Communist ideology. But of course that wasn't the point. The issue creeping up on Hollywood was not the means and manner by which the studios did their business, but what ended up on the screen as a result. When Riskin conceded that the overseas bureau had had to make decisions about sending certain films to particular countries during the war, he thus inadvertently placed this narrative within the realm of censorship, which was the sort of position now being easily construed by some as Communist. He nevertheless concluded his statement in the debate by reiterating his conviction that an agency that could work to spread American values around the world in this new age of global communication would be enormously valuable.[5]

In hindsight, Riskin's position appears somewhat paradoxical. Given his astute assessment of what was about to happen in postwar Europe, his comments in the broadcasts boasted quite a naïveté about the threat at home. Right-wingers were already identifying the propaganda they saw as Communist inspired and therefore "un-American," and films like *Mission to Moscow* were about to be exposed in the same light as features like *The North Star* and *Song of Russia*. Curtiz's film, based on Ambassador Joseph Davies' mission to Moscow, had been virtually the final film that the Bureau of Motion Pictures had passed judgment on in 1943 before its windup. Its production, as well as *The North Star*'s, had been prompted by the White House.[6] In many respects, then, it was remarkable that Riskin—closely associated with Rooseveltian opinion and agencies like the Bureau of Motion Pictures, which was already becoming tainted with accusations of Communist conspiracy—never became more embroiled in the purges that followed. In fact, after these public declarations, Riskin kept his counsel to himself, possibly self-consciously, so as not to draw attention to such views as the more vociferous debates gathered pace in Hollywood. Later, his failing health would play a considerable part in helping him to avoid the inquisition of the early 1950s.

Though Riskin's comments seem to reveal naïveté about the situation at home, they may actually have been part of a strategy to distance himself from his colleagues in Hollywood whom he knew to be more determinedly left-wing, some even Communist Party members. This plan may have been prompted by Riskin's experiences with the Screen Writers Guild before the war, in which his instinct had been to pull the union toward a moderate liberal position, rather than by any underlying premonition about the Communist backlash that would be unleashed in the United States after 1945. The writers' congress of 1943 at UCLA had already produced a new determination in Hollywood to look forward after the war to a very different kind of film industry. Darryl Zanuck's comments to the delegates of the congress had summed up this view: "We've got to start making movies that entertain but at the same time match the new climate of our times. Vital, thinking men's blockbusters. Big theme films." Although Riskin was not present, he would surely have endorsed the notion that Hollywood, many of whose patrons had been deeply affected by the experience of war, had a responsibility to reflect social and political change. Ian Hamilton describes the mood as "elevating," manufactured out of a kind of "abstract sincerity" on the part of the screenwriters and other filmmakers looking toward a more hopeful, even idealistic world after the war.[7]

Nevertheless, whether it was intentional or not, Riskin remained wary of people who wanted to use such gatherings to further more extreme political aims. Fay Wray remembers that, during one of Riskin's visits to California during the war, some of the people who would later be among the Hollywood Ten, but who at the time represented the Hollywood Writers' Mobilization (a group drawn up out of the 1943 congress), came by the Beverly Wilshire Hotel to speak with him. Riskin listened intently to what they had to say but never took further their ideas or offers of help within his role at the OWI.[8] It was a position that confirmed Riskin's awareness that some of these writers had dabbled in the Communist Party organization, and thus involving them in any official government capacity might result in problems for him and them. He didn't disapprove, necessarily, though it would be remarkable if Riskin did not consider them misguided; he simply thought any greater liaison would become imprudent at some point in the near future. And, by chance or calculation, Riskin's instincts proved to be right. For without the distance that he had established between himself and the more activist writers, the investigations that were about to descend on Hollywood in 1947, when his health was not yet an issue, might have drawn him much further into the center of the maelstrom hovering over the film community.

Robert Riskin Productions and the Struggle for Independence

In November 1945, Hollywood's anti-Communist nightmare was still some way off. Riskin had major plans following his return to California, and he took out a full-page advertisement that month in the *Hollywood Reporter* to announce the formation of Robert Riskin Productions. Fay Wray became the first vice president, and Riskin appointed Bill Holman as studio manager and Lester Roth as secretary. Three films were slated for release the following year, confirming that Riskin was back in movies and intent on making a big splash—although which three movies the company would produce became a source of some discussion and confusion over the following months. The production that remained constant was the very first that Riskin wanted to shoot: a story adapted from his own original screenplay *The Magic City*. The story of this initial film had been circulating for a while; Riskin had revealed to the *New York Times* as early as July the title and broad themes of the production, which was not going to be, as he had first thought, about Europe.[9] A further announcement, in the January 7, 1946, *Hollywood Reporter*, stated that Riskin had signed a deal to distribute his films through RKO, a company that had already signed Leo McCarey's Rainbow Productions, as well as, interestingly, Frank Capra's new independent company, Liberty Films.

It had long been assumed in Hollywood that Capra and Riskin would work together again, even though, as already suggested, warning signs about this presumption had appeared as far back as 1939. Capra was a regular visitor to the Riskin household, a social arrangement that continued well into the late forties, and there remained an obvious closeness and respect. But some tension persisted, whether it was over recognition, the dimensions of some new partnership in the wake of the unsuccessful Frank Capra Productions venture, or the types of films they wanted to make. In Paris in December 1944, Riskin had given an interview for French newspapers discussing his relationship with Capra. Riskin explained that he got an idea, went away to the country for a few months, came back, met Capra in a small café in Manhattan where they had extraordinary Italian wine, told him the idea, and then "all I have to do is wait a few weeks and then be present at the opening of this new film of Frank Capra."[10] Riskin reportedly presented this tale with a hint of mischief in his eyes. Nevertheless, whether his comments reflected envy, frustration, or sarcasm, or perhaps a combination, the little fable left an acidic taste that couldn't be washed away and suggested that the reuniting of Hollywood's most successful team was anything but a done deal.

Joseph McBride's account of this period adds piquancy to the partnership's postwar story. After Liberty Films was incorporated in April 1945, Capra supposedly asked Riskin to join him in the venture; some reports "presumed" that Riskin would team up with his old sparring partner. But Fay Wray refuted the claim that her husband was ever asked.[11] McBride's recounting of events comes from later interviews with both Capra and Wray, so this discrepancy between the two stories raises some questions. Both parties had reasons to stick to what they thought were positive adjudications of those actions and discussions further on in life, when other disputes concerning authorship and ideas in the pair's films arose. But the incident dealing with Riskin's supposed rejection of an offer to join Liberty is not mentioned in either Capra's or Wray's autobiography. Wray, in her account, swiftly moves on to talk about her husband's first independent film, and Capra notes that he considered Riskin for the writing of *It's a Wonderful Life*, only to remember that he now had his own production company.[12]

If Capra did ask Riskin to join the new company, his old writing partner clearly refused, and by the beginning of 1946, Robert

Riskin Productions and Liberty Films found themselves side by side under the umbrella of RKO. On January 15, the *Hollywood Reporter* claimed that Riskin had two more productions ready to follow *The Magic City*. *Johnny Appleseed* was to be a biographical tale of the "fighting father of the western orchard" and his adventures on the frontier, while *Impact* was cited as a sociological drama of big business and American society. The three films were to have a combined budget of $5 million.[13]

All seemed to be well, but within a month, this roster of films had changed. In February 1946, it was reported that Riskin's company had also bought the rights to the Michael Uris comedy *The Girl from Bogardus*, and it would become the second film from the new company.[14] A month later, another change occurred. Riskin announced that his dramatic account of the work of the OWI, *Now It Can Be Told*, highlighting the courage of the people who worked in the organization during the war, was to be the second feature after *The Magic City*, a production that was due to go before the cameras that month, March 1946.[15]

Riskin was clearly nervous about the reception the films would receive, the attitudes of the postwar audience, and his ability to accomplish what he and Capra had failed to do at the height of their success in 1941: initiate a successful independent venture in Hollywood. But he also faced a misfortune that made him change his mind about the kinds of movies he wanted the company to pursue and the sort of competition he was likely to face. In February, it was revealed that Disney intended to make an animated version of the Johnny Appleseed story. The last thing Riskin Productions needed as a new company was competition with one of the biggest names in Hollywood. The Johnny Appleseed project was quietly dropped, hence the reason for at least one of the alterations in the production schedule.

The Magic City did eventually go before the cameras, but not until the summer of 1946. In between time, Riskin contributed some dialogue, not credited on the screen, to Lewis Milestone's new film, *The Strange Love of Martha Ivers* (1946), for Paramount and Hal Wallis Productions. Riskin had personal connections with a number of people associated with the film, any one of whom could have persuaded him to work on the script. The eponymous star of the movie was longtime Capra-Riskin favorite Barbara Stanwyck, who was now playing degenerate femme fatales in the emerging film noir tradition in Hollywood. Stanwyck was coming off her successful Oscar nomination for Billy Wilder's *Double Indemnity* (1944) and would later receive the same accolade for Anatole Litvak's *Sorry, Wrong Number* (1948). Litvak had codirected a number of the *Why We Fight* documentaries with Capra only a few years previously (and had quite possibly been alerted to Stanwyck's talent and versatility by the director), and the *Sorry, Wrong Number* role—a scheming invalid who hears a murder plot over the telephone—was virtually written for the star.

Riskin had also known Milestone and producer Hal Wallis for a long time, though it is not clear how well he knew the screenwriter for *The Strange Love of Martha Ivers*, Robert Rossen. Rossen had become involved in some of Hollywood's most stridently left-wing politics during the late thirties and had certainly been a member of the Communist Party then. He became disillusioned with the party's views, however, and severed all ties before the war ended. Whether he met up with or had cause to talk to Riskin during this period is not known, but his similar upbringing offered the prospect of some connection. Rossen's parents, like Riskin's, were Russian Jews, his early life was spent on the mean streets of New York City's Lower East Side, and his origins as a writer were in fairly unsuccessful Broadway plays. He even boxed professionally for a while, a scene Riskin had plenty knowledge of in the New York of the twenties.

Whatever the reasons for Riskin's association with *The Strange Love of Martha Ivers*, Rossen's script surely gave him a renewed enthusiasm for the craft following his return to Hollywood. Based on John Patrick's novel—which would win the Oscar for best original story—the film offered a distinctly postwar twist to the small-town/big-city tales Riskin had wrapped around his prewar stories. Combining murder, blackmail, predatory females, and local politics, Rossen put darkness and revenge into the tale of the earlier death of the termagant Mrs. Ivers, a wealthy spinster whose family founded and still dominates Iverstown, the film's setting. The young orphaned Martha of the title is the culprit. Having clubbed her grandmother down the stairs with a candlestick, she concocts a plan, with the help of her weak-willed friend Walter O'Neil (Kirk Douglas), to cover up the manslaughter. O'Neil's lawyer father, a man who is desperate for his son to get on in life, finds Mrs. Ivers at the bottom of the sweeping staircase with the front door wide open, helps to establish the alibi for all concerned, and eventually sends an innocent man to the gallows for the crime. Later, however, O'Neil senior kills himself, broken by the guilt and the need to protect his son, who stands to inherit the family fortune if he sticks with Martha.

Seventeen years later, the boy Martha had made a promise to escape town with on the night of the killing, Sam Masterson (Van Heflin), passes through Iverstown on his way west. Sam has grown up to be an opportunistic grifter, but one who aligns himself on just the right side of any moral dilemma. "You've killed people, Sam, it says so on your record," laments Martha, trying to explain her actions late in the film. "I've never murdered," Masterson counters. Early in the picture, he meets up with a glamorous but destitute girl, Toni Marachek (Lizabeth Scott), on her way out of town, and falls for her in an elaborate series of provocative encounters. But Toni is herself evading the law, having arrived in Iverstown while on probation for an earlier offense. Masterson, meanwhile, discovers the fate of the two young people he left all those years ago, seeing in the posters all over town that Walter is running for reelection as district attorney. Masterson, thinking that Walter could help Toni, contacts the now-married Martha (Stanwyck) and Walter. But the couple, in their panic, think that Sam is looking to extort money from them over Mrs. Ivers's death; they first try to find out what Sam knows and frighten him, then seek to pay him off to keep him quiet about the events of nearly two decades before.

This was principally Rossen's script, and Riskin received no screen credit at the time for the modicum of dialogue he wrote on *The Strange Love of Martha Ivers*.[16] The closure of the film, when Walter tumbles down the stairs just as Mrs. Ivers did eighteen years earlier and Martha urges Sam to finish him off so they can be together, is brutally taut. But Sam helps Walter to recover from the fall and walks away as Martha threatens him with a gun; then, as Masterson trudges out of the driveway, the couple enter a virtual suicide pact because they can stand the torment of their illicit lives no longer. All this ratcheting up of the characters' moral failures was far more indicative of Rossen's tough, hard-boiled writing than Riskin's. Likewise, Toni is a classic noir construction; that she has "been away for a while" suggests to the audience just how loose, manipulative, and desperate she can be. She is the sort of female protagonist that Riskin had written for before, like Gloria Stone in *Lost Horizon*, and though he may have given Toni a little fortitude and a more hopeful outlook, she remains far more gritty and granite-like than was Riskin's taste. Nevertheless, when Walter observes that Martha has been his pet project their whole lives and that she has always acted "like a bird in a cage," one sees the resemblance to Stew Smith's "bird in a gilded cage," Anne Schuyler, whose similar constraints and personal torment Riskin developed to comic effect in *Platinum Blonde*.

Some of the personal and ideological concerns of *The Strange Love of Martha Ivers* also seeped into Riskin's ongoing script for *The Magic City*. Rip Smith in the latter story and Sam Masterson in the former are ragged, troubled characters in their own ways, although Masterson has the hard-knocks, tough-guy persona that became endemic in the noir genre. Both crave money and believe the "fast buck mentality" is their route to success in the modern America of the late forties. Further, both towns, Grandview in Riskin's story and Iverstown in Rossen's, are sentimentalized by some of the protagonists, but in fact they're rather uncomfortable, uncertain places: one is hiding secrets of past misdeeds, and the other is just hiding from society's inexorable progression. Each film in its way threw up a less-than-appetizing facet of postwar society and its assertive individual aims. *The Strange Love of Martha Ivers*, however, had the benefit of being at the vanguard of the noir genre fixation that dominated Hollywood in the immediate postwar years, and so had a ready-made audience appreciative of its ideas and players. Its cinematography is frequently dark, dominated by recurrent nightscapes, while bus stations and bars are often lonely terminuses for troubled, enigmatic characters. Riskin knew how to write these types of people from his earlier work, and while it is difficult to pinpoint exact contributions, one can appreciate his awareness of Stanwyck's performance. Martha is obsessed and greedy but also craves attention and understanding. Her relationship with the increasingly drunken and hollow wreck that is Walter echoes Florence Fallon from *The Miracle Woman* and even Lulu Smith from Capra's story *Forbidden*. *The Strange Love of Martha Ivers* takes its time to reach a denouement, but along the way, it constructs atmosphere and melodrama with ease. For Riskin, it was a bold and successful return to the Hollywood fold, and it pushed him to work diligently on his own material.

In *The Magic City*, however, he was attempting to tackle subtler, more complicated social relations than in *Martha Ivers*. Riskin was bravely trying to push himself in the script to address other social developments in America, including the rising influence of public opinion and modern advertising techniques, a task that the film never quite pulls off, although not for want of trying.

On the face of it, Robert Riskin Productions' first film had

Director William Wellman and his crew shooting *Magic Town*, 1946. (Reproduced by permission from BBC Worldwide Publishing.)

all the necessary ingredients for success. Riskin wrote the script with his old friend and reliable partner from the overseas bureau of the OWI, Joseph Krumgold. Acting as his own producer, he acquired one of the actresses of the moment, Jane Wyman, as the leading lady. Wyman had recently appeared in Paramount's Academy Award–nominated *The Lost Weekend* for director Billy Wilder, and she had been nominated for an Oscar herself just a few months before for her role in MGM's *The Yearling* as a struggling farmer's wife, opposite Gregory Peck. Riskin was also delighted to have James Stewart, recently returned from service in Europe, as the star. Stewart had in fact signed with all three of RKO's independents, not wishing to tie himself down to a studio after the war. Indeed, RKO made some play in its publicity for Riskin's film by highlighting Stewart's recent credits, notably his work on Capra's film for Liberty, *It's a Wonderful Life*. Riskin, having vowed never to return behind the camera, also had a director for his first independent movie: the renowned William Wellman, a man who had made such classics as *Wings*, *The Public Enemy*, and, more recently, *The Story of G.I. Joe*.

Riskin and Krumgold's plot for what was quickly renamed *Magic Town* is contemporary, engaging, romantic, and pretty funny in places. It is the tale of a marketing executive—perhaps a sly dig at some of the characters floating around the OWI in its later years—who discovers the perfect American small town for polling, in terms of its demographics and its inhabitants' responses to questions. The invasion of the quiet, respectable idyll of Grandview by the rather cynical corporate world was not an alien narrative concoction for Riskin. However, *Magic Town* took the bold stance of trying to present community, rather than individual characters such as Longfellow Deeds and John Willoughby, as the wise adjudicator of values and ideals. Riskin attempted to grapple with the notion of a town that was communal and aware of its proud traditions while at the same time seemingly at odds with prevailing norms and developments in postwar society. He aimed to make Grandview a contemporary site, not some antique backwater that existed in the past, but one confronting the possibilities of the modern world, a small tableau for a wider American dilemma. Ironically, it was a task not dissimilar to the

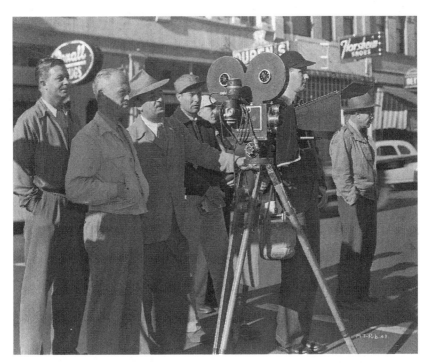

Director William Wellman lines up a shot for a street scene from *Magic Town*, 1946. (Reproduced by permission from BBC Worldwide Publishing.)

one that Capra had set for himself in the recent *It's a Wonderful Life*, though it is often forgotten that the story of the Baileys and Bedford Falls is a retrospective rites-of-passage fable covering the period between the world wars. Riskin wanted the postwar world to be very much apparent and insistent in *Magic Town*, and to some degree, he and Krumgold succeeded.

The pollster, Rip Smith (Stewart), initially an ambitious city type, moves into the town he has discovered perfectly represents average American views, thanks to his old friendship with local schoolteacher Mr. Hoopendecker (Kent Smith). He intends to make money providing accurate data to companies but falls under the charms of the local paper's editor, Mary Peterman (Wyman), who, just to complicate matters further, wants the town to modernize and become part of the new American century. She discovers that Rip is not here to sample the quiet life

James Stewart as "Rip" Smith and Ned Sparks as Ike Sloan in *Magic Town*, 1947.
(Reproduced by permission from BBC Worldwide Publishing.)

and make his home in the perfect American town but wants to
exploit it for his failing business and make a name for himself
with the polling elite in New York. The film offers an enticing
cast, including Ned Sparks, who virtually reprised his role as
the cynically deadpan, taciturn Happy McGuire from *Lady for
a Day* fourteen years before. Given most of the best lines in that
film, here he practically steals the show as Smith's business partner, Ike Sloan. His dry repartee, delivered in the well-loved and
much-mimicked monotone that was his signature, works almost
as well in this story as it did in *Lady for a Day* and acts as a conscious foil to Rip's increasingly confused intentions for the town
and his romance with Mary. Ike is Rip's humanist conscience. He
constantly reminds him of the better things in life, of enjoying
oneself, making a family, and living a normal existence instead
of chasing illogical and distant dreams.

When Rip insists that Grandview is the perfect microcosm of American opinion, Sloan replies that it sounds as if he is talking about a utopia. The line is a wonderfully resonant counterpoint to Riskin's much-vaunted prewar utopias: the Mandrake Falls of *Mr. Deeds Goes to Town*, the Millville of *Meet John Doe*, and the fantastic Shangri-La of *Lost Horizon*. Here, though, utopia is no more than a set of statistics that Rip rattles off to Ike, a mathematical exactitude of how postwar American society is supposed to look and think. Rip's dreams are therefore not ideological, transcendental, or metaphysical: they are about equations and numbers that will acquire for him wealth and position. Mary, her mother Ma Peterman (Ann Shoemaker), and Hoopendecker help Rip to shake off these stark, specific objectives, but more than that, as the narrative progresses, Grandview gets into Rip's blood, with its pride, tradition, and ambition.

Riskin sensed that *Magic Town* had the makings of a perfect Capraesque story with a modern twist. Ike, Mary, Ma Peterman, and the mayor (Harry Holman) brilliantly recalled Capra and Riskin's classic cast of characters. Riskin cleverly updated some of the characters, practically telling the tales of their lives since the early films. Ike, for example, is Happy McGuire, grown up and respectable. Riskin included Regis Toomey and Ann Doran playing Grandview's archetypal couple, the Weavers, as a direct updating of their roles as Millville's loyal residents the Hansons in *Meet John Doe*. All these elements seemed to pave the way for a renewal of the Capra-Riskin formula, but Riskin didn't have Capra around. Capra, though, rather thought he did.

Joseph McBride's account of the film cites Capra's extraordinary assertion that he and Riskin both worked on the script but Riskin wanted to finish it for himself to prove he could do it, and so went ahead, even directing the movie. Then, Capra insisted, Riskin's brother Everett stepped in when it was clear the picture just wasn't working and pleaded with Capra to finish it. Capra refused but, "as a favor," asked Wellman to shoot the last week or so of the film. McBride balances this claim with Fay Wray's statement that Wellman was the only director and Riskin simply never considered helming the movie. Wellman, in a 1975 interview, confirmed that he directed from beginning to end but also said that Capra and Riskin had a big row about the picture, intimating that they were originally in line to work on it together.[17]

There is no evidence to support Capra's contention, but it does seem unlikely that they were not talking about each other's projects, if they were maintaining a healthy social banter. Capra does not claim in his biography that he asked Riskin to write *It's a Wonderful Life*, which was already well into production by the time *Magic Town* had started filming, nor does he claim any input on *Magic Town*. According to a story now much more commonly relayed, the divisions between Capra and Riskin were set in train by the battle over screenwriting credit for *It's a Wonderful Life*, which a Screen Writers Guild arbitration awarded to Capra, much to the chagrin of the main writers, Albert Hackett and Frances Goodrich. Hackett believed that Capra's claim on *It's a Wonderful Life* was part of the director's larger quest for writing credit on all his films, including those with Riskin, although it is not clear whether Hackett communicated this idea to Riskin himself.[18] Regardless, this was a sign of what was to follow two years later, in the dispute over writing credit for *Riding High*, the remake of *Broadway Bill*.

The difficulties surrounding *Magic Town*, even without Capra's interjection, did not help the production. Even by his own admission, Wellman was not the right choice for the film. Riskin spent many hours tinkering with the script, trying to map comedic value and social message into the narrative. He found a way to win the town's loyalty to Rip, by making him coach the school basketball team, whose members repay Smith at the close by encouraging parents and elders to carry out their plans for development even after their newfound fame has destroyed Rip's polling data. But Riskin was aware that the promise of the movie's first half fell away as he inched toward a resolution. Any inquisition into America's corporate and scientific postwar social paradigm was undermined by the need to resolve relationships and rediscover the soul of Grandview's community. In short, Riskin was back in a situation he had vowed not to repeat after the experiences of *Meet John Doe* and, to a lesser degree, *The Thin Man Goes Home*. The *Magic Town* screenplay underwent a first redraft on September 6,

James Stewart and Jane Wyman consult a map of the United States in a publicity shot for *Magic Town*, 1947. (Reproduced by permission from BBC Worldwide Publishing.)

1946, with revisions on October 3, 5, and 6 and December 17 and 18, by which time the last thirty pages of the script had been virtually rewritten and the film was already well into production.[19]

By the picture's release in May 1947, Riskin had grown very uneasy about the quality of the piece. But, taking as its cue Stewart's portrayal of Rip Smith, RKO went into overdrive, selling the film to theaters with pictorial reviews of the characters and story, a teaser poster campaign based on the word "magic," and even a cartoon strip that gave away portions of the narrative.[20] *New York Times* reporter John Harkins, who followed Riskin and Fay Wray to one of the film's sneak previews (by now part and parcel of studios' publicity drives), reported how nervous Riskin was at the screening, though Wray confided that he always got that way at such events. The screening was not a great success, and Riskin and Wray were further unnerved at the number of children in the audience, who seemed to make noise all through the film.[21] The audience's reaction, regrettably, set the tone for the public's response. The picture met with a lukewarm reception from the critics and fans, which was somewhat undeserved. The film did have some sparkling moments, and it read much better on the page than it played on the screen. The scene in the office late at night in which Wyman discovers Rip has ulterior motives for being in Grandview, just after she has let her guard down and is falling in love with him, is a more noirish romantic scenario than many Riskin wrote at other points in his career. And Wyatt plays Mary as a perfect foil for Riskin's obsession with career women and the legacy of responsibility. But Wellman tended to make the scenes too flat, the comedy never flows in quite the manner it should, and some of the characters are not given enough sparkle and personality on screen to interest the audience. Riskin's fears about the production company were coming to pass; he knew if he did not achieve a big hit for Riskin Productions with *Magic Town*, he would have to face the prospect of folding when he had barely started.

He had in fact hinted at this scenario in an interview for the *Motion Picture Herald* the previous December, as he was struggling through various drafts of the movie. Riskin professed happiness that there were other high-quality pictures because it reflected well on the industry and on his ability and judgment. He astutely realized that, in the new postwar Hollywood, one had to set oneself apart from other filmmakers, to create a brand with one's films that audiences would recognize and return to see. This philosophy hinted at the coming breakup of the studio system and prophesied the rise of actor influence. "I think there will be fewer and better pictures in Hollywood," he said. "The trend is towards quality rather than quantity."[22] The comments were a rehash of the work ethic Riskin had already spoken of when making *Meet John Doe* and, indeed, dated back to his early experiences at Columbia. Writing could not be done to order, he insisted again, but this was an acute observation that, in the changing Hollywood, a single film could sustain creative and commercial popularity for a greater period than it could have a decade before. No longer was there the need to churn out another hit picture within six months of the last. He wanted his first independent film to achieve that kind of sustainability.

But releasing *Magic Town* in the middle of 1947 proved an unfortunate step. The cold war was finally catching up with Hollywood, in the form of the House Un-American Activities Committee (HUAC). The headlines were no longer about the films or the stars, but about Communists operating in the heart of America's cultural capital. In May, at almost exactly the same moment that Riskin's movie was premiering, HUAC was moving into the Biltmore Hotel in Los Angeles to begin preliminary hearings into the infiltration of Hollywood by Communists. The Motion Picture Alliance for the Preservation of American Ideals offered several movies as evidence of subversive tendencies. Its executive director, Dr. John Lechner, formed a welcoming party with a list of features that, according to the alliance, were culpable left-wing propaganda. One of the films was *The Strange Love of Martha Ivers*.[23] Ian Hamilton points out that the talk of "big theme" pictures that had been so desirable only a couple of years before was now subversive rhetoric.[24] Hollywood had adopted the very same arguments that Crisp and McGuinness had laid before Riskin in their debate just two years beforehand.

If the labeling as subversive of a film that he had worked on—even without a screen credit—didn't create a delicate enough situation for Riskin, then working within a studio, RKO, that was now seen as having some of the most radical proponents of left-wing, anti-American thought was certainly cause for concern. This was the studio where Edward Dmytryk and Adrian Scott had portrayed overt racism in the military with *Crossfire*, and where other writer-directors like Kazan, Polonsky, and Rossen worked. Dalton Trumbo was, in 1945–46, the editor of the Screen Writers Guild's official magazine, the *Screenwriter*, pushing for the establishment of the American Authors' Authority to protect writers' interests.[25] Riskin's friend and colleague Philip Dunne was on the editorial board of the magazine with Trumbo and Ring Lardner Jr. In 1945 and '46, the *Screenwriter* had followed in the footsteps of the writers' congress and pushed for stronger campaigns within the union. The December 1946 issue included an article by Dunne in which he highlighted the need to "always keep pertinent political issues before the guild."[26]

But this kind of talk had serious ramifications a year later. The Motion Picture Alliance, clearly emboldened by the Republican capture of Congress in 1946 and the passing of the Taft-Hartley Act, which forced union members to swear an oath denying Communist affiliation, pressed for the exposure of those within its midst who it felt were subversives. In his visit to Hollywood in May and June, the chair of HUAC, J. Parnell Thomas, interviewed fourteen witnesses, all of them sympathetic to the aims of the committee. They included director Sam Wood, writer Rupert Hughes, and actors Adolphe Menjou, Gary Cooper, and Robert Taylor. Taylor actually said that he had to wait until he finished spouting red propaganda in *Song of Russia* to enter the navy. On the basis of Thomas's "conversations," nineteen people were named as Communists and were issued subpoenas to appear before the committee in Washington in October 1947.

In the beginning, Hollywood laughed this threat off and even set up protests and meetings, the Committee for the First Amendment being the most famous group to counter the Motion Picture Alliance. But there was some dissension among the liberals who supported those called before HUAC. Within the Committee for the First Amendment, prominent members such as John Huston and William Wyler, as well as Philip Dunne, were uneasy about the refusal to answer the leading question, "Are you now, or have you ever been, a member of the Communist Party?" Riskin and Dunne were very close, and their postwar comments had already intimated that their feelings on this issue were likely to be virtually identical: yes, it was okay to refuse to answer HUAC, but the accused should then go before a judge, the press, or someone else to answer the question to deflate speculations. Meanwhile, before the hearings began, Parnell Thomas attempted to parry the arrival in Washington of stars belonging to the Committee for the First Amendment, like Bogart, Bacall, Sinatra, Fonda, and Hepburn, by announcing that the studios had already agreed to blacklist Communist sympathizers. But Eric Johnston, the president of the Motion Picture Association, pledged that anything as un-American as a blacklist would never be instituted in Hollywood.[27]

Of the nineteen who appeared before the committee in October 1947, ten were cited for contempt: Alvah Bessie, Herbert Biberman, Lester Cole, Edward Dmytryk, Ring Lardner Jr., John Howard Lawson, Albert Maltz, Samuel Ornitz, Adrian Scott, and Dalton Trumbo. For a week or so after the hearings, the Ten seemed to claim a victory of sorts. Most of Hollywood looked to be on their side. Rallies and broadcasts were scheduled trumpeting that democracy had won the day. The *Nation*'s legendary Washington correspondent I. F. "Izzy" Stone concluded that "the committee is out to give the moguls of the industry no rest until they not only take from the screen what little liberal and social content it has, but turn to making films which would prepare the way for fascism at home and abroad." He went on, "The inquiry must be fought by all men of good-will."[28] But confidence in the defense soon crumbled. Many in Hollywood were not impressed by the Ten's conduct on the witness stand; Huston and Dunne especially thought that the tactics were poor. They wanted them to say straightforwardly that they refused to answer the principal question on the grounds that Congress could not ask a citizen's political beliefs, and they believed this would have been applauded. But some of the Ten lost their dignity, thought Huston and Dunne, by trying to worm around the question and make themselves out to be smarter than the committee. The stars of Hollywood were quietly tipped off to distance themselves from the Ten, although it is unlikely that Riskin ever needed such advice. Meanwhile, the battle in Hollywood hurt the industry where it felt it most, in its pocketbook. There was a serious slump in cinema attendance (between 1946 and 1948, a drop from eighty million to sixty-two million a week[29]), and the last thing the studios wanted was to battle the American Legion and Washington. Plans were drawn up to dump the Ten.

On November 24, 1947, fifty members of the Motion Picture Association met at the Waldorf-Astoria Hotel in New York; two days later, they issued a statement that Hollywood believed in free speech but was determined to rid itself of subversives. They stated that they deplored the actions of the Ten and would not knowingly engage Communists. Eric Johnston's declaration that Hollywood would never resort to anything as divisive as a blacklist proved to be false. The list emerged, and loyalty oaths followed in its wake. The Ten, meanwhile, went to prison, most for a year, and eventually the Screen Writers Guild was compelled to hand over files dating back to the mid-thirties to aid further investigation. Any help former colleagues were giving to the Ten, or indeed to any other left-wingers, remained clandestine. This malignant period was rounded off by the irony that the grand inquisitor, J. Parnell Thomas, joined two of the Ten, Ring Lardner Jr. and Lester Cole, in the Federal Correctional Institution in Danbury, Connecticut, for payroll padding.[30]

To what extent Riskin—and, similarly, his old partner Capra— was caught up in this furor is a tricky question. Joseph McBride lists the various files that were kept on Capra, by HUAC and the FBI, among others, though none amounted to anything like evidence of Communist conspiracy. Fay Wray writes that she believes Riskin was investigated at some point. She claims, though, that when he was briefly under scrutiny, his penchant for wearing hats, particularly in his wartime work, was greatly in his favor, because Communists, she learned, apparently never wore hats.[31]

The initial investigation by HUAC largely passed Riskin by, as it did Capra. But Riskin noted a change in his friend and an unsavory attitude that had crept into Hollywood behavior in general. One night during a dinner party between the families, Capra mentioned that he knew the son of a mutual friend to be a Communist. The young man was later investigated by the authorities, although it was not clear that Capra had anything to do with the check.[32] For Riskin, the obvious response to the recent events in Hollywood was not to ignore them, but to refrain from dignifying the hysterical accusations and feverish hand-wringing with a response. Hence Capra's willingness to raise the subject and make accusations, as though somehow to confirm that he himself had the right credentials in the current atmosphere, troubled Riskin. McBride suggests that the distance that had begun to separate Capra and Riskin might well have had something to do with attitudes toward certain writers and Riskin's association with the more progressive faction of the Screen Writers Guild. This is possible, but as already stated, Riskin was equally wary of and unsympathetic to some of those groups. That he never became embroiled in the events and never had to testify or compromise loyalties may have been partly because he never spoke of party affiliations in public, partly because his independent company distanced him from the political troubles within the major studios, and partly because he had little contact with the publicly outed Communists.

The Dangers of Going out of Business

Magic Town was not the success Riskin had hoped for in 1947, and it was not clear whether his company could immediately get any further productions off the ground. Some time after the movie's release, Riskin spoke of his position in the postwar Hollywood hierarchy to Thomas Pryor of the *New York Times*. Pryor's article was prompted by reports at the end of the forties that Britain was about to slap a 75 percent import tax on Hollywood films, a move that would obviously have negative ramifications for independent companies like Riskin's, which were already working with tight margins and therefore needed overseas rentals to haul in additional revenue. Riskin put up a combative defense, bullishly replying, "The independents have been around a long time. They built up this industry and there is no danger of them going out of business now. They are in a much better position than the majors because they are not burdened by expensive operating costs."[33] He was, however, operating barely inside the margins of his company budget. In truth, Riskin had spent too much money on the production of *Magic Town* and was now suffering as a result.

The *New York Times* article made clear how much Riskin had been affected by the changes in Hollywood since the end of the war. Pryor quoted him as being taken aback by the number of "new big shots" who were calling themselves independent producers but who didn't seem to know the first thing about filmmaking. Dismissing their influence, Riskin called them nothing more than promoters and said the moment they were on the outside looking in, the better it would be for all concerned. But in these comments sounded a note of disappointment, if not desperation. If Hollywood was losing its sense of discipline and beginning to stray from the confines of studio control, then Riskin was no better example of the trend. But he was astute enough to ponder whether it was unsettling him as much as it was the film community in general. Capra, Cohn, Jo Swerling, Sam Briskin, and others in his past had all focused his craft and reigned in his wanderlust tendencies. Riskin could handle the necessary business dealings and producing chores, as he had shown on other projects. But these tasks had also tended to divert his attention, because, unlike the "big shots" he now identified around the studios, Riskin always wanted the job done properly. *Magic Town* demonstrated the quality and professionalism that his production company had to offer Hollywood, but he also felt pulled in different directions, obliged to keep an eye on every facet of the operation. If he was frustrated, it was because these responsibilities distracted him from what he considered to be the most important legacy of any film: the script.

As if to remind himself of the importance of the writing, Riskin concluded his interview with Pryor by adding a bit of self-promotion, highlighting two pictures he described as in preparation at his own company. One of these was the much-touted *The Girl from Bogardus*, Michael Uris's story that had headlined the opening of Riskin Productions nearly four years earlier but only now had a screenplay, by newcomer Liam O'Brien. The other script was Riskin and O'Brien's original story about a newspaper reporter returning to America from Europe after the war, *You Belong to Me*. Neither of these stories, unfortunately, would be made by Riskin. No sooner had he talked up his future prospects than he was forced to fold his independent operation in 1949, liquidating the assets and selling the one completed script, *You Belong to Me*. Whether Riskin could have fought harder to keep the company is difficult to judge. The impulse to write again without the pressures that had surrounded him for much of the decade, within first Capra's company and then his own, certainly had some effect. But ultimately, he was modest enough to recognize where his talents lay. Within a few short months of the collapse of Riskin Productions, his and Liam O'Brien's script for *You Belong to Me* would have a new champion. This development would pave the way for one of the last major acknowledgments of his screenwriting career, for the script found its way into the hands of a familiar figure: Frank Capra.

CHAPTER SEVEN

THE WRITER

Riskin liquidated the assets of his production company in 1949, much as Frank Capra had done with his Liberty Films early in 1948. Capra sold Liberty to Paramount and concluded a three-picture directing deal with them that he hoped might resurrect his career. It may seem strange now to state that Capra was looking to reestablish his credentials when one of his previous two films for Liberty had been *It's a Wonderful Life*, but that movie did not do as well at the time as its now-revered status would imply.[1] The second and final film he made under the Liberty banner, *State of the Union*, paved the way for his move to Paramount, as it was a complicated deal between the studio, Liberty, and MGM. Although not well liked or regarded in comparison with his other movies, *State of the Union* was one of the most intriguing and demonstrative political statements of Capra's career, and its business at the box office was substantial, reflecting the loyal fan base that still existed for the director's pictures.[2]

As a result of his early failure to get a number of projects off the ground at Paramount, however, together with the studio's ambivalent attitude toward its supposed star recruit, Capra's career then hit a crisis.[3] Giving up on some of his original pet projects, Capra pushed the studio to buy the rights to his and Riskin's 1934 hit *Broadway Bill*. He had the idea of remaking the movie under a new title, *Riding High*. In fact, desperate to have a hit at the studio, Capra suggested to Paramount that he could fashion the new *Broadway Bill* into a musical comedy, with Bing Crosby in the role of Dan Brooks. The studio went for the project largely because it seemed to guarantee that Capra wouldn't spend the kind of money that his later Columbia projects and his independent features had cost. Capra brokered a deal whereby the studio sold a story he was intent on filming—*A Woman of Distinction*, eventually directed by Eddie Buzzell—to Harry Cohn in exchange for the rights to *Broadway Bill*. The deal was concluded in October 1948, and Capra insisted he could bring the project to the studio with a budget under $2 million.

Perhaps as a consequence of the cost cutting, or perhaps to differentiate the two films entirely, Capra then embarked on the screenwriting endeavors that would become so controversial and that almost certainly contributed to his drifting apart from his old writing partner. Riskin refused Capra's appeals for a shared screenplay credit on the film, and the Screen Writers Guild backed this claim. The guild insisted that only Riskin should be acknowledged as the screenwriter, and that Melville Shavelson and Jack Rose, who had been the two main adapters of *Riding High*, as well as Capra, should be given credit for additional dialogue, with the original story nod going to Mark Hellinger. The guild was right: Capra didn't give birth to a new film with his plans for a radical overhaul of the script or his engagement of Bing Crosby. Yes, there were songs in the movie now, and Crosby played Brooks as a carefree bachelor rather than a married man looking to live his dream. But Capra engaged eight members of the original cast, including Raymond Walburn to play down-on-his-luck gent Colonel Pettigrew and Clarence Muse as the stable hand Whitey. He also shot new footage at Tanforan Racetrack outside San Francisco, in order to combine new and old shots.

Running at 112 minutes compared to its original 90, *Riding High* was very moderate fare. It recouped a mere $2.35 million at the box office on its belated general release in April 1950, enough for a very modest profit but less than *State of the Union* had made two years before.[4] Moreover, the alterations to the script had made the film obvious and the characters one-dimensional, and the whole project lacked the deft touch that for so long had been Capra's trademark on screen.

The controversy between Capra and Riskin concerning the credits for *Riding High* was certainly serious and disappointing for the writer. As Pat McGilligan takes pains to point out, however, their reactions did not make evident any concerted breakdown in their relationship. Indeed, their social liaisons continued quite unhindered in the early part of 1950, as if both were determined not to be put off by anything as distasteful as a squabble over authorship rights. Fay Wray expressed as much surprise as anyone at Capra's later remark that the two had quarreled. Yet it seems clear that any thoughts the pair had of reuniting, which McGilligan and others believe was possible, were quickly fading into the distance as the picture hit the screens in the spring of 1950.[5]

When Riskin was forced to liquidate the assets of his production company, one completed story remained on the books. *You Belong to Me* was the tale of a reporter, naturally, who returns to the States from Italy with four orphaned children in his care. He plans to win over the girl he refused to marry a few years before, spurred on by her parting note in the form of a gramophone recording, in which she tells her former love that she is waiting for him no longer and is about to marry a rich businessman. Riskin had concocted the story with Liam O'Brien, the young writer he had contracted to Riskin Productions as a kind of apprentice and who he hoped would be part of the next generation of talented scribes.

Riskin sold the story to Paramount, now Capra's home. It was originally going to be a vehicle for Bob Hope, with Irving Asher producing, but accounts suggest Capra heard it was a Riskin story and jumped in, keeping Asher but taking over the production in August 1950. Why and how Capra "heard" of the film but never seemed to discuss it with Riskin is simply unknown. If the team were ever going to reunite, there was surely no more opportune time than the summer of 1950 for them to bury any lasting arguments over *Riding High* before the disputes took hold of their long friendship. The screenplay for *You Belong to Me* was to be completed during the late summer, and filming finished in time for an early 1951 release. In fact, the film would not be released until September, a year and a half after *Riding High*, and in the meantime Capra and Riskin seemed to have little or no further contact. When, in the middle of shooting the picture, Riskin collapsed from a stroke, the chance was lost, and the two never communicated again.

And yet no mention has ever been made of Capra's asking, or Riskin's seeking, before this turn of events, to adapt Riskin and O'Brien's story. McGilligan claims that six writers went to work on the script for *You Belong to Me*, although the production credits only three: Virginia Van Upp, who was a talented and influential figure at Columbia in the thirties as a scenarist and producer; Capra's old friend and confidant Myles Connolly; and Liam O'Brien.[6] If O'Brien, having taken leave of his mentor's production company, was one of the main writers, why was Riskin himself not? Since Riskin fell ill only after filming began, Hollywood's most successful team seemed to have had one last opportunity to collaborate.

There is in fact a good explanation as to why Riskin didn't pilot his own story to the screen, even without assuming that the arguments over the *Broadway Bill* remake dashed the chance of any reunion. Riskin could not participate because no sooner had he wound up his company than he signed a contract with his longtime friend Darryl Zanuck at Twentieth Century–Fox. Zanuck set Riskin to work on two scripts very quickly, and therefore he was obliged to fulfill the duties of his new contract ahead of any other project. No intimation that Capra and Riskin even attempted to collaborate on *You Belong to Me* has ever been expressed. It seems reasonable to conclude that both thought that too much time had passed since they had last worked together; the chemistry could not be rekindled, and their interests had diverged considerably.

Judging by what Capra did to Riskin and O'Brien's story, the last point might be crucial. The screenwriting duo had drafted the tale as another vehicle for Jimmy Stewart. The reporter was to be smart, lighthearted, but with an unabashed romantic streak. Riskin and O'Brien were looking to recast Stewart as a boyish and yet sensitive composite of Tony Kirby, Jefferson Smith, and Rip Smith—someone like Capra's George Bailey from *It's a Wonderful Life*. At Paramount, however, Capra brought in Bing Crosby, whom he had just worked with on *Riding High*; Jane Wyman, who, ironically, had worked with Stewart and Riskin on *Magic Town* three years earlier; and Franchot Tone. The director then transformed the story into his second straight musical comedy and adopted the title *Here Comes the Groom*. This drift from the original story was an even more curious development than *Riding High* had been. But the picture was successful in that it made

an Oscar-winning standard out of songwriters Hoagy Carmi-
chael and Johnny Mercer's "In the Cool, Cool, Cool of the Evening," reprised more than once in the movie. And, amazingly,
Riskin and O'Brien received an Academy Award nomination for
original story, over O'Brien's contribution with Upp and Connolly, which failed to feature in the screenwriting category. It was
to prove the last nomination of Riskin's career.

But while Riskin could feel satisfied that his work was still
drawing attention, the movie itself lacked cohesion and character involvement in many places. Peter Garvey, the reporter on
assignment in what had become the remnants of war-torn France
rather than Italy, a country now being rebuilt by the Marshall
Plan, does have more than a little of Riskin's protagonists' usu-
al charm and affection for life. The change of location and the
taking in of only two orphans probably did little to alter Riskin
and O'Brien's story, but in their tale there were personal connections in the relationships between the reporter and the children
that suggested resonance in Riskin's own experiences in Italy
during the war, as though he knew of some real-life example.
In addition, the story looked set to offer a subtle contemplation
of America's place in the postwar world that quickly got lost in
the movie. Still, Garvey's attempts to escape the clutches of his
longtime sweetheart, Emmadel Jones (Wyman), have a considerable touch of autobiographical conceit. This is Riskin, one might
suggest, revisiting the apprehensions about commitment he had
before his marriage to Fay Wray. Crosby plays Garvey with his
emotional heart beating in all the right places, no more so than in
the "selling" of blind orphan Theresa (Anna Maria Alberghetti)
to a wealthy American couple looking to adopt a child to take
back to the States. Garvey brings them together because he sees
the musical ability of the child tied to the fame of the conductor
husband. But Crosby's stab at depth of character indicates that
he was much more suited to *Road to . . .* movies with Bob Hope.

The duel that is built up between Pete Garvey as the wisecracking gadfly and Wilbur Stanley (Tone) as the elegant Bos-
ton Brahmin who has won over Em's affections is simply not
convincing. Charles Maland suggests that Stanley represents a
serious personality turn in Capra's movies, a wealthy businessman whose charm, eloquence, and willingness to sort out dif-

ficulties—the confusion with the house let for Pete is the classic scene—detach him completely from the ruthlessness of the Kirbys, Taylors, and Nortons of earlier pictures.[7] Hence the sense of confrontation (and resolution) between Garvey and Stanley is so diluted throughout the film that they almost have a grudging regard for each other. In addition, the story is nearly concluded before the other possible object of Wilbur's affections, Winifred (Alexis Smith), is revealed as so distant a cousin (we are firmly assured) that this need not worry us as a "family liaison" any further. And the resolution, in which Stanley suddenly achieves moral clarity and steps aside at the drop of a hat so Garvey can marry Em, the children are not sent back to France, and Stanley can pursue almost-not-related-at-all Winifred, is convenient in the extreme.

There are some nice touches, particularly Robert Keith's deft performance as Garvey's editor, George Degnan. "We've shared some things over the years," exclaims Pete as he tries to turn Winifred into a predatory female so she can catch Wilbur and he can have Em. "We've never shared this," retorts George, giving Win a deadpan glance. Winifred's "coming out" as a woman with romantic, not to say sexual, intent also reminds us of what was once daring and sublime in Capra and Riskin's films. She follows an arc that is reminiscent of Ellie Andrews's but lacks some of the intricacy and humor that so charged the social revolution exposed in It Happened One Night. Even in Winifred's transformation, as Ray Carney observes, the relationship between the sexes has also now been reduced to a "comedy of manners, a choice of acting strategies," rather than an exploration of human emotion.[8] Although this keenly expressed determination to square up to class and sexuality as sparks fly between society's haves and have-nots is an endemic theme of two decades of Capra's films, and although it survives the story's alteration here, Riskin would have found layers of exposure and dealt much more finely with cultural attitudes and mores than the finished screenplay managed to do.

Capra clearly found it difficult to pull off the slapstick construction, and the technique in some scenes of speeding the dialogue until it became excessive, over-laden noise just didn't work. As in Riding High and, to an extent, It's a Wonderful Life, prewar sensibilities existed in a postwar materialist world in *Here Comes the Groom*. It's a telling scene when, at night, Pete and Em go to the building where she works and prowl the wide-open spaces of empty office interiors: their sparseness, modernism, and size suggest the new look of American global economic intent. The scene could have mixed comic and poignant moments in contemplation of the future and the world they are leaving behind. Instead, Capra opts for Johnny Mercer's song, a dance routine, and a brief farewell outside at the car, leaving the viewer somewhat nonplussed about the motivation for the scene.

Here Comes the Groom, whatever its faults, was still another moderate hit for Capra, primarily achieved on the strength of Bing Crosby's popularity.[9] Reviews like that in *Variety* generously called the picture a "top-notch piece of comedy" and claimed that Riskin and O'Brien had provided a "merry yarn" for Capra's direction.[10] Even respectable commentaries like this, however, were not enough to assuage Capra's doubts. The whole production was an experience the director clearly wasn't keen to repeat, and he never felt entirely comfortable at Paramount. On set, Capra even confided to actress Alexis Smith that he was considering walking away from movies altogether. "It just wasn't fun anymore," he lamented.[11] The insertion of songs at certain junctures in the film to show off musical talent rather than to advance the story highlighted how little control Capra had over final cut, a decided change from his prime years at Columbia.[12] He left the studio after this, only the second film of a three-picture deal. Although he made one more minor film during the late fifties—*A Hole in the Head* (1959) starring Frank Sinatra, for United Artists—and a small series of television adaptations and writing, Capra would do nothing significant for a decade, until he remade *Lady for a Day* as *Pocketful of Miracles* in 1961.

Riskin, meanwhile, completed two scripts very quickly for Fox. The first and better tale was *Mister 880*, the story of an elderly New York counterfeiter who comes to trial, based on the notes of St. Clair McKelway, who wrote up the real-life story for the *New Yorker*. McKelway's account of the tale, "Old Eight Eighty," appeared in the Annals of Crime in the late August and early September 1949 editions of the magazine. Riskin used the story but went back to the original case as well, reviewing the minutes of the September 3, 1948, court hearing for the Southern District of New York versus Emerich Juettner.[13] Riskin had barely set foot inside the doors of Fox before he took the working title *Old Eight Eighty* and sat down to write a screen treatment of the court case that had now become quite a famous news item. By February 1950, a first draft of the story, now called *Mr. Eight Eighty*, had arrived on Darryl Zanuck's desk. As the drafts appeared, Zanuck personally made notes, and his assistant Michael Abel commented—very favorably—on the style of writing. A final revised draft, dated April 5, 1950, reached Zanuck with an endorsement from Abel, and the movie was subsequently slated for production under the direction of Edmund Goulding.[14]

Goulding's career dated back to the early silent era, and he had made his name at MGM in the 1920s. Having spent time at Warner Brothers before arriving at Fox, he was renowned as a filmmaker who slipped easily into different styles, a talent Zanuck may have been looking for to make the most of Riskin's multidimensional themes. Goulding's two most recent successes had both been vehicles for Tyrone Power, but *The Razor's Edge* (1946) was a flying romance (based on Somerset Maugham's story) while *Nightmare Ally* (1947) was, of all things, a brutal circus story. Goulding certainly picked up on Riskin's inferences in the screenplay. Riskin converted the tale into part noir detective story (an admiring nod to *The Strange Love of Martha Ivers*) and part lighthearted comedy, with Edmund Gwenn playing fraudster Skipper Miller and a young Burt Lancaster as treasury agent Steve Buchanan, looking to track down the counterfeit bills in circulation.

In the story, Buchanan is the latest Secret Service agent charged with solving the ten-year-old case of a small-time fraudster who hands over only a limited number of one-dollar bills at a time, making tracing him virtually impossible. Buchanan does trace one of the bills to Ann Winslow (Dorothy McGuire), a woman who knows Skipper but is unaware of his illicit activity. Buchanan realizes she is an innocent courier of the dollar bills and decides to use her to track down Miller on the pretext of courting her, but he ends up falling in love with her. When Ann realizes that Miller has been passing the bills to her out of kindness, he is finally caught, but she makes sure he is not harshly treated.

David Thomson accurately describes the film, which locks the crime chase together with a nostalgic romance, as a "weird mixture of Fox's postwar realism and grass-root sentimentality."[15] The *Monthly Film Bulletin* describes Miller, who is a throwback to Riskin's earlier reactionary characters, like the colonel in *Meet John Doe* and even Longfellow Deeds, as a "character portrayed with unremitting whimsicality, which is a keynote of the film as a whole."[16] Even in the forgery racket, Riskin appears to state, there can be honor among thieves, respect for those who need help, and some slack cut for the benign and misguided, as opposed to the outright evil and contemptible. In Riskin's narrative setup, Miller's world is fading fast and the modern realities are closing in, but Buchanan, who is Miller's nemesis in this respect, also gets time enough to learn a little humility and feel nostalgia himself while gently closing the door on a society relegated to America's past. Riskin even took some time in the screenplay to reclaim a part of his own past. Key scenes refer to Flatbush, the New York neighborhood where Riskin grew up and learned to love the theater. It was almost as if, through Miller, Riskin was making an attempt to reconcile the past and pay homage to those struggling, penniless years.

Once again, however, it was through the female lead that Riskin established many of the themes and much of the philosophical contemplation in the picture. Ann is the epitome of the postwar American woman. Working at the United Nations as an interpreter, she is intelligent, independent, and incisive. When she discovers the truth about Buchanan, she happily toys with him by laying clues to indicate that she knows who he is and what he is after. It is Ann who first comes to the realization of who her neighbor Skipper is, and she makes Steve see the implications of sending an old man to prison for the rest of his life. Riskin gave her character an enlightened, internationalist, and forward-thinking position in postwar society, and thus Ann became the last in a long line of his female protagonists who revolutionized the roles of women in movies and gave them poise, purpose, and, importantly, a voice.

Variety was very complimentary of the film on its release, and Riskin's return foray into the studio system looked set to be a hit. "Here is a film of gentle humor, pathos and entertainment," wrote the trade paper. It went on to praise Riskin's authentic treatment of the original stories and concluded, "Never has there been so enchanting, so benevolent a fraud . . . it can't miss at the box-office."[17] The film did capture a reasonable audience and was a pretty successful outing for writer and director. Edmund Gwenn won a nomination for best supporting actor at the Academy Awards of 1950, and he won the Golden Globe award in the same category. The film also helped to make Burt Lancaster a major name, and the film's recognition seemed to portend a profitable relationship between Riskin and Zanuck.

Riskin wrote his second screenplay for Fox very swiftly on the back of *Mister 880's* success. *Half Angel*, based on another real-life case, unfortunately had inferior dialogue, casting, and structure from inception to screen. It was also the only film Riskin was associated with during his lifetime that was made in Technicolor. The story's central character possesses multiple personalities: she sleepwalks by night, making an exhibition of herself, but by day is unable to remember anything. Riskin constructed the outline of *Mister 880* and *Half Angel* almost in tandem, but this second story was far too quickly assembled and went before the cameras with far too little rewriting and polishing.

Riskin had always been drawn to the biography of his characters, and both screenplays in their shooting script form give attention to the interactions between players and the formation of their relationships. But Riskin's talent for mixing sharp language with even sharper cultural references was simply not as apparent as it once was. Still, there is a curious underplay of radical social commentary in both screenplays, especially in *Half Angel*. A sense of economic and political dislocation is very much implied in each screenplay and on screen—Goulding's set in *Mister 880*, for example, represents change and progress with the construction work that surrounds Skipper and Ann's apartment building. It is entirely possible that Riskin had become wary of his ideological engagement in light of the anti-Communist purges hovering over Hollywood. *Mister 880* did follow the trend of adapting recent sensational stories for the screen. *Call Northside 777* (1948), *The House on 92nd Street* (1945), and *Boomerang* (1947) had all recently used such a tactic; in the first film's case, Jimmy Stewart played it straight, to striking effect. The docudrama genre that Hollywood had cobbled together from various forms of particularly European neorealist cinema was one Riskin felt quite comfortable with, following his own wartime documentary efforts, and *Mister 880* copied the above films' socially investigative structures and institutional examinations, especially in the voiceover narration that opens the story.

Half Angel, by contrast, makes for very light froth indeed. Director Richard Sale, more at home cowriting pieces for the screen, seemed unsure what to make of the characters. Loretta Young, Riskin's onetime romantic partner, was not strong enough to carry off the part of the sleepwalking Nora, who, while asleep, makes advances toward former boyfriend John Raymond (a horribly miscast Joseph Cotten) but, when awake, denies that she is in love with him.

The film disappeared quite rapidly after its release and was, without question, the biggest disappointment of Riskin's career in both artistic and commercial terms. Why did he pursue two projects so quickly, one after the other, particularly in light of his comments in the last few years about writers' needing time to contemplate their scenarios? He probably wanted to demonstrate to Zanuck, and impress his new studio, that he could produce to order. But by mid-1950, when *Half Angel*'s screenplay was being completed, he possibly already knew that he was becoming ill and hence didn't continue to rewrite and polish his drafts with quite the same care as before. There is also some sense that a social and cultural formula was being rehashed in his films. The distinctiveness of *Magic Town* within Riskin's postwar output was that it directly played to the practical rebuilding and conceptual remodeling of American society after the war. Grandview was certainly a touch sentimental, but that sentiment had a purpose. It balanced progress and corporate conformity with personal ambition and attainment. It also managed to be funny and playful in the tradition of Riskin's best work. David Thomson's description of *Mister 880* applies also to *Half Angel*: both were a bit too whimsical and a little too obviously nostalgic. They had some classic Riskin dialogue, but the latter film in particular seemed mechanical, which Riskin had never been in his writing.

As if driven to complete as much material as he could, Riskin continued to write all the way through 1950. He delivered one more script to Zanuck by the close of the year: *Belvedere*, a story written for actor Clifton Webb. Webb was becoming an established star, having already been nominated for Oscars for Otto Preminger's *Laura* (1944) and Goulding's *The Razor's Edge* (1946). He had also already played Mr. Belvedere, a pompous babysitter, in *Sitting Pretty* (1948) and *Mr. Belvedere Goes to College* (1949), and Riskin's tale was presumably one more script in the series; indeed, Webb went on to do *Mr. Belvedere Rings the Bell* in 1951. Why Riskin agreed to jump into another series of films after his experience with the *Thin Man* series is hard to understand. It can only be assumed that the writing was an assignment from Zanuck, who must have felt Riskin was the man to keep up the impetus of this established comic series. Riskin sent the script to Zanuck only days before the onset of his illness.[18]

A Career Curtailed

On December 27, 1950, Riskin had a major stroke that put an end to his professional career. He was only fifty-three years old at the time, still in the prime of life, still with much to give to the movies, and with a young family whom he adored. It is to the benefit of all that Riskin had established a catalog of work that arguably could not be surpassed by any other screenwriter in its critical and commercial accomplishments.

Fay Wray devoted herself to her husband's care for nearly five years. Friends and family came by on a regular basis. Fay jotted down thoughts, conversations, and little asides that Riskin rehearsed, talked about, and dug up from his past. The war, friends, and associates—some long gone—went through his mind as the stroke and medication fought to control his senses. The family still keeps the notes Fay wrote as she kept a vigil, the papers accumulating through the months. Sadly, the words and conversations jotted down on yellow legal notepaper were not those of Riskin in the present, of how he could and should have been. Yet they represent Bob Riskin entirely. The talk is witty and humorous; the memories involve care and concern for others.

Many occasions are tied up with Riskin's flirting and joking with the nurses and with Fay in his comfortable, charming, graceful way. For Fay and the family, the five years leading up to Riskin's death in September 1955 were hard, no doubt filled with a sense of injustice and disbelief that such a condition should afflict such a positive spirit. Yet those days and the words Fay wrote down so diligently now stand as a very positive testament to the man's humility, his vigor and his zest for life, and his voracious appetite for words.

James Cain, one of the many young Hollywood writers to whom Riskin had offered advice, wrote to Fay after Riskin's passing to say that her husband had helped him to "be my own man" when it came to telling stories. Riskin had told him that a story had to be "a living, individual thing," and Cain remembered how much Riskin's words had made him think about the state of his own writing.[19] This fellow writer's praise is a telling assessment not just of the help Riskin offered but of his generous spirit and general good humor.

Riskin's legacy also lived on in the movies themselves. A 1956 remake of *It Happened One Night* entitled *You Can't Run Away from It* and Capra's own remake of *Lady for a Day* as *Pocketful of Miracles* in 1961, starring Glenn Ford, were satisfactory eulogies to Riskin's ability—if only because, while most critics thought them not bad, many remarked how inferior they were to his original scripts. It is easy to take a similar position with respect to director Steven Brill and actor Adam Sandler's 2002 attempt to remake *Mr. Deed Goes to Town* as *Mr. Deeds*. To be fair, a number of contemporary people could have done a better and more honest job of the adaptation than did Brill and Sandler (the Coen brothers, Gary Ross, Nicolas Cage, Tobey Maguire, George Clooney, Joan Allen, and Reese Witherspoon all spring to mind as having directed or starred in Riskin-like features). But one can find solace in that the comparison of the two movies stands as one of the clearest examples in Hollywood history of an original movie's trumping its updated version in every conceivable aspect, be it humor of the script, rounded characters, pathos, heart, narrative pace, cinematography, or style.

The reason for the failure of the new *Mr. Deeds* is something that Hollywood, by and large, finds it very difficult to admit to-day: even as far back as the 1930s, filmmakers like Robert Riskin set the bar enormously high. The quality of the filmmaking that set apart Riskin, Capra, and the Swerlings, Buchmans, Hacketts, and Hechts of that time has been proven by a longevity that has only brought more evidence of their skill and ability. Too many screenwriters of Hollywood's golden age have suffered from ne-glect when their work deserves the industry's thanks for their belief in quality, their craftsmanship, and their contribution to the art of cinema. That Robert Riskin was a leader among this committed band of writers and filmmakers only makes his cause more deserving and his recognition among a wider community that much more overdue.

EPILOGUE

Donald Ogden Stewart, Dudley Nichols, Robert Riskin . . . I
didn't know of many others. And I didn't admire too many.
—Julius J. Epstein, *Casablanca* writer, when asked
to name screenwriters he knew of or admired

Hardly a man here is in the big money who has not a best-
seller or some striking stories or a successful play to his credit. (A few exceptions to this are John Lee Mahin and Robert
Riskin, who are among the half dozen best picture writers in
the business.) But the rule still stands.
—F. Scott Fitzgerald

In his narrative account of postwar Hollywood, *The Story of Cinema*, David Shipman spends a few moments detailing Robert
Riskin's 1947 production of *Magic Town*. He describes the film as
interesting and quite good in places, but nevertheless remarks on
how the movie's perceived limitations reflected Riskin's dependence on his directorial mentor, Frank Capra.[1] Charles Maland
offers the view that Riskin's early influence in their partnership helped introduce to Capra the "cynical urban types" that
suffused his stories. He also improved the dialogue Capra had
been getting by on with other writers, and he tightened story
construction. Nevertheless, while Riskin operated as a sounding
board for the director, he did not, according to Maland, "create
Capra's social vision."[2] Stephen Handzo, in an article titled "Un-

239

der Capracorn" that dated to the renaissance in the director's work during the 1970s, likewise argues strongly for the lucid quality of the narratives and dialogue that Riskin brought to Capra's pictures. But the "undisciplined mawkishness" of *Magic Town* and the poorly directed *When You're in Love*, in Handzo's estimation, provide ample evidence that Riskin was "dependent on a strong director."[3]

Any assessment of Robert Riskin's career seems to be filled with such statements. Only Patrick McGilligan's succinct appraisal in an introduction to six of Riskin's leading screenplays, as well as the first edition of this book, portion Riskin off from Capra in any meaningful way. Much of the lingering critical and scholarly appreciation, all of it tied to wider assessments of Capra, has remained grudging. Where a critic or scholar hands out a slice of praise, a discordant remark about the writer's work is almost always sure to follow. And the sticking point has forever been the persuasive presence of the man with the name above the title of their films. Even when Riskin's other credits got some attention, as with Handzo, they were often trampled by the weight of the Capra collaborations, which by virtue of their reputation were somehow automatically more worthy than Riskin's additional stories and work. Handzo's appraisal, so close in time and tune with Capra's own self-reverential reassessment of his movies, pours more oil on the fire by claiming that the director's "most effective and visually sophisticated films—*It's a Wonderful Life, Mr. Smith Goes to Washington, The Bitter Tea of General Yen*— are all non-Riskin, suggesting that Riskin's virtue and limitation was his conception of film narrative in playwrighting and novelistic terms," rather than any overtly cinematic spectacle.[4]

Yet Handzo mentions and seemingly endorses the Riskin style in *The Whole Town's Talking* and *Mister 880*, which were without Capra. He also shies away from talk of the "visual sophistication" in *American Madness, Lost Horizon*, or *Meet John Doe*, which the pair made together, and which are as technically striking and visually spectacular as anything Hollywood produced at the time. What this compartmentalization of movies along the lines of directorial authority means is a lesson long in the making, and not just for Riskin's career but for all screenwriters in

Hollywood's history. They became victims of a convenient historical lethargy that too easily dismissed their contribution and happily paraded the director's intent. The difference with some who were later able to tell their tale and set the record straight is that Riskin was not around long enough to defend his work or to contest the assessments of it.

But it wasn't simply that screenwriters needed to survive into retirement to retrospectively make their case for status. Additionally, while the studios sometimes adopted the tactic of assigning projects to teams of writers, or replacing one with another on occasion as if to confirm the scribes' disposable nature, there was the formality of employment itself to overcome, as Ronny Regev notes. The loss of authorship was written into screenwriters' contracts: the material they assembled was the legal property of the studio. Regev describes how Benjamin Kahane, vice president at Riskin's own studio, Columbia, laid out such a relationship in his 1937 testimony to the National Labor Relations Board. The NLRB was investigating the conditions of employment in Hollywood, and Kahane painted a picture of an industry that privileged the producer as the orchestrator of projects. He—for it was almost always a "he"—was the one who engaged the writer(s) to dream up the studio's screenplay, and who needed to be satisfied of a script's quality once it was finished.[5]

Oscar-winning screenwriter Philip Dunne, who was Riskin's colleague at the Office of War Information during the 1940s, saw in a producer's command of the "properties" a studio had at its disposal a lack of trust in judgment about unknown quantities. Adapted material was a far safer bet, and this made original screenplays much harder to come by than one might imagine. Producers tended to acquire already popular stories that had been tried and tested elsewhere. That was why, in Dunne's opinion, the most successful screenwriters like Riskin already had too much on their plates, adapting others' plays, novels, and short stories to write original material for a studio lukewarm about their ideas, although Riskin managed to achieve both.

Yet originality appeared on screen whatever the pedigree of the story filmed. Dunne championed the writers' cause naturally, but more vociferously when the designation "a film by . . ." at

the start of a movie gave so much attention to the director's auteur credentials, even though the premise of the most successful
(adapted) scripts grew out of the imaginings of the writer. "Critics are fond of ruminating on the styles of directors, completely
ignoring the fact that screenwriters make a far more important
stylistic contribution," he said.[6]

Studio control of the rights, process, and credit for scripts
made for a demanding environment, an environment that someone like Dunne only began to shine a spotlight on much later—in
his case during the 1980s—when recollections were in demand
for stories and memories from the Golden Age. Riskin was never
afforded that moment of recall. For more than four years at the
start of the 1950s, residing at the Motion Picture Home in Woodland Hills, Riskin battled his stroke and deteriorating condition.
This difficult time was occasionally punctuated by flashes of lucidity that allowed him to dictate story ideas to Fay Wray, who,
diligently writing down her husband's thoughts in scrapbooks,
hoped and prayed for the day the Bob Riskin she knew would
reemerge. Accounts continued to stress Riskin's wit and mod-
esty. In the spring of 1955, the Screen Writers Guild that Riskin
had helped to found presented him with its Laurel Award for
lifetime achievement. Fay accepted on his behalf, and when she
took it back to Riskin, he managed one of his typical quips, asking, "Do I get to keep it?" It turned out to be the last honor be-
stowed upon him in his lifetime. On September 20, 1955, Riskin
finally succumbed to his illness and died at Woodland Hills. He
was fifty-eight years of age.

Riskin's funeral at the Grace Chapel, Inglewood Park Ceme-
tery, on September 23 drew many film stars, directors, and producers. Riskin's genius was much commented upon, and his
importance to the screenwriting profession was never in doubt
at the time of his death. His friend George Jessel gave the eulogy.
"The story of Robert Riskin is in three acts," he said. "You can
write the first two on a joyous note; you will have to write the last
with a tear."[7] The *Los Angeles Examiner* described the occasion
and drew particular attention to the galaxy of film "notables"
who turned out to pay their respects.[8] Significantly, the report
mentioned one man who wasn't there. He had been absent for
the last five years and, on the day of Riskin's funeral, Frank

Capra still failed to show up.

The reasons for Capra's mysterious absence from the final years of Riskin's life have been speculated about periodically. Victoria Riskin, in her memoir of her mother's and father's lives and careers, surmised that Capra may have still been trying to come to terms with the death of his own son, at a young age, and/or that the debilitating illness of his friend was just too tough a blow to deal with. Ultimately Vicki Riskin felt that working out Capra's motivations and insecurities had taken her a lifetime, when in fact, she realized, it had only taken her father five minutes.[9] Capra found poverty hard to deal with in his younger life but discovered fame and the spotlight even harder to compute when celebrity and influence were his to bestow. Bob Riskin saw that battle play out in Capra's creative impulses time and again. It no doubt influenced Capra's plea for writing credit on *Riding High* in 1950, perhaps in a personal struggle to match what Riskin had once written and prove he could do it himself. Vicki Riskin recounts a tale that her father's fellow writer Sidney Buchman remembers, of how he and Riskin had that ability to take the one "astounding" idea Capra would have out of a multitude of them written down on scraps of paper, and make a gem of a screenplay from it. Capra could have the notion; he just couldn't fashion the fictional world around that idea, and it troubled him to his dying day.[10]

Capra's triumvirate of writers at Columbia, Swerling, Buchman, and Riskin, could access such worlds and created almost a studio manifesto endorsing sharp, sprightly, socially informed dialogue.[11] Riskin's astute sense of Capra's diffidence toward his own writing prowess did little for Riskin's recognition, however. The Capra no-show on the day of Riskin's funeral in September 1955 set a marker for his partner's fading from the scene that Capra did little to halt throughout the rest of his life, and succeeding histories have not only been reluctant to accept rehabilitation but have actively discouraged it on occasion.

At the turn of the millennium, Vito Zagarrio's full-frontal assault on Joe McBride's revisionist thesis of Capra in *Frank Capra: The Catastrophe of Success* confirmed the way Riskin's stock as a screenwriter was tossed around without too much regard for his fundamental place in Hollywood's artistic firmament and industrial structure. In the chapter "It Is (Not) a Wonderful Life" in his and Robert Sklar's edited collection *Frank Capra: Authorship and the Studio System*, Zagarrio suggests that when Capra gets the dates wrong for his aborted attempts to make *Soviet* for MGM, in the preproduction phase of *Lady for a Day* in 1933, that is the extent of McBride's evidence for destroying Capra's authorship of the films the pair made, in favor of Riskin's. Zagarrio goes on to call David Rintels's arguments from the *Los Angeles Times* of 1977 (outlined in the prologue of this book) unworthy of credit because, as McBride mentions only in parentheses, Rintels later married Victoria Riskin. He concludes by stating that the Capra-Riskin dispute was not discovered by McBride but is part of a broader debate on the relations between directors and their fellow artists.[12]

There are all manner of arguments one might use to counter these points, not the least of which is that Zagarrio cites *Lady for a Day* as opening in 1934 when the picture was released in September 1933 (perhaps just to emphasize that anyone can confuse dates). One might add that Vicki Riskin and David Rintels, while acquainted socially, had been out of touch for two or three years when his *Los Angeles Times* article appeared, and so the insinuation of collusion to defend her father in print against Capra is unfounded too. Zagarrio is right that the debate over authorship was not new to McBride's thesis, but Capra's sole-author claim had not, as the works above help to demonstrate, been really tested in the literature before McBride stepped in.

The real underlying element of this historical cut and thrust is that Riskin once again ended up on the wrong side of history, an outlier only occasionally inserting his influence into Capra's oeuvre. It was all too easy with Riskin to keep playing a parlor game of defense and attack, claim and counterclaim, to test the validity of one interpretation over another. This process is the responsibility of the historian, of course, but over the years, with no right of reply, Riskin's absent voice confounded analysis and concealed further rich, historical testament that would have told us a lot about him, and about the screenwriting fraternity more generally. As previously stated, it is not the purpose of this book to condemn Capra for not acknowledging Riskin enough. In truth the charge against Capra is that, rather like other directors with their writers, he did not always understand what he had with Riskin, did not truly comprehend the symbiotic nature of their relationship. The evidence cited in this work does show that Capra was keenly supportive and widely generous in his praise when they worked together, and while it is clear that aspects of that appreciation altered in later years, there are some mitigating circumstances that explain Capra's inability to acknowledge the dynamic that both fed off in each other's company, at least to some degree.

Relationships as personal and professional as Riskin and Capra's often become hugely intricate, delicate affairs over the course of many years. What was once natural teamwork later becomes myopic reminiscence. In a 1980s American Film Institute appreciation of the director, Vicki Riskin heard Capra speak about the origins of some of his and her father's films. *Mr. Deeds Goes to Town* was brought up, and Capra proceeded to talk about its narrative and plot development. He then mentioned "pixilated," a word Riskin had the sisters Jane and Amy Faulkner use to describe Longfellow as slightly quirky in his behavior and manner. But Capra noted in the talk that it had been his idea to use the word. Vicki Riskin exclaimed in our interview about this event that she just hadn't known what to make of the comment. How could Capra have forgotten who originated the word's use? What would be the point of pushing to claim more of the screenplay than he had actually contributed, particularly when he won the Oscar for best director for that movie while Riskin failed to take away the award for best screenplay?[13] Rather like Capra's rebuttal to David Rintels in 1977, it seemed impenitently harsh.

Still, Capra's demeanor suggested that mixed emotions were in play at the very least and were reflected in characters and situations that ran right across his movies. As McBride recognized in his own work on Capra, the sunnier side of Capraesque tended to conceal darker inhibitions and fears, the "emotional peaks and valleys" that the fabled optimistic idealism buried away for a long time in assessments of the director.[14] That Capra liked the attention too, that the twilight of a career sometimes makes it easier to enhance one's reputation at the expense of other contributors, also helps us understand how those contradictory turns in his career left him nervous about a legacy. Capra had spent more than a decade on the sidelines before his autobiography was published, and in Hollywood terms he had been virtually condemned to the "What ever happened to . . . ?" columns. *The Name above the Title* drew acclaim, the tendency toward auteur theory within film scholarship accelerated his newly established classic status, and—unjust as it sounds—Riskin was not there to provide any comeback.

But Riskin's absence from this debate was metaphorical as well as literal. It was the absence and diminution of the screenwriting collective as well as the depreciation of their art. Respect for Riskin's own work had not grown in Hollywood in the time since his death, but that was true for several of his contemporaries too, whether they wrote autobiographies or otherwise. As McBride states, Riskin, together with Jo Swerling and Sidney Buchman, offered what many screenwriters proffered to their directors: they gave Capra something to say and paved the way for his career as a socially conscious filmmaker. Even Capra knew that his writers brought some mesmeric value to the art being created that he couldn't quite capture himself. He confided in McBride that his best films in some way "live forever and they're beyond you. I look at 'em and they don't seem to be mine."[15]

The fact was that Hollywood's attitude toward screenwriters had over decades changed little from Riskin's heyday. As Pat McGilligan points out in *Backstory*, when Leo Rosten surveyed the screenwriters in Hollywood for his groundbreaking work *The Movie Colony* in 1938, he found only seventeen screenwriters who earned more than $75,000 a year, compared to forty-five directors, fifty-four producers and executives, and eighty actors who were in that salary bracket.[16] Back in those days, the final say of directors and the troubled history of the guild that quickly acquired a reputation for activism—never a good thing in a town suspicious of unions—took their toll on the screenwriting business. Writers were permanently undervalued, screenwriters' professional reputations were besmirched, and careers were abridged at the drop of a hat. It should come as no surprise, therefore, to see screenwriters' memoirs as tending to look back embittered or aggrieved. The debate over the relationship and authorial claims of Capra and Riskin, energized by *The Name above the Title*'s success in the 1970s and continuing to the present, is but one precious fragment of a wider, scarred landscape. The American Film Institute has never given a Life Achievement Award to a single screenwriter, except for hyphenates: the brilliant Orson Welles, John Huston, Billy Wilder, Warren Beatty, and Mel Brooks—and it is fair to assume that many filmgoers would identify all five as directors or, in the case of the latter two, actors before they would call them writers. In addition, throughout the Academy's history, honorary Oscars have been given only five times to screenwriters, the most recent of whom, Spike Lee, might also be thought of as a combined writer-director-producer.[17]

The evidence above should be reason enough to reaffirm Riskin's place in the history of Hollywood, not just scriptwriting, in no uncertain terms. His was a status based on trust and respect rather more than blatant ambition and politicking. Riskin felt, in fact, that the latter rarely worked at the studios anyway. It was one of the reasons why Riskin defended his position, explained his actions, and set out his views on writing and the industry on only a few occasions. His caustic and revealing article in the *Hollywood Reporter* following the defection of the so-called "four horsemen" from the Screen Writers Guild to their own Screen Playwrights union in 1936 is perhaps the most outspoken example of such practice.

The piece appeared at one of the few points in Riskin's career, before his government role in the war, at which he felt compelled to stridently defend his beliefs. There were many other times, however, when Riskin's sense of decency, restraint, and respect for his colleagues prevented him from bellowing his opinions or screaming injustice at the studio, on the pages of magazines, or elsewhere. Indeed, the most famous tale of Riskin's career—that he dumped 120 pages of blank typewriter paper on Capra's desk one day and said, "Here! Let's see you give that the Capra touch!"—is apocryphal. As Vicki Riskin confirmed, it would have been a move wholly in keeping with some of her father's most feisty characters, but so untypical of the man himself.[18]

This view of refinement and diplomatic dexterity is reinforced by the near absence of Riskin from *King Cohn*, Bob Thomas's account of Harry Cohn's reign at Columbia. In Thomas's wildly entertaining tale, Riskin never shows up in heated arguments, slamming doors, or losing his temper in the face of Cohn's domineering personality, as colleagues like Sidney Buchman, Dore Schary, and Herman Mankiewicz do. Even though Riskin at times resented his boss's tone as much as these writers did, his dispassionate demeanor seems to reside somewhere just on the periphery of Thomas's stories, observing them with a wry humor. Indeed, Thomas has only one tale to tell of Riskin's mischievous side. Another of Columbia's leading scribes, Dorothy Parker, remarked to Jo Swerling that for four cents she would have Cohn replaced by the studio's security guard, Cap Duncan. In jest, Swerling and Riskin went about setting up a fund for the promotion of Duncan, coffers which quickly swelled on the sympathetic Columbia back lot. Cohn finally got wind of the stunt when the two tried to gamble the lot at Dunes Casino in Palm Springs and the manager added more to the pot.[19] That was Riskin's style: adventurous, clever, witty, and inoffensive even when he might be laughing at others' expense.

As the story suggests, Riskin commanded respect and admiration from his colleagues even in the most lighthearted of moments. And when the tone became more serious, such attitudes never wavered. His role in the formation and establishment of the Screen Writers Guild and his equanimity in the face of potential disaster and uprising—because of the breakaway he then rebutted—helped define his career as an industry spokesperson. But fellow scribes also simply wanted to hear what he had to say about writing, how he managed to construct scenes effortlessly and make the interaction between his players natural and unhindered by clunky words spoken in less than convincing situations. In *Billy Wilder in Hollywood*, author Maurice Zolotov takes a moment to ponder Riskin's laid-back style and easygoing working routine. Wilder was one of Riskin's visitors when he arrived at Columbia as a fledgling writer. Zolotov suggests a flair and confidence in Riskin's appearance that impressed and influenced the young Wilder, and he describes Riskin's habit of sitting on the porch of the back lot at Columbia, writing on his yellow legal pad. "He was not competitive; he wanted every writer to do well," observed the soon-to-be legendary filmmaker, slightly bemused.[20]

It was this generosity of spirit that endeared Riskin to others and, as with Wilder, most likely mystified them too. In a business such as Hollywood, how could someone afford to be so magnanimous to those who were, after all, the likely competition for his screenplay ideas? But Riskin had already fought his way up the studio ladder, knew the perils and pitfalls, and recognized the authority of his position. After all, there were few that came before him. Screenwriters of previous decades worked in silent film, a very different form, and Riskin belonged to a relatively small band of writers who were at the forefront of the "talkie" culture from the start of the 1930s. The pioneering spirit impressed fellow authors simply with what he put on the page, and the rest he felt no need to justify. He probably never told anybody that he had worked his way into Harry Cohn's affections at the studio by tearing apart his own play, *Bless You, Sister*, in that famous screen conference in which he first encountered Capra. He certainly never felt compelled to offer that dicey strategy as the way to win success in Hollywood. Riskin more likely emphasized his apprenticeship, turning out dialogue and stories almost on request in his first couple of years, learning the craft, respecting the talent, and earning a reputation for himself.

<a>The Screenwriter and History

<txt / fl>In the years leading up to and since the first edition of this book, some greater attention has been paid to screenwriters in the annals of Hollywood's past. As well as classic studies by Richard Corliss and Nancy Lynn Schwartz, Steven Maras and Marc Norman have added to the reevaluation of writers and their contribution to the industry. Maras points to the difficulty of revisionism when screenwriting has been caught up in critical waves of analysis on other areas of film, such as reception, and on business theory concerning Hollywood's mass production ethos.[21] Norman's *What Happens Next* is by far the most sweeping history of writers, and Norman's own skill and experience in the profession equip him well for detailing the writer's position as "industrialized . . . typecastable . . . overalled line workers."[22]

In what is in effect a biographical resume of screenwriters and the directors, producers, and moguls that "ran" them, Norman is all too aware of the brilliant talents that came and went in the thirties and forties, amid the pressures for creativity on demand. Few fashioned more dramatic, more striking, and more cutting-edge stories than Ben Hecht (who was *the* Hollywood screenwriter, according to Richard Corliss), Nunnally Johnson (the busiest screenwriter), Jules Furthman (who wrote half of the most entertaining pictures in Hollywood, claims Pauline Kael), and Dudley Nichols (one of the most acclaimed and respected screenwriters of the thirties and forties, suggests Tom Stempel), and Norman gives such talent their due in much the same way as these earlier critics.[23]

But Norman is also careful to single out Samson Raphaelson with Ernst Lubitsch and Riskin with Capra as "profound and re-spectful" partnerships that contested the assumption that a "pla-toon of screenwriters was necessary" to make a movie work.[24] The problems came when the director got all the press, and the more so when their memoirs left the collaborators behind alto-gether. Most of the writers above left some legacy somewhere, whether it was in files, boxes, or interviews where some of their own opinions at least contributed to a growing tapestry of work on writing for the screen. Over the period of a decade, rough-ly 1931–41, however, nobody was more consistently successful, or more contemporarily articulate about the art of screenwrit-ing, than Robert Riskin. Julius Epstein once described Riskin as a very literate writer. "And if he hadn't died," he said, "I think Robert Riskin would have lasted and lasted and lasted."[25]

For Epstein, there was a sophistication and an immediacy in Riskin's dialogue that made it urbane and contemporary, that came from and was about street life. "Dialogue" is a word that comes up time and again in association with his work. Asked what it was about the British film industry that was different from Hollywood in the thirties, W. R. Burnett, who wrote the original story upon which Riskin based *The Whole Town's Talking*, replied that in Britain, filmmakers were interested in telling a story. But in Hollywood, he said, "Dialogue, dialogue, dialogue! Quip, quip, quip! Even in the great American films of that peri-od, like those of Robert Riskin, you'll find the same thing—you had to have a quick reply."[26] Capra put it another way: "Robert Riskin was a very talented man with a fine ear for dialogue. The ear for dialogue was what really intrigued me about Riskin. People always sounded real when he wrote their dialogue, and I worshipped that."[27] To be able to not only write but construct dialogue that was appropriate for each character was much underrated. To be able to do that and use dialogue to tell the story of the times, to document history through the players, was Riskin's gift.

And while many cared deeply and rightly about recognition, and political and creative freedom, as well as regard and financial reward for their work, nobody cared more about screenwriting as a profession than Riskin did. The manner, method, and meticulousness of writing are almost as important to his career as the screenplays themselves. He generated respect through his generosity and admiration of others, but also through his search for perfection within himself. He demonstrated compassion for those he tutored early in their careers, and they recognized his imprint on their later writings. He was liked for the way he deflected attention from his own talent and the spirit with which he dealt with his later illness.

There will be many who will never see John Ford's *The Whole Town's Talking* as being in the same class as *Lady for a Day*, see *Ann Carver's Profession* as nearly as good as or better than *You Can't Take It With You*, consider *Magic Town* as brilliant as *Meet John Doe* or *Mister 880* comparable to *Mr. Deeds Goes to Town*. These may well not be as good films, but in some respects it hardly matters. What each picture demonstrates is that Riskin's work stood independently of any of the directors he worked with, even Capra. Riskin's writing shone when he and Capra shared some of the responsibility for dialogue, character, and pitch, in *Mr. Deeds*, *Lost Horizon*, and *Meet John Doe*, for example. Certainly with Ford's film, with *Magic Town*, and even with *Mister 880*, the success came down to Riskin's script as much as any other component. If these films didn't resonate or sparkle quite as much as the Capra pictures, it was because they operated in the social comedic screwball genre of which Capra was the acknowledged master. Ford, Wellman, and Goulding, with great respect to their individual talents, were not in the same league when it came to that category. If Riskin had gotten the chance to write with Preston Sturges or Billy Wilder, the result might have provided a comparative test with his scriptwriting for Capra. But even without that comparison, the individual accomplishments across the length and breadth of Riskin's work remain astonishing.

Riskin's greatest achievement, though, his most satisfying and arguably finest legacy, was established without Capra: his work in World War II for the OWI. To create, produce, assemble, and endorse the body of work that Riskin did with the *Projections of America* series for the Motion Picture Unit of the OWI's Overseas Bureau was an astonishing feat. To be able, in addition, to say something idealistic, and to add to the considerable reputation of the documentary form, was nothing short of miraculous. The films lay dormant in the vaults of the National Archives and in one or two special collections for years, apart from *Toscanini*, and even that short documentary, once widely available on video, fell into obscurity. Until, that is, I was lucky enough to be part of a filmmaking team, led by director Peter Miller and producer Antje Boehmert, that resurrected the films and Riskin's wartime story in the PBS documentary *Projections of America* (2015). Uncovering previously lost footage, photography, and testimony, *Projections* reassembled Riskin's defining career moment and created an entirely different picture of the way some Allied propaganda worked in the war. Most of the twenty-six films that we spotlighted for the first time in seventy years have only fragmentary imprints of Riskin's writing style, but the signs of his craft and the precision with which he went about his production and managerial business are ingrained in every one of those wartime shorts and left an indelible mark across a documentary we were deeply proud of. Taken as a whole, Riskin's OWI series formed a disquisition on government propaganda, on attitudes toward America at home and overseas, and on the state of the world during its darkest hour. The collection is a legacy worthy of the man's character and capability.

Riskin never worried too much about that legacy, though of course he was not afforded the opportunity to evaluate his career in any meaningful way. Life showed him that when one thing had run its course—characters, stories, partnerships, the war—

you had to move on to the next and not waste time looking back. Riskin moved on from Broadway, from Columbia, from the OWI, and, in the end, from Capra. He did these things not to abandon his place or stake in the role he had but to make progress toward something new. The Capra relationship has marked that progression, but it never clouded Riskin's own judgment of it. Whatever tensions surfaced within their partnership during his career, Riskin's appreciation of Capra's skill was never in doubt. "To be associated with a director who has a keen understanding for your 'outpouring' and who, at the same time, is master of his own craft, is the acme of every screen writer's ambition. A singular experience for a writer is to see his characters come to life on the screen in their true and unmarred form. This Frank Capra accomplishes for you in his masterful and individual way . . . and, generally, just for good measure, throws in some little tidbit of his own, to heighten and clarify your original conception."[28] Riskin made this statement in an article that appeared just as he was finishing the publicity rounds for *Meet John Doe*. He couldn't have been aware that he was closing his partnership with Capra, but his comments do have something of a valedictory sentiment.

No one should be surprised, therefore, that Riskin went in search of another challenge after Capra and put himself in harm's way during the war, for reasons that might seem overly idealistic. But nowhere in his comments, articles, reviews, or interviews is there any indication that Riskin ever wavered in his idealism. His hope for a peaceful world after the war, the oft-remarked-upon sentimentality of some of his stories and characters, his constant delight in helping his friends and family and putting others first—nowhere is there any evidence that this was false sincerity, merely a pretense for those around him.

After all their years apart, and after his mystifying absence during Riskin's period of illness, Capra summed up his relationship with the person he had known best throughout his professional career: "We were good friends. We saw each other a great deal—went out together. It was a very wonderful relationship."[29] Similar feelings of loyalty, affection, and camaraderie for Riskin abound in those who came across him during their careers. If any of that standing and respect dissipated in the years after his death, it was because Hollywood lost him far too soon, before anyone had a chance to take stock and evaluate his colossal contribution to scriptwriting. But the survival of the films, and the continual reworkings of plots and characters that add phrasing, style, and performance to modern scripts by screenwriters as talented and diverse as Aaron Sorkin, Steven Zailian, Elaine May, Phil Alden Robinson, Grant Heslov, Greta Gerwig, and more, mean that, even today, the Riskin touch survives.

Eric Smoodin observes that some of the reverence for Capra's movies, if anything, gathered pace in the aftermath of his death in the early 1990s. While filmmakers as varied as Stephen Frears, the Coen brothers, and Spike Lee imitated scenes and stories from the Capra canon—many of them iconic moments that came from non-Riskin-scripted features, *Mr. Smith* and *Wonderful Life* especially—the writer's oblique poise and prose is there regardless in the work of these contemporaries.[30] The career of Robert Riskin is ultimately a story that existed in the shadows for far too long. On one level, Riskin trod a familiar path of triumph and tragedy that mirrored Hollywood's golden era. Many of cinema's classic generation that left too soon had tales to tell of dramatic excess and heartrending loss. Such extremes were never quite the arc of Riskin's life. But in his pursuit of Hollywood fame as well as in accomplishing a run of screenplays that remain virtually unparalleled in their consistent quality, he has as much right as anyone to claim a significant place in the mythology of American cinema. For Robert Riskin was simply one of the finest screenwriters of Hollywood's finest age.

FILMOGRAPHY

Riskin as Writer

Mr. Deeds (2002) (film *Mr. Deeds Goes to Town*)

Pocketful of Miracles (1961) (story)

You Can't Run Away from It (1956) (also earlier screenplay)

Here Comes the Groom (1951) (story)

Half Angel (1951)

Mister 880 (1950)

Riding High (1950)

Magic Town (1947) (story) (written by)

The Strange Love of Martha Ivers (1946) (uncredited)

The Thin Man Goes Home (1945) (story)

Meet John Doe (1941)
. . . a.k.a. Frank Capra's *Meet John Doe* (USA: complete title)
. . . a.k.a. *John Doe, Dynamite* (UK)

You Can't Take It with You (1938) (screenplay)

Lost Horizon (1937) (screenplay)
. . . a.k.a. *Lost Horizon of Shangri-La* (USA: TV title)

When You're in Love (1937)
. . . a.k.a. *For You Alone* (UK)

Mr. Deeds Goes to Town (1936) (screenplay)

The Whole Town's Talking (1935)
. . . a.k.a. *Passport to Fame* (UK)

Carnival (1935) (also story)
. . . a.k.a. *Carnival Nights* (UK)

Broadway Bill (1934)
. . . a.k.a. *Strictly Confidential* (UK)

It Happened One Night (1934) (screenplay)

Lady for a Day (1933) (screenplay)

Ann Carver's Profession (1933)

Ex-Lady (1933) (story)

Virtue (1932)

Vanity Street (1932) (uncredited)

Night Club Lady (1932)

American Madness (1932)

Shopworn (1932)

The Big Timer (1932) (also story)

Three Wise Girls (1932)

Men in Her Life (1931)

Platinum Blonde (1931) (dialogue)

The Miracle Woman (1931) (play: *Bless You, Sister*)

Arizona (1931) (adaptation) (dialogue)
. . . a.k.a. *Men Are Like That*
. . . a.k.a. *The Virtuous Wife*

Illicit (1931)

Many a Slip (1930) (play)

Riskin as Producer

Magic Town (1947) (producer)

The Real Glory (1939) (associate producer) (producer)

They Shall Have Music (1939) (associate producer)
. . . a.k.a. *Melody of Youth* (UK)
. . . a.k.a. *Ragged Angels* (USA: reissue title)

Riskin as Director

When You're in Love (1937)
. . . a.k.a. *For You Alone* (UK)

Office of War Information

Between 1942 and 1945, Riskin supervised, coproduced, and codirected twenty-six features for the Bureau of Overseas Motion Pictures, Office of War Information. Notable titles in this Projections of America series include the following:

Swedes in America

The Town

Toscanini

Valley of the Tennessee

Autobiography of a Jeep

NOTES

Prologue

1. Fay Wray, *On the Other Hand: A Life Story* (New York: St. Martin's Press, 1989), 239.

2. Ibid., 241–45.

3. Hersholt fell seriously ill during his own career, on the set of von Stroheim's masterpiece. After two months on location in Death Valley, he found himself in the hospital with a hemorrhage brought on by temperatures of 132 degrees in the shade. Ian Hamilton, *Writers in Hollywood, 1915–1951* (New York: Carroll and Graf, 1991), 25.

4. Marc Norman, *What Happens Next: A History of American Screenwriting* (London: Aurum, 2008), 484.

5. Joseph McBride, *Frank Capra: The Catastrophe of Success* (London: Faber and Faber, 1992), 550.

6. McBride cites Richard Breen, Barney Dean, and William Morrow as writers with whom Capra also tried to work and/or who added some finishing touches to the script of *Riding High*. Ibid., 550.

7. Pat McGilligan, introduction to *Six Screenplays* by Robert Riskin (Berkeley: University of California Press, 1997), lxvi.

8. McBride, *Frank Capra*, 619.

9. David W. Rintels, "Someone's Been Sitting in His Chair," Calendar, *Los Angeles Times*, June 5, 1977; Frank Capra, "'One Man, One Film'—The Capra Contention," Calendar, *Los Angeles Times*, June 26, 1977.

10. David W. Rintels, "'Someone Else's Guts'—The Rintels Rebuttal," Calendar, *Los Angeles Times*, June 26, 1977.

11. Leland Poague asserts that Capra included his thoughts on the personal auteurist vision of his films in two articles: "A Sick Dog Tells Where It Hurts" (*Esquire*, January 1936) and "Sacred Cows to the Slaughter" (*Stage*, July 1936). Leland Poague, *Another Frank Capra* (Cambridge: Cambridge University Press, 1994), 2, 246.

12. Sarris took his cue from the French magazine *Cahiers du Cinéma*'s ini-

tial 1955 list of what the magazine's critics considered to be the sixty greatest American directors to that point, Capra among them. Andrew Sarris, "The Auteur Theory and the Perils of Pauline," *Film Quarterly* 16, no. 4 (Summer 1963): 26–33.

13. James Childs, "Capra Today," *Film Comment* 8, no. 4 (November 1972): 22–23.

14. Virginia Wright Wexman, *Hollywood's Artists: The Directors Guild of America and the Construction of Authorship* (New York: Columbia University Press, 2020), 31.

15. Capra, "One Man, One Film."

16. Wray's remarks were confirmed in the author's interview with Riskin and Wray's daughter, Victoria Riskin, Los Angeles, July 15, 2003.

17. Lewis Jacobs, "Film Directors at Work: Frank Capra," in "Meet John Doe": *Frank Capra, Director,* ed. Charles Wolfe (New Brunswick, NJ: Rutgers University Press, 1989), 200–202.

18. Joseph McBride, *Frankly: Unmasking Frank Capra* (Berkeley, CA: Hightower, 2019), 33–34.

19. McBride, *Frank Capra,* 619.

20. Wray recounts that, among others, Lew Wasserman, Jack Benny, Edward G. Robinson, and Irving Berlin all came to see Riskin, but she makes no mention of Capra. Wray, *On the Other Hand,* 245.

21. Tom Stempel, *FrameWork: A History of Screenwriting in the American Film,* 3rd ed. (Syracuse, NY: Syracuse University Press, 2000), 63–69.

22. Ibid., 65.

23. Richard Corliss, *Talking Pictures: Screenwriters in the American Cinema* (New York: Penguin, 1974), 5.

24. Ibid., 218.

25. "Film Review—Lady for a Day," *Variety,* December 31, 1932, https://variety.com/1932/film/reviews/lady-for-a-day-1200410740/.

1. The Miracle Man

1. Victoria Riskin, personal communication with the author, January 1, 2004.

2. McBride, *Frank Capra,* 235.

3. McGilligan, introduction to *Six Screenplays,* xv.

4. Riskin gave an account of his early life, as close to anything about his pre-Hollywood days as there is in existence, to *Collier's.* Jerry D. Lewis, "Top Story Man," *Collier's,* March 29, 1941, 21, 83–84.

5. McGilligan, introduction to *Six Screenplays,* xv.

6. McBride, *Frank Capra,* 235.

7. Charles Maland says that Riskin did indeed attend Columbia, while McGilligan notes only that others claim he did. Charles Maland, *Frank Capra* (New York: Twayne, 1995), 64; McGilligan, introduction to *Six Screenplays,* xvi.

8. *New York Times,* "Sunny Spain for Mr. Riskin," November 4, 1937. The unsigned article discusses Riskin's early career in the context of his later work.

9. Fay Wray, "Biography of Robert Riskin as Screen Writer" (unpublished manuscript), 2.

10. McGilligan, introduction to *Six Screenplays*, xv.

11. Ibid., xvi.

12. In both Maland's and McBride's accounts, the play (and later the film) was based on the more famous evangelist, Aimee Semple McPherson. Maland, *Frank Capra*, 54; McBride, *Frank Capra*, 227.

13. Victoria Riskin, personal communication with the author, January 1, 2004.

14. *New York Times*, "Woman Evangelist in Bless You, Sister," December 27, 1927; *Herald Tribune*, December 27, 1927; *New York Telegraph*, December 27, 1927; *Variety*, December 27, 1927; *Brooklyn Times*, December 27, 1927. In the film, Bickford played the part of Timothy Bradley, the Bible salesman turned impresario for Mary who makes her a star. Bickford received rave notices for his performance.

15. McGilligan, introduction to *Six Screenplays*, xviii. Later in Riskin's career, Fitzgerald periodically came back into the picture and was sometimes known as the "ex-wife" in the press. Why Riskin, who must surely have read at least some of the reports, never put out an official account of their relationship for the press remains a mystery.

16. Burns Mantle, ed., *The Best Plays of 1929–30 and the Year Book of the Drama in America* (New York: Dodd, Mead, 1930). The book officially reports the number of performances at fifty-six, although McGilligan attributes twenty-four in his analysis. He also quotes the *New York Times* review of *Many a Slip*, which described some of the humor as "labored and obviously manufactured to snare easy laughs" but acknowledged the play had "moments [which] cause you to sit up and wonder." McGilligan, introduction to *Six Screenplays*, xviii.

17. Pat McGilligan, *Backstory: Interviews with Screenwriters of Hollywood's Golden Age* (Berkeley: University of California Press, 1986), 4–5.

18. Corliss, *Talking Pictures*, 219.

19. Victoria Riskin added a little more to the tale. She suggested that Riskin, thinking his bold plan had backfired, kept pretending to press the down button on the elevator for some minutes, until the Warner Brothers attorney emerged with a higher offer. Victoria Riskin, interview with the author, July 14, 2003. There is a story, later included in Riskin's profile, that he had tried to get into Hollywood first. Legend has it that he had only $1.25 in his pocket after the crash (probably at the end of 1929 or perhaps early in 1930) and that he used this to send a wire to Budd Schulberg at Paramount to ask for a job. Schulberg is supposed to have replied that he was "overmanned," a word Riskin never forgot in alluding to his work ethic as a scribe. The problem is that while Schulberg was indeed a prodigy at Paramount, he didn't join the studio until he was seventeen, sometime in 1931, at which time Riskin was most probably already on the West Coast. It is possible that he made contact with Schulberg (a New Yorker himself) just as he arrived in Hollywood or immediately prior to being offered a job at Columbia. See Virginia Wright, *Los Angeles Daily News*, September 9, 1947.

20. McGilligan, introduction to *Six Screenplays*, xviii.

21. Ibid. McGilligan uses the "boy prodigy" phrase to describe Riskin's developing reputation on Broadway, which the Hollywood studios' East Coast offices were spotting.

22. McGilligan, *Backstory*, 5.

23. Bernard F. Dick, *The Merchant Prince of Poverty Row: Harry Cohn of Columbia Pictures* (Lexington: University Press of Kentucky, 1993), 9. See also Bob Thomas's no-holds-barred account of Cohn's life and times. Thomas paints a picture of Cohn's almost patriarchal treatment of his writers, punctuated by moments when he would simply scream, "You are stealing my money!" because no new scenes or scripts were forthcoming. Bob Thomas, *King Cohn: The Life and Times of Hollywood Mogul Harry Cohn* (Beverly Hills: New Millennium Press, 2000), 80–86.

24. Wright, *Los Angeles Daily News*, September 9, 1947.

25. Lewis, "Top Story Man," 83–84.

26. Maland, *Frank Capra*, 63.

27. Ethan Mordden, *The Hollywood Studios: Their Unique Styles during the Golden Age of Movies* (New York: Fireside, 1988), 179.

28. Ibid.

29. Maland, *Frank Capra*, 63.

30. In his book, Bergman emphasizes his belief in Capra's importance by devoting a whole chapter to him. Andrew Bergman, "Frank Capra and the Screwball Comedy, 1931–1941," in *We're in the Money: Depression America and Its Films* (Chicago: Ivan R. Dee, 1992), 132–48.

31. Ray Carney, *American Vision: The Films of Frank Capra* (Hanover, NH: Wesleyan University Press, 1986), 137–52.

32. Dick, *Merchant Prince*, 49.

33. Vito Zagarrio, "It Is (Not) a Wonderful Life: For a Counter-reading of Frank Capra," in *Frank Capra: Authorship and the Studio System*, ed. Robert Sklar and Vito Zagarrio, 83 (Philadelphia: Temple University Press, 1998).

34. Capra spoke of courage and eternity being revealed to him and seemed to take stock of his own religious experiences earlier in life in writing about the film. Frank Capra, *The Name above the Title: An Autobiography* (New York: Macmillan, 1971), 130–31.

35. Riskin and Swerling's friendship persisted to the very end of Riskin's life. Swerling's own career has been unfairly neglected in Hollywood history. In addition to the films Swerling made with and for Capra and Riskin, he penned *Washington Merry-Go-Round* (1932), *Pennies from Heaven* (1936), *The Westerner* (1940), *The Pride of the Yankees* (1942), and *Lifeboat* (1944) and wrote the play that became the musical *Guys and Dolls*, to name only a few of his credits. He thoroughly deserves to have more retrospectives of his films and a memoir of his career documented and brought to wider attention.

36. McBride, *Frank Capra*, 231.

37. Carney, *American Vision*, 138.

38. Edward Bernds, *Mr. Bernds Goes to Hollywood* (London: Scarecrow Press, 1999), 143–45.

39. By 1940, the play was being made again in Hollywood, this time as *His Girl Friday*, directed by Howard Hawks and starring once more Cary Grant, together with Ralph Bellamy and Rosalind Russell.

40. Capra, *Name above the Title*, 134.

41. An exception to this rule is Riskin's much later film, *Magic Town*; the reasons for that rural setting are discussed further in chapter 6.

42. Richard Maltby, "*It Happened One Night*: The Recreation of the Patriarch," in Sklar and Zagarrio, *Frank Capra*, 134.

43. Carney, *American Vision*, 152.

44. Carney quotes Derrida here in offering the view that Smith, at the conclusion of the picture, sees for the first time the "structurality of structure," or in other words the possibility of actually becoming a playwright and not having to belong to one of the social systems or structures that he has been subject to so far in the film. Ibid., 149–50.

45. Poague, *Another Frank Capra*, 78.

46. Joseph McBride points out that the script was tinkered with by many hands at Columbia and therefore emerged as quite a muddled piece. McBride, *Frank Capra*, 229–30.

47. Ibid., 240, 233. Stanwyck actually went on to divorce Fay in 1935 and, in 1939, married actor Robert Taylor.

2. The Big Timer

1. *Los Angeles Examiner*, "'Arizona' Powerful Drama Enhanced by Fine Cast," July 24, 1931.

2. These three early scripts are held in Robert Riskin Papers, Scripts, box 2, Fay Wray Collection, Cinema-Television Library, University of Southern California, Los Angeles.

3. For a review of *Night Club Lady*, see *Hollywood Reporter*, "Good Yarn Hurts 'Painted Woman,'" August 4, 1932.

4. McBride relays a 1937 report from the *New York Times* that suggested Riskin was on the verge of being sacked prior to *Platinum Blonde*. McBride, *Frank Capra*, 232.

5. McGilligan, introduction to *Six Screenplays*, xxi n. 17.

6. *Herald Tribune*, June 9, 1933; *New York Times*, June 9, 1933.

7. The script for *Ann Carver's Profession* with Riskin's personal changes is held in Robert Riskin Papers, Scripts, box 2, Fay Wray Collection, Cinema-Television Library, University of Southern California, Los Angeles.

8. Hamilton, *Writers in Hollywood*, 112.

9. Bergman, *We're in the Money*, xi.

10. The Gianninis are often cited in the literature as inspiration for Tom Dickson. The comparison seems fair, but the actual evidence from Riskin that Dickson was meant to represent the Bank of America founders is at best sketchy. See McGilligan, introduction to *Six Screenplays*, xxvi, and Maland, *Frank Capra*, 70.

11. *Collier's*, March 29, 1941, 21.

12. Somewhat confusingly, Joseph McBride seems to hint at both scenarios

for Riskin: original story and studio assignment. In the space of two pages, he first writes that Riskin put the finishing touches on his original story while Capra was away in Europe, and then writes that, having been assigned the job of writing the tale, Riskin went to see Doc Giannini. McBride, *Frank Capra*, 247, 249.

13. Andrew Sarris, *"You Ain't Heard Nothing Yet": The American Talking Film; History and Memory, 1927–1949* (New York: Oxford University Press, 1998), 104.

14. Lary May, *The Big Tomorrow: Hollywood and the Politics of the American Way* (Chicago: University of Chicago Press, 2000), 86–87.

15. Ibid., 89.

16. Capra, *Name above the Title*, 137.

17. McBride, *Frank Capra*, 252; Rochelle Larkin, *Hail, Columbia* (New Rochelle, NY: Arlington House, 1975). McBride quotes Capra from a 1973 interview with Richard Glatzer. He also cites the Larkin assessment that Capra had come up with the narrative for *American Madness*.

18. McBride, *Frank Capra*, 241–51.

19. Capra, *Name above the Title*, 129.

20. Corliss, *Talking Pictures*, 219; Poague, *Another Frank Capra*, 110.

21. Poague, *Another Frank Capra*, 112.

22. Eric Smoodin, *Regarding Frank Capra: Audience, Celebrity, and American Film Studies, 1930–1960* (Durham, NC: Duke University Press, 2004), 29–36. See also Laura Mulvey, "Visual Pleasure and Narrative Cinema," *Screen* 16, no. 3 (Autumn 1975): 6–18, and Jackie Stacey, *Star Gazing: Hollywood Cinema and Female Spectatorship* (London: Routledge, 1994).

23. Smoodin, *Regarding Frank Capra*, 35.

24. Mulvey, "Visual Pleasure and Narrative Cinema," quoted in Joanne Hollows, Peter Hutchings, and Mark Jancovich, eds., *The Film Studies Reader* (London: Arnold, 2000), 242.

25. Corliss, *Talking Pictures*, 215.

26. Richard Corliss, "Capra & Riskin," *Film Comment* 8, no. 4 (November 1972): 18.

27. Carney argues that the economic savings that Capra achieved for Columbia using this tactic differed markedly from practices at, say, Warner Brothers, where lots of generic, rather imprecise sets were used over and over again for a variety of settings. Carney, *American Vision*, 114.

28. Capra, *Name above the Title*, 139–40.

29. McBride, *Frank Capra*, 252.

30. Carney, *American Vision*, 115.

31. The *New York World* review (August 10, 1932) compared the picture to the recent *Washington Masquerade* starring Lionel Barrymore, also a feature about economics, this one mixed with politics. It thought *American Madness* daring and plausible. The *Christian Science Monitor* (August 10, 1932) described *American Madness* as a "thriller without an offending note," while the *Cleveland Plain Dealer* (August 10, 1932) thought President Hoover should give Columbia Pictures a hug for the "melodramatic sermon it preaches."

32. Colin Shindler, *Hollywood in Crisis: Cinema and American Society, 1929–1939* (London: Routledge, 1996), 74–75.

33. McBride cites Rapf as the man who came up with the title, though Capra credits himself and Riskin ("We called our first effort . . ."). McBride, *Frank Capra*, 252; Capra, *Name above the Title*, 137.

34. Thomas Schatz, "Anatomy of a House Director: Capra, Cohn, and Columbia in the 1930s," in Sklar and Zagarrio, *Frank Capra*, 20.

35. Robert Sklar, "A Leap into the Void," in Sklar and Zagarrio, *Frank Capra*, 59.

36. Schatz describes Columbia's 1929–30 budgets for its films to show how Cohn protected his assets and grew slowly and carefully. While the studio's most comparable rivals, Paramount and Universal, regularly gave over to $500,000 and even $1 million budgets at this time, Columbia stayed in the $50,000 to $150,000 range, with only an occasional foray into costs of $200,000. Schatz, "Anatomy of a House Director," 16.

37. Ibid., 21.

38. Capra, *Name above the Title*, 140.

39. Robert Riskin, *Los Angeles Herald*, October 1, 1932.

40. *Los Angeles Herald*, "Undersea Tale to Star Holt," September 12, 1932.

41. Riskin's one proviso in handing over *The Bottom of the Sea* to the studio was that he kept dramatic rights. It is not clear whether this became a dispute over the script. *Los Angeles Evening Herald and Press*, "Columbia May Get Robert Riskin's 'Confield' Play," August 31, 1932; James Mitchell, "Dr. Millikan's Life Will Be Basis for Film," *Los Angeles Examiner*, August 31, 1932. Interestingly, these reports were filed on the same day, and both cited conversations with Riskin. He may have been smart enough to believe he wanted to give an exclusive to both papers. Either way, his name was now widely known around the studios.

42. *Los Angeles Evening Herald and Press*, "Columbia May Get Robert Riskin's 'Confield' Play."

43. Some accounts suggest that the film was banned in Britain, but McBride points out that it was passed by the British Board of Censors after a few additional cuts. McBride, *Frank Capra*, 282.

44. The copy of the script in Riskin's papers goes under a number of headings, including *Apple Annie* and *Beggar's Holiday*, both of which are scribbled out on the title page and finally replaced with *Lady for a Day* in Riskin's own hand. Robert Riskin Papers, Scripts, box 2, Fay Wray Collection, Cinema-Television Library, University of Southern California, Los Angeles.

45. McBride, *Frank Capra*, 289–91.

46. Eileen Creelman, "Picture Plays and Players," *New York Sun*, September 13, 1934.

47. *New York Telegraph*, March 1934, quoted in McBride, *Frank Capra*, 290.

48. Thomas, *King Cohn*, 88.

49. Carney, *American Vision*, 231.

50. Damon Runyon to Robert Riskin, September 8, 1933. Robert Riskin Papers, Fay Wray Collection, Cinema-Television Library, University of Southern California, Los Angeles. See also McGilligan, introduction to *Six Screenplays*, xxxi.

51. Donald C. Willis, *The Films of Frank Capra* (Metuchen, NJ: Scarecrow Press, 1974), 140.

52. McBride, *Frank Capra*, 295.

53. Capra, *Name above the Title*, 149.

54. For a comparison of the two films, see Dick, *Merchant Prince*, 111.

55. Bernds, *Mr. Bernds*, 170.

56. McBride, *Frank Capra*, 236.

57. Orson Welles, for whom Mankiewicz wrote *Citizen Kane*, summed up Mank's attitude and much of the screenwriting fraternity in Hollywood when he said, "The big studio-system often made writers feel like second-class citizens, no matter how good the money was. They laughed it off of course, and provided a good deal of the best fun—when Hollywood, you understand, was still a funny place. But basically, you know, a lot of them were pretty bitter and miserable. And nobody was more miserable, more bitter, and more funny than Mank . . . a perfect monument of self-destruction." David Thomson, *Rosebud: The Story of Orson Welles* (London: Abacus, 1997), 147.

58. Richard Meryman, *Mank: The Wit, World, and Life of Herman Mankiewicz* (New York: Morrow, 1978), 171, quoted in Hamilton, *Writers in Hollywood*, 96.

59. Hamilton, *Writers in Hollywood*, 95–96.

60. Ian Hamilton's account of the guild's battle for recognition is forceful and instructive. Ibid., 93–103.

61. Maland, *Frank Capra*, 79.

62. McGilligan, introduction to *Six Screenplays*, xxxv; McBride, *Frank Capra*, 303.

63. McGilligan, introduction to *Six Screenplays*, xxxi.

64. The profession of reporter seems, in retrospect, an obvious choice, but it wasn't at the time. Either Riskin was aware that he was already beginning to typecast some of his leading characters, or else he just wanted to do something different with Warne's character. Warne started off as an artist before becoming an inventor until, finally, Riskin stuck with his already tested profession. Bernds, *Mr. Bernds*, 219.

65. McGilligan relates the tale from Capra's autobiography but makes sure to acknowledge that Riskin knew when to take on board ideas from outside and how to use them. It may not have been entirely his own ploy to convert Warne and Andrews, but it was his dialogue and manipulation of the story that consolidated such a successful change. McGilligan, introduction to *Six Screenplays*, xxxii.

66. Bergman, *We're in the Money*, 133.

67. Ibid.

68. McBride has Riskin pitching the story to Cohn as a hit and mentions a number of other actresses, including Bette Davis and Loretta Young, as candidates for the role of Ellie. McBride, *Frank Capra*, 303–5.

69. McGilligan, introduction to *Six Screenplays*, xxxvii.

70. Sklar argues that *Ladies of Leisure* fits his thesis because it has something of a "false" happy ending, Kay Arnold's suicide leap from the boat ultimately failing. Sklar, "A Leap into the Void," 39–46.

71. Riskin, *Six Screenplays*, 312–13.

72. Capra owed $4,950 in back taxes. *Los Angeles Examiner*, August 20, 1934.

73. Hellinger's story was originally titled "On the Nose." The gist of the story appears later in one of Hellinger's columns, a thank-you piece that shows the author's appreciation for Riskin and Capra's adaptation. (Hellinger himself, or an associate, must have earlier provided Riskin with the story.) Mark Hellinger, "All in a Day," *New York Daily Mirror*, 1934.

74. California remained one of the few places in the United States where racing survived and, indeed, thrived in the first couple of decades of the twentieth century, an era when Prohibition and anti-gambling movements had lent a restrained, morally conservative atmosphere to many parts of the country, including parts of the West Coast. Tanforan was one of the few tracks to maintain a healthy business turnover. For a nice summary of the era, see Laura Hillenbrand, *Seabiscuit: The Making of a Legend* (London: Fourth Estate, 2001), 3–21.

75. Maland, *Frank Capra*, 85.

76. *Los Angeles Examiner*, October 21, 1934; *Hollywood Reporter*, July 1, 1935.

77. *Los Angeles Examiner*, "6 Best Film Stories Named," December 21, 1934.

78. Maland, *Frank Capra*, 67.

79. Carney, *American Vision*, 155–222.

80. Martin Rubin, "The Crowd, the Collective and the Chorus: Busby Berkeley and the New Deal," in *Movies and Mass Culture*, ed. John Belton (London: Athlone, 1996), 82–83.

81. Maland, *Frank Capra*, 65.

3. The Partnership

Epigraph quoted from the version of the shooting script with the signatures of Capra, Cooper, and Jean Arthur on the inside front page and held in Robert Riskin Papers, Scripts, box 2, Fay Wray Collection, Cinema-Television Library, University of Southern California, Los Angeles.

1. Magazines as ideologically far apart as *Time* and *New Masses* thought *Mr. Deeds* the "funniest and most spiritually nourishing" film of the season, a "social film" with realistic portrayals of the unemployed. *Time*, April 27, 1936, 36; *New Masses*, April 28, 1936, 29.

2. McBride, *Frank Capra*, 318.

3. Robert Riskin, "The Canine Era," *Hollywood Reporter*, December 31, 1934, 59, 103.

4. Garrett D. Byrnes, "Film 'Carnival' Shows Riskin's Narrative Skill," *Providence (RI) Bulletin*. The clipping, held in Riskin's papers, is undated but is almost certainly from March 1935, the film having opened only a few days after *It Happened One Night* won a full set of Oscars at the ceremony for 1934, held on February 27, 1935. Robert Riskin Papers, box 4:21, Fay Wray Collection, Cinema-Television Library, University of Southern California, Los Angeles.

5. Bernds, *Mr. Bernds*, 254–55.

6. For an account of Cowan's relations with Columbia, see Dick, *Merchant Prince*, 131–34.

7. "W. R. Burnett: The Outsider as Interviewed by Ken Mate and Pat Mc-Gilligan," in McGilligan, *Backstory*, 63–64. See also Scott Eyman, *"Print the Legend": The Life and Times of John Ford* (New York: Simon and Schuster, 1999), 188.

8. Andrew Sinclair, *John Ford* (New York: Dial Press, 1979), 59.

9. Tag Gallagher, *John Ford: The Man and His Films* (Berkeley: University of California Press, 1986), 107.

10. Jean Mitry, *John Ford*, 2nd ed. (Paris: Editions universitaires, 1964), quoted in Gallagher, *John Ford*, 108.

11. Gallagher, *John Ford*, 111.

12. Ibid., 110.

13. "W. R. Burnett: The Outsider," 64.

14. Sarris, *American Talking Film*, 178.

15. Stephen Handzo describes Jean Arthur's role in *The Whole Town's Talking* as a "proto-*Deeds*" character. Stephen Handzo, "Under Capracorn," in *Frank Capra: The Man and His Films*, ed. Richard Glatzer and John Raeburn, 167 (Ann Arbor: University of Michigan Press, 1975).

16. Unsigned review of *The Whole Town's Talking*, directed by John Ford, *Variety*, reprinted in Derek Elley, ed., Variety *Movie Guide 1997*, 1050 (London: Hamlyn, 1996).

17. Coombs argues that *"The Whole Town's Talking* lightly anticipates and combines a style and a theme that would subsequently go their separate ways in Ford: the expressionism of his morality plays (*The Informer, The Long Voyage Home, The Fugitive*) and the notion of an ideal realm conjured up through the dream mechanism of cinema already taking shape in films like *Judge Priest* and *Steamboat Round the Bend* to reach its culmination in *The Sun Shines Bright*." Richard Coombs, review of *The Whole Town's Talking*, directed by John Ford, *Monthly Film Bulletin* 47, no. 556 (May 1980): 99–100.

18. Grace Wilcox, "From Poverty Row to Riches," *Screen and Radio Weekly*, July 18, 1935.

19. McBride, *Frank Capra*, 328.

20. "'Opera Hat' Replaces 'Horizon' for Capra on 35–36 Program," *Hollywood Reporter*, July 1, 1935.

21. McBride, *Frank Capra*, 334.

22. Louis B. Mayer was even more blatant than Cohn: he sent down a memo to his employees that simply said, "Stop Sinclair!" Nancy Lynn Schwartz, *The Hollywood Writers' Wars* (New York: Knopf, 1982), 35–39.

23. Ibid., 71.

24. McBride, *Frank Capra*, 237.

25. Schwartz, *Hollywood Writers' Wars*, 71.

26. Robert Riskin, "I Was Going Along Minding My Own Business," *Hollywood Reporter*, May 7, 1936.

27. For some time, Mahin defended his position by claiming that the screenwriters had wanted another union, which Riskin's article contradicts, coming from the inside of the process, as it were. However, Tom Stempel's work quotes Mahin from a 1968 UCLA oral history project in which he admits that his boss

at MGM, Irving Thalberg, who detested the thought of a guild antithetical to the interests of the studios, suggested that the right-wing faction start its own organization, ultimately the Screen Playwrights. Stempel, *FrameWork*, 139.

28. Larry Ceplair and Steven Englund, *The Inquisition in Hollywood: Politics in the Film Community, 1930–1960* (Berkeley: University of California Press, 1983), 38.

29. Schwartz, *Hollywood Writers' Wars*, 64.

30. *Hollywood Reporter*, "Bob Riskin Upped to Producer Rank," June 24, 1936.

31. McBride, *Frank Capra*, 237–38.

32. Corliss, *Talking Pictures*, 221.

33. Bergman, *We're in the Money*, 142.

34. Dudley Early, "Mr. Capra and Mr. Riskin Go to Town," *Family Circle*, October 23, 1936, 14–17, 22.

35. As Bob Thomas explains, Capra and Riskin were allowed to prepare scripts without interference, and Cohn scarcely ever visited them on the set. Thomas, *King Cohn*, 118.

36. Early, "Mr. Capra and Mr. Riskin Go to Town."

37. McGilligan, introduction to *Six Screenplays*, xlii.

38. McGilligan points out that Kelland would, in 1942, become publicity director of the Republican National Committee. Ibid., xlv.

39. Riskin, *Six Screenplays*, 461.

40. Ibid., 422.

41. Unsigned review of *Mr. Deeds Goes to Town*, directed by Frank Capra, *Variety*, reprinted in Derek Elley, ed., Variety *Movie Guide 1993*, 468 (London: Hamlyn, 1992).

42. Carney, *American Vision*, 6.

43. Riskin, *Six Screenplays*, 456.

44. For a further discussion of West's Hollywood contributions, see Hamilton, *Writers in Hollywood*, 157–65.

45. For a further elaboration of the presidential motif in Capra's films, see Ian Scott, "Populism, Pragmatism, and Political Reinvention: The Presidential Motif in the Films of Frank Capra," in *Hollywood's White House: The American Presidency in Film and History*, ed. Peter C. Rollins and John E. O'Connor, 180–92 (Lexington: University Press of Kentucky, 2003).

46. McBride, *Frank Capra*, 348.

47. Alistair Cooke's statement has been quoted a number of times, notably in McBride's biography and Bergman's assessment of thirties films. McBride, *Frank Capra*, 350; Bergman, *We're in the Money*, 144.

48. Robert Sklar, *Movie-Made America: A Social History of American Movies* (New York: Random House, 1975), 196.

49. Charles Maland, "*Mr. Deeds* and American Consensus," *Film and History*, February 1978, 9–15; Lois Self and Robert Self, "Adaptation as Rhetorical Process: 'It Happened One Night' and 'Mr. Deeds Goes to Town,'" *Film Criticism*, Winter 1981, 58–69. Maland engages the ideas of literary theorist John Cawelti,

who argues that popular stories symbolically portray tensions in society but that Hollywood manages to fashion satisfying conclusions out of these stories while at the same time reflecting and shaping cultural values. It is not difficult to see how cultural and social influence were attributed to Capra and Riskin when Hollywood was selling seventy-five million to ninety million tickets per week, asserts Maland. Maland, "*Mr. Deeds* and American Consensus," 9–15; John Cawelti, *Adventure, Mystery, and Romance: Formula Stories as Art and Popular Culture* (Chicago: University of Chicago Press, 1976).

50. Maland, "*Mr. Deeds* and American Consensus," 9–15.

51. Kevin Starr, *The Dream Endures: California Enters the 1940s* (New York: Oxford University Press, 1997), 269.

52. McBride, *Frank Capra*, 341.

53. Carney, *American Vision*, 265.

54. Ibid., 267.

55. Riskin gets only three references in the entire course of Carney's book, and little more than a page in relation to the partnership the two created, although Carney does refer to them as a pair when it comes to *Mr. Deeds*. Here, perhaps not surprisingly, Riskin is referred to only as an underling, Capra's cowriter, even though Capra never did enough to receive a writing credit from the Screen Writers Guild for the pair's films. Ibid., 290.

56. Ibid., 273.

57. Capra, *Name above the Title*, 187.

58. McBride, *Frank Capra*, 329–30.

59. *New York Daily News*, "Film Writer Kayoes Colleague in Third," April 14, 1936; *New York Post*, "Brawls Mark Easter Film Folk Parties," April 14, 1936; *Los Angeles Evening News*, "It Happened Again: Another Hollywood Comedy," April 13, 1936.

60. Robert Donat's performance in the lead role would win him an Academy Award in Sam Wood's 1939 screen version of Hilton's novel *Goodbye, Mr. Chips*.

61. Sam Frank, "*Lost Horizon*: A Timeless Journey," *American Cinematographer* 67, no. 4 (April 1986): 31.

62. McGilligan, introduction to *Six Screenplays*, xlv.

63. Frank, "*Lost Horizon*: A Timeless Journey."

64. McGilligan, introduction to *Six Screenplays*, xlix.

65. Creelman, "Picture Plays and Players," quoted in McGilligan, introduction to *Six Screenplays*, xlvi.

66. Sarris, *American Talking Film*, 487.

67. Frank, "*Lost Horizon*: A Timeless Journey," 33.

68. Poague, *Another Frank Capra*, 127; Maland, *Frank Capra*, 101.

69. McBride, *Frank Capra*, 354. At this point, the film ran to 10,472 feet, or 116 minutes, 21 seconds, according to Sam Frank. Cohn simply got a studio editor to cut more footage before its general release to theaters. Sam Frank, "*Lost Horizon* Losses Restored," *American Cinematographer* 68, no. 7 (July 1987): 46.

70. McBride gives *Lost Horizon*'s total profits as $5,295,546 as of October

1985, even before the film got more exposure on video and, now, DVD. Mc-Bride, *Frank Capra*, 353.

71. Ibid., 354. Sam Frank quotes Gene Milford as saying that, despite rumors of a higher figure, there was no more than 29,000 feet of film, or around five hours of screen time. Frank, *"Lost Horizon*: A Timeless Journey," 38.

72. Frank also notes that it wasn't until 1969 that the American Film Institute gave any thought to restoring the film to its near-original cut. At that time, Columbia had only one decomposing nitrate print of the picture left in its vaults, and the institute acquired this. More prints were later found, and the task of reassembling all the available Capra footage began. Frank, *"Lost Horizon* Losses Restored," 47–48.

73. Poague, *Another Frank Capra*, 126–27.

74. Ibid., 127; Elliot Stein, "Frank Capra," in *Cinema: A Critical Dictionary; The Major Filmmakers*, ed. Richard Roud, 1:187 (London: Secker & Warburg, 1980).

75. Robert Riskin, "Has No Fixed Rules for Writing Scenarios," *Cincinnati Times-Star*, July 31, 1936.

76. McBride, *Frank Capra*, 359; McGilligan, introduction to *Six Screenplays*, li.

77. George McCall, "$750,000 Panic for Riskin," *Los Angeles Evening Examiner*, February 21, 1937.

78. Rose Pelswick, "Famous Writer, Europe Bound, Bares Woes in Making Film," *New York Journal*, April 1, 1937, quoted in McGilligan, introduction to *Six Screenplays*, lii.

79. Hollis Wood, "Riskin Quits Capra-Riskin Team to Collaborate with Self on Grace Moore's Picture," *Richmond (VA) News-Leader*, February 23, 1937.

80. *Los Angeles Examiner*, July 5, 1939.

81. Wood, "Riskin Quits Capra-Riskin Team."

82. Rufus B. von KleinSmid to Robert Riskin, August 1938, Robert Riskin Papers, box 4:38, Fay Wray Collection, Cinema-Television Library, University of Southern California, Los Angeles.

83. [Robert Riskin], "The Theme's the Thing," [1937–38].

84. Virginia Wright, "Cinematters," *Los Angeles Evening News*, April 28, 1938.

4. The Idealist

1. *Variety*, "Bob Riskin Muses on 'Lost Horizon' and Wisecracking to a B'way Chorine," April 7, 1937.

2. Capra is supposed to have burned the first two reels of the picture in the studio's incinerator as a symbolic gesture against the trouble those twenty minutes of film had caused him for months with preview audiences, as well as with Cohn and the New York executives, who were not happy with the picture. Capra, *Name above the Title*, 201. McBride suggests that not only was this not the whole story of saving the movie, but that aspects of the first twenty minutes were reincorporated into later moments during the film, advancing the notion

that *Lost Horizon*'s recut following its tough initial previews was a massively complicated reassignment of scenes to different parts of the picture. McBride, *Frank Capra*, 361.

3. Thomas, *King Cohn*, 119–21.

4. *New York Evening Post*, "Capra, Riskin Britain Bound," April 15, 1937.

5. Capra, *Name above the Title*, 212. McBride is as dismissive of Capra's version of events in Russia as anything that is to be found in his biography of the director, including Capra's attempts to match up events with films in the revised paperback edition of *The Name above the Title*. McBride, *Frank Capra*, 367–68. Capra's comments about Riskin's admiration for socialism and his "committed pacifism" also don't quite tally. Riskin was more moderately left-wing than socialist, as his actions within the Screen Writers Guild testify to. Further, his willingness to contribute to the war effort in 1941 in Britain and later in 1942 within the American government, while not refuting his belief in peaceful coexistence, reveals that he was not a pacifist in the face of Nazi tyranny, which he knew had to be defeated.

6. G. Alexandrov and V. Nilson, "How American Films Are Made," *Izvestia*, May 10, 1937 (trans. Robert S. Carr).

7. Schatz, "Anatomy of a House Director," 29.

8. McGilligan, introduction to *Six Screenplays*, liii.

9. Robert Sklar, "The Imagination of Stability: The Depression Films of Frank Capra," in Glatzer and Raeburn, *Frank Capra*, 129.

10. Carney's explanation for the similar moments in the two films is predicated upon his belief that the scenes are somewhat long and pointless. Carney argues that the scenes are included to contrast most directly with the bureaucracy of modern life and the technology of economic control; for a moment, they break the spell of smooth narrative exposition. Carney, *American Vision*, 274.

11. McBride, *Frank Capra*, 384.

12. This draft of the shooting script is held in Robert Riskin Papers, Scripts, box 2, Fay Wray Collection, Cinema-Television Library, University of Southern California, Los Angeles.

13. *Motion Picture Daily*, "Capra-Riskin Team Likely to Join UA," June 11, 1938; *Time*, "Columbia's Gem," August 8, 1938.

14. McBride, *Frank Capra*, 394–400.

15. Thomas Schatz's analysis concentrates on this possible deal for Capra without intimating that Goldwyn was also interested. In Joseph McBride's assessment, the liaison between Capra and Selznick was born out of correspondence that suggested Capra wanted to direct *Gone With the Wind*, knowing Selznick to be unhappy with his director of the time, George Cukor. Schatz, "Anatomy of a House Director," 28–29; McBride, *Frank Capra*, 404–5.

16. Dick, *Merchant Prince*, 117–18.

17. McBride, *Frank Capra*, 405.

18. Thomas, *King Cohn*, 147–48. McBride suggests that the Chopin project dated back to 1936, when Cohn announced that it would be the follow-up to

Lost Horizon, with both Buchman and Riskin writing the script. McBride, *Frank Capra*, 360–61.

19. Unsigned review of *The Real Glory*, directed by Henry Hathaway, *Variety*, reprinted in Elley, Variety *Movie Guide 1997*, 773.

20. McBride, *Frank Capra*, 425, 412–15.

21. Nelson Bell, *Washington Post*, May 4, 1939.

22. Loyd Wright was becoming an influential figure in Hollywood circles. Not only did he represent a number of stars, but he was also set to become the president and general counsel of the Society of Independent Motion Picture Producers.

23. *Los Angeles Examiner*, "Capra and Riskin Form Film Firm," October 3, 1939.

24. McGilligan, introduction to *Six Screenplays*, liv.

25. McBride, *Frank Capra*, 426.

26. The budget was made up by Jack Warner's giving Frank Capra Productions a $500,000 loan and the Bank of America's giving a $750,000 loan at 6 percent interest. McBride, *Frank Capra*, 430.

27. Warner Brothers Pictures memorandums, November 28, 1939, *Meet John Doe*, box 2, file 12935B, Warner Bros. Archives, Cinema-Television Library, University of Southern California, Los Angeles.

28. McBride only suggests that the screen treatment was "handed to Riskin." Charles Wolfe reports only that *The Life and Death of John Doe* was rewritten in the spring of 1939 and then bought by Capra and Riskin in November of that year. McBride, *Frank Capra*, 429; Charles Wolfe, "Authors, Audiences, and Endings," in Meet John Doe: *Frank Capra, Director*, 6–7.

29. R. J. Obringer to Morris Ebenstein, July 21, 1941. *Meet John Doe*, Legal Files, Warner Bros. Archives, Cinema-Television Library, University of Southern California, Los Angeles. See also Wolfe, "Authors, Audiences, and Endings," 8–9.

30. *Hollywood Reporter*, "Capra-Riskin Dissolving Corporation," April 23, 1941. This report cites that Capra and Riskin had also been working very closely with Bill Holman, who had been appointed the company's production executive, having previously been Columbia's studio manager for many years.

31. Charles Wolfe notes that the name and behavior of Swerling's character owed something to the kinds of characters director Preston Sturges was inventing in his own satirical features; one might also see a link to the Marx Brothers. Wolfe, "Authors, Audiences, and Endings," 5.

32. *Motion Picture Daily*, "Capra-Riskin Team Likely to Join UA."

33. *Los Angeles Examiner*, "Starts on Trip, Lands in Jail," May 1, 1940.

34. Louella Parsons, "Fay Wray Weds Robert Riskin," *Los Angeles Examiner*, August 24, 1942.

35. Charles Wolfe's account states that the script was complete as early as April 1940, but even if it was intended as a shooting script, it quickly became nothing more than another draft; tinkering and alteration continued until the finish of the shoot. Wolfe, "Authors, Audiences, and Endings," 11.

36. McBride reports that Ann Sheridan was another choice for the role but was vetoed by the studio because she was in a contract dispute. Stanwyck signed on as late as May 31 for shooting beginning in July, although the cameras did not actually begin to roll until the beginning of August. McBride, *Frank Capra*, 430.

37. A version of the script dated January 26, 1941, used these names. *Meet John Doe*, file 12689, Warner Bros. Archives, Cinema-Television Library, University of Southern California, Los Angeles.

38. Memorandum by Herman Lissauer to William S. Holman, August 22, 1940. *Meet John Doe*, file 2808, Warner Bros. Archives, Cinema-Television Library, University of Southern California, Los Angeles.

39. Wolfe, "Authors, Audiences, and Endings," 11.

40. Glenn Alan Phelps, "Frank Capra and the Political Hero: A New Reading of 'Meet John Doe,'" *Film Criticism*, Winter 1981, 49–50.

41. Ibid., 52.

42. Maland notes that while Long John is not the "idealistic Capra hero" at the start of the film, it is Capra who "created him" to embody many of his own principles. Maland, *Frank Capra*, 113–14. Willis calls Long John a "Capra hero" who is at the same time susceptible to corruption, not a common trait of his characters. Willis, *Films of Frank Capra*, 46.

43. Wolfe, "Authors, Audiences, and Endings," 10–11.

44. In the script in the Warner Bros. Archives, this line is revised to "I'm beginning to understand a lot of things." Some of the other changes are not in the script but are included in the dialogue transcript, indicating that the lines might well have been made up on the set of the reshot scenes. *Meet John Doe*, file 175, Warner Bros. Archives, Cinema-Television Library, University of Southern California, Los Angeles.

45. These publicity materials are held in *Meet John Doe*, files 175 and 665, Warner Bros. Archives, Cinema-Television Library, University of Southern California, Los Angeles.

46. The file on *Meet John Doe* and the moral rearmament movement is held in *Meet John Doe*, box 2, Warner Bros. Archives, Cinema-Television Library, University of Southern California, Los Angeles.

47. Peter J. McCoy to Warner Brothers Pictures, April 18, 1941, *Meet John Doe*, file 2808, Warner Bros. Archives, Cinema-Television Library, University of Southern California, Los Angeles.

48. Warner Brothers Pictures memorandum, November 12, 1941, *Meet John Doe*, box 2, file 12935B, Warner Bros. Archives, Cinema-Television Library, University of Southern California, Los Angeles.

49. Memorandum by Finlay McDermid to Morris Ebenstein, December 22, 1941, *Meet John Doe*, box 2, file 12935B, Warner Bros. Archives, Cinema-Television Library, University of Southern California, Los Angeles.

50. John T. McManus, "'Meet John Doe' Pictures a Fascist Putsch in the U.S.A.," *PM's Weekly*, March 2, 1941, 51–53. A number of stills from the movie

are included in the article, at least two of which capture scenes that did not make it to the final cut.

51. *Hollywood Reporter,* "'Meet John Doe' Terrific Hit for Capra and Riskin," March 13, 1941.

52. Bosley Crowther, review of *Meet John Doe,* directed by Frank Capra, *New York Times,* March 13, 1941; Edwin Schallert, "'Meet John Doe' Hailed as Capra Victory," review of *Meet John Doe,* directed by Frank Capra, *Los Angeles Times,* March 31, 1941. Both reviews are reprinted in Wolfe, Meet John Doe: *Frank Capra, Director,* 221–25.

53. Warner Brothers Pictures financial statements, October 31, 1942, *Meet John Doe,* box 2, file 12935B, Warner Bros. Archives, Cinema-Television Library, University of Southern California, Los Angeles.

54. Lewis, "Top Story Man," 84.

55. McBride, *Frank Capra,* 440–41.

56. An invoice for £2000 ($8,050) paid by Warner Brothers Pictures to Riskin is held in *Meet John Doe,* box 2, file 12935B, Warner Bros. Archives, Cinema-Television Library, University of Southern California, Los Angeles.

57. Grant had an interesting stipulation in his contract whereby Warner Brothers was to donate a total of $100,000 to the Red Cross, the United Service Organizations, and the British War Relief Association of Southern California. Frank Capra Papers, file 2817A, Warner Bros. Archives, Cinema-Television Library, University of Southern California, Los Angeles.

5. The Liberator

1. McGilligan, introduction to *Six Screenplays,* lx.

2. David Shipman, *The Story of Cinema,* vol. 1 (London: Hodder and Stoughton, 1982), 469.

3. Wray, *On the Other Hand,* 217.

4. Riskin was handling business for Frank Capra Productions now that Capra had left (in early 1942) to become an officer in the Signal Corps and to make propaganda films himself. A letter acknowledging this fact came from the Frank Capra Productions office that had been set up at 247 South Beverly Drive in Beverly Hills. Chester Sticht to Mr. Shernow, February 16, 1942, *Meet John Doe,* file 1624, Warner Bros. Archives, Cinema-Television Library, University of Southern California, Los Angeles.

5. Shipman, *Story of Cinema,* 1:469.

6. Robert Riskin to Fay Wray, May 13, 1942, private collection of Victoria Riskin.

7. The scripts are held in the MGM Collection, Cinema-Television Library, University of Southern California, Los Angeles.

8. Unsigned review of *The Thin Man Goes Home,* directed by Richard Thorpe, *Variety,* reprinted in Elley, Variety *Movie Guide 1993,* 704.

9. Wray, *On the Other Hand,* 215.

10. W. J. Donovan to Fay Wray, February 28, 1942, private collection of Vic-

toria Riskin. The telegram read, "Thanks for the note, have asked Sherwood if he thinks Riskin could be of service, you sound as if everything were well with you. Good luck."

11. Secretary of War Henry Stimson wrote to Roosevelt in support of Donovan's work, prompted in no small part by the general himself. John Morton Blum, *V Was for Victory: Politics and American Culture during World War II* (New York: Harcourt Brace, 1976), 34–35.

12. Clayton R. Koppes and Gregory D. Black, *Hollywood Goes to War: How Politics, Profits and Propaganda Shaped World War II Movies* (New York: Macmillan, 1987), 54.

13. Ibid., 55.

14. Koppes and Black offer a classic La Guardia quote as evidence of an attempt to refute the irrefutable: "'There are three reasons why it is not [a propaganda agency],' the mayor said. 'The first is that we don't believe in this country in artificially stimulated high-pressure, doctored nonsense, and since we don't, the other two reasons are unimportant.'" Ibid., 55–56.

15. Ibid., 57.

16. Clayton R. Koppes and Gregory D. Black, "What to Show the World: The Office of War Information and Hollywood, 1942–1945," in *The Studio System,* ed. Janet Staiger, 279 (New Brunswick, NJ: Rutgers University Press, 1995).

17. Ibid., 280.

18. Thomas Doherty, *Projections of War: Hollywood, American Culture, and World War II* (New York: Columbia University Press, 1993), 47.

19. The BMP's weightiest tome was *The Government Informational Manual for the Motion Picture.* A copy is held in RG208, National Archives.

20. Mellett referred to misguided people in the Senate who, only a year before, had accused Hollywood's pro-British movies of stimulating a mood of intervention in America. Pearl Harbor broke the spine of this argument, which had been perpetuated by the Senate investigation committee led by Gerald P. Nye of North Dakota and Burton K. Wheeler of Montana. Richard R. Lingeman, *Don't You Know There's a War On? The American Home Front, 1941–1945* (New York: Capricorn Books, 1976), 171–72.

21. Doherty, *Projections of War*, 44.

22. Doherty shows how resentful the film community was, not only of the BMP's interference, but also of the demands of the military and the Office of Censorship in attempting to control Hollywood product. Ibid., 44–49.

23. Fay Wray to Bob Riskin, [May–June 1942], private collection of Victoria Riskin.

24. Wray, *On the Other Hand*, 220.

25. Ibid., 221.

26. Doherty, *Projections of War*, 51.

27. Robert Riskin to Ulric Bell, January 8, 1943, Office of War Information Records, box 3510, RG 208, National Archives. For an account of the debate over *Casablanca*, see Koppes and Black, "What to Show the World," 287–90.

28. Wray, *On the Other Hand*, 253.

29. *Hollywood Reporter*, January 14, 1943.

30. *Hollywood Reporter*, March 4, 1943. The *British Film Centre Documentary Newsletter* described *Mrs. Miniver* as existing in "a world of giggling housemaids with their bucolic young men." The writer went on to claim that audiences would be "disgusted by its gross misinterpretation of character and types," although he couldn't help but admit that Londoners had been brought to tears by its sentimentality, precisely the kind of reaction that Riskin was looking for. Quoted in Lingeman, *Don't You Know*, 192.

31. *Hollywood Reporter*, March 4, 1943.

32. The March 18, 1943, release, *At the Front in North Africa*, particularly pleased the overseas bureau, for it contained some of the most outstanding and disturbing combat footage of the war. The film broke with War Department policy by showing American casualties, but it offered success at a cost. The bureau consistently pointed out the need for dynamic, convincing footage to be shown, for example, to doubters in Latin America, where, they argued, similar German combat features were generating sympathy among some of the population. Doherty, *Projections of War*, 237.

33. *Motion Picture Herald*, "116 Films Are Sent to North Africa," March 13, 1943.

34. *New York Times*, quoted in *Motion Picture Herald*, "OWI Films to Tell World How U.S. Folk Behave," March 13, 1943.

35. News of the deal with Brigadier General Osborne, head of Special Services, Fifty-ninth Division, was reported in *Daily Variety*, "Riskin Sets Deal with Army on Capra Picture," March 15, 1943.

36. Doherty writes, "More than any other government moviemaking, *Why We Fight* was decisive in impact." Doherty, *Projections of War*, 71. While it is hard, for the most part, to criticize the scale and quality of Capra's propaganda series, Doherty's study, like others, does not once mention the *Projections of America* series, Riskin's influence upon these films, or their importance to the war effort.

37. Bill Nichols, *Introduction to Documentary* (Bloomington: Indiana University Press, 2001), 49.

38. *New York Times*, "British to See OWI Short Film," October 8, 1943. This particular endorsement of the documentary must have been quite gratifying to the bureau. The OWI had conducted a survey during 1943 about wartime prejudice, and even for the time, the extent of racial intolerance among Americans was quite astonishing. The need to combat such views as seen from outside the country was regarded as a priority. Doherty, *Projections of War*, 205–6.

39. *Motion Picture Herald*, "OWI Films to Tell World How U.S. Folk Behave," March 13, 1943.

40. Three noted features were *New Britain* (1940), *London, Autumn 1941* (1941), and *Ordinary People* (1941). While it is not clear that Riskin had any input into these propaganda efforts, it is inconceivable that he wouldn't have known or seen them while he was in Britain working for the government. Richard M. Barsam, *Non-Fiction Film: A Critical History*, rev. ed. (Bloomington: Indiana University Press, 1992), 184.

41. Paul Arthur, "Jargons of Authenticity (Three American Moments)," in *Theorizing Documentary*, ed. Michael Renov, 110–17 (New York: Routledge, 1993).

42. The BMP maintained a Washington office, but it did nothing more than liaison work for the remainder of the war. Lingeman, *Don't You Know*, 188.

43. Koppes and Black provide a comprehensive assessment of the congressional investigation into the OWI during 1943. They point out that the result was that many remaining members of the Domestic Branch moved into overseas operations, strengthening its program, and the single unit benefited from improved relations with Hollywood as well. Koppes and Black, *Hollywood Goes to War*, 134–41.

44. *Variety*, "Opposition Grows in Congress to OWI Overseas Division," October 20, 1943.

45. *Variety*, "Toscanini Makes Gratis OWI Pic," January 12, 1944.

46. *London Evening Standard*, "Mr. Deeds Here," November 30, 1943.

47. Memorandum by William D. Patterson to Robert Riskin, February 25, 1944, Office of War Information Records, entry 6D, box 2, RG 208, National Archives.

48. Memorandum by William D. Patterson to Robert Riskin, February 23, 1944, Office of War Information Records, entry 6D, box 2, RG 208, National Archives.

49. Memorandum by William D. Patterson to Robert Riskin, February 26, 1944, Office of War Information Records, entry 6D, box 2, RG 208, National Archives.

50. Memorandum by William D. Patterson to Robert Riskin, March 11, 1944, Office of War Information Records, entry 6D, box 2, RG 208, National Archives.

51. Ibid.

52. *Motion Picture Herald*, "Rank-Riskin," February 26, 1944.

53. *Hollywood Reporter*, "Riskin Outlines Plans for Film Invasion of Europe," April 11, 1944. In this article, Riskin is quoted as saying that he thought motion pictures had become more effective among the Italian public than newspapers for their ability to create a dramatic emotional impact.

54. *Motion Picture Herald*, "U.S. Films Playing in 300 Houses in Italy, Says Riskin," April 15, 1944.

55. Robert Riskin to Edward Barrett, August 12, 1944, quoted in Koppes and Black, "What to Show the World," 292–93.

56. *Hollywood Reporter*, "Bob Riskin May Quit OWI for Pix," April 19, 1944.

57. *Hollywood Reporter*, "OWI Films Interesting," May 17, 1944.

58. Bosley Crowther, "Speaking Up for America," *New York Times*, May 21, 1944; Virginia Wright, *Los Angeles Daily News*, May 22, 1944.

59. Crowther, "Speaking Up for America."

60. Koppes and Black, *Hollywood Goes to War*, 230–33.

61. Crowther, "Speaking Up for America."

62. *New York Times*, "Russians Cheer U.S. Play," June 1944.

63. Memorandum by Robert Riskin to William D. Patterson, April 3, 1945, Office of War Information Records, entry 6D, box 2, RG 208, National Archives.

64. *Hollywood Reporter*, "OWI to Produce until War Ends," January 8, 1945.

65. *Motion Picture Daily*, "OWI to Halt All Filmmaking by June 30," December 13, 1944.

66. *Le Franc-Tireur*, 1945, quoted in *New York Times*, January 14, 1945.

67. It was at this time, after Riskin returned to France at the beginning of 1945, that an interesting memo cropped up at the OWI, written by John Snedader, the head of the Egyptian division of the bureau. Snedader commented that reports in a French newspaper being published in Cairo stated that Riskin had been killed in France, although the source of the reports could not be located. Memorandum by John Snedader to Lillian Pearlman, January 25, 1945, Robert Riskin Papers, Publicity, file 4:45, Fay Wray Collection, Cinema-Television Library, University of Southern California, Los Angeles.

68. *Hollywood Reporter*, March 6, 1945.

69. *Motion Picture Daily*, "Industry Film Project to Go On," April 25, 1945.

70. The final film was a short commending the foresight of a French farmer who had taken to growing rice as a food supply rather than just raising bulls on his land.

71. Barsam, *Non-Fiction Film*, 228.

72. Koppes and Black, *Hollywood Goes to War*, 324.

73. Gerd Horten, *Radio Goes to War: The Cultural Politics of Propaganda during World War II* (Berkeley: University of California Press, 2002), 3, 5.

74. Bosley Crowther, "Destination Abroad: Something about the Pictures Which the OWI Is Sending Overseas," *New York Times*, August 29, 1943.

75. Richard Dyer McCann, "Documentary Film and Democratic Government: An Administrative History from Pere Lorentz to John Huston" (PhD dissertation, Harvard University, 1951), quoted in Barsam, *Non-Fiction Film*, 220.

76. Arthur L. Mayer, "Fact into Film," *Public Opinion Quarterly* 8, no. 2 (Summer 1944): 221.

6. The Producer

1. Victoria Riskin, personal communication with the author, January 1, 2004.

2. *Exhibitor*, "Riskin Emphasizes Documentaries' Value," May 30, 1945.

3. "Should Hollywood Make Movies Designed to Influence Public Opinion?" *Town Meeting of the Air*, ABC, September 6, 1945.

4. Ibid.

5. *The Reviewing Stand*, Northwestern University on the Air, September 23, 1945.

6. Hamilton, *Writers in Hollywood*, 227.

7. Ibid., 275.

8. Wray, *On the Other Hand*, 231.

9. *New York Times*, "Random Notes about Hollywood," August 5, 1945.

10. A transcript of this conversation is held in Robert Riskin Papers, Public-

ity in Paris, file 4:14, Fay Wray Collection, Cinema-Television Library, University of Southern California, Los Angeles.

11. McBride, *Frank Capra*, 506.

12. Wray, *On the Other Hand*, 235; Capra, *Name above the Title*, 378.

13. *Hollywood Reporter*, "'Johnny,' 'Impact' on Riskin's Sked," January 15, 1946.

14. *Hollywood Reporter*, February 27, 1946.

15. *Hollywood Reporter*, "Riskin Puts OWI Pic Second on Independent Sked at RKO," March 11, 1946.

16. The script was Rossen's in the main, but one can sense where Riskin's dialogue is used. Today, filmographies (the Internet Movie Database, for instance), as well as some versions of the DVD of the film, officially include Riskin's name in the credits.

17. McBride, *Frank Capra*, 506–7.

18. Ibid., 511–22.

19. The script for *Magic Town* is in Robert Riskin Papers, Scripts, box 2, Fay Wray Collection, Cinema-Television Library, University of Southern California, Los Angeles.

20. These publicity materials are held in the Pressbook Collection, Cinema-Television Library, University of Southern California, Los Angeles.

21. John Harkins, "Sneak Preview and a Mild Nightmare," *New York Times*, May 18, 1947.

22. *Motion Picture Herald*, "Good Picture Benefits the Entire Industry, Riskin Believes," December 7, 1946.

23. Schwartz, *Hollywood Writers' Wars*, 254.

24. Hamilton, *Writers in Hollywood*, 278.

25. Ibid., 283.

26. Philip Dunne, "The Issue of 'Politics,'" *Screenwriter* 11, no. 7 (December 1946): 1.

27. Hamilton, *Writers in Hollywood*, 294.

28. I. F. Stone, "The Grand Inquisition," *Nation*, November 8, 1947, reprinted in Carl Bromley, ed., *Cinema Nation: The Best Writing on Film from* The Nation, *1913–2000*, 163–67 (New York: Thunder Mouth Press/Nation Books, 2000).

29. Danny Miller and Jarnal Shamsie, "The Resource-Based View of the Firm in Two Environments: The Hollywood Film Studios from 1936 to 1965," *Academy of Management Journal* 39, no. 3 (1996): 529.

30. Hamilton, *Writers in Hollywood*, 295–96.

31. McBride, *Frank Capra*, 708, 710; Wray, *On the Other Hand*, 225, 231.

32. Victoria Riskin, interview with the author, July 14, 2003.

33. Thomas M. Pryor, "Robert Riskin Looks into the Crystal Ball," *New York Times*, October 5, 1949.

7. The Writer

1. *It's a Wonderful Life* had revenues of $3.3 million, making it twenty-seventh in *Variety*'s list for 1946–47. That was, however, $480,000 short of the costs of making and marketing the film. McBride, *Frank Capra*, 530.

2. *State of the Union* took $3.5 million at the box office in 1948. Ibid., 547.

3. Maland cites *Friendly Persuasion* and *Roman Holiday* as films Capra tried but failed to get made (both were later directed by his friend William Wyler). Maland, *Frank Capra*, 161.

4. The film had received previews as early as the previous August, but audiences had not reacted well. Capra and the studio took a long time to recut and try to inject some pace into the picture. McBride, *Frank Capra*, 551.

5. McGilligan, introduction to *Six Screenplays*, lxiv.

6. Ibid., lxv.

7. Maland makes the point that early-Capra reporter characters would have written a scathing account of wealthy landlords' exploiting their clients but that Pete chooses instead to set up a virtual competition with Stanley, humorously, we are led to believe, in the battle for Em's hand in marriage. Maland, *Frank Capra*, 164–65.

8. Carney, *American Vision*, 483.

9. The film finished nineteenth on *Variety*'s list of top-grossing films for the year, taking $2.5 million. Maland, *Frank Capra*, 166.

10. Unsigned review of *Here Comes the Groom*, directed by Frank Capra, *Variety*, reprinted in Elley, Variety *Movie Guide 1993*, 307.

11. McBride, *Frank Capra*, 559.

12. Carney's analysis of the film includes a nice story about Capra's reaction to news in the 1970s that *Lost Horizon* might be remade as a Bacharach and David musical. Capra responded that it could be an opera but never a musical. Carney makes a similar point about Capra's attempts at musicals: they paved the way for the man and woman to get together in the story, but his films had always looked to develop so much more emotional content, social engagement, and romantic illusion. Carney, *American Vision*, 482–83.

13. A copy of the minutes of the court hearing is held in Robert Riskin Papers, *Mister 880*, file 4:29, box 4, Fay Wray Collection, Cinema-Television Library, University of Southern California, Los Angeles.

14. Four main drafts of the script were written between February 14 and April 4, 1950. All the bound drafts are held in *Mister 880*, file 1, MGM Collection, Cinema-Television Library, University of Southern California, Los Angeles.

15. David Thomson, *The New Biographical Dictionary of Film*, 4th ed. (London: Little, Brown, 2002), 348.

16. The review adds that there were one or two "excellent touches of comedy" and that the film, overall, was "agreeable." Unsigned review of *Mister 880*, directed by Edmund Goulding, *Monthly Film Bulletin* 17, no. 20 (October 1950): 150.

17. Unsigned review of *Mister 880*, directed by Edmund Goulding, *Variety*, August 23, 1950.

18. Fay Wray remembers a memo with the first draft of the script that read, "Dear Darryl: Season's Greetings. All I can give you for Christmas is the script for 'Belvedere.' I hope it is just what you wanted from Santa." Wray, "Biography of Robert Riskin," quoted in McGilligan, introduction to *Six Screenplays*, lxvi.

19. Wray, *On the Other Hand*, 252.

Epilogue

The first epigraph is quoted in McGilligan, *Backstory*, 177. The second epigraph is drawn from *The Letters of F. Scott Fitzgerald* and is quoted in McGilligan, *Backstory*, 241.

1. David Shipman, *The Story of Cinema* (London: Hodder and Stoughton, 1984), 2:202.

2. Maland, *Frank Capra*, 65.

3. Handzo, "Under Capracorn," 167.

4. Ibid.

5. Ronny Regev, *Working in Hollywood: How the Studio System Turned Creativity into Labor* (Chapel Hill: University of North Carolina Press, 2018), 60.

6. Philip Dunne, *Take Two: A Life in Movies and Politics* (New York: McGraw-Hill, 1980), 243–45.

7. McGilligan, introduction to *Six Screenplays*, by Robert Riskin, lxvi–lxvii; *Los Angeles Examiner*, "Rites for Robert Riskin Draw Film Notables," September 24, 1955.

8. *Los Angeles Examiner*, "Rites for Robert Riskin."

9. Victoria Riskin, *Fay Wray and Robert Riskin: A Hollywood Memoir* (New York: Pantheon, 2019), 328.

10. Ibid., 328–29.

11. Ian Scott, "Columbia Pictures and the Great Depression: A Case Study of Political Writers in Hollywood," in *Hollywood and the Great Depression: American Film, Politics and Society in the 1930s*, ed. Iwan Morgan and Philip John Davies (Edinburgh: Edinburgh University Press, 2016), 63.

12. Zagarrio's argument does not actually make a wholesale attack on previous literature relating to Capra. His chapter overall is in fact an interesting advancement of the notion that a dark, tragic element pervaded much of Capra's work, and this influenced other, more contemporary directors as well. This makes it all the stranger that he somewhat blatantly denounces McBride only to make the point that autobiographies—like/especially Capra's—are fairly unreliable documents and that he is therefore choosing to use the films themselves as material. For the discussion on Riskin, see Zagarrio, "It Is (Not) a Wonderful Life," 69–72.

13. Victoria Riskin, interview with the author, Los Angeles, July 14, 2003.

14. McBride, *Frankly: Unmasking Frank Capra*, 22.

15. Ibid., 100.

16. McGilligan, *Backstory*, 6.

17. Ibid., 9.

18. Victoria Riskin, interview with the author, Los Angeles, July 14, 2003. Tom Stempel also cites the incident in his book, although he acknowledges Capra's own take on the story, which was that "Bob was too much of a gentleman to come up with that corny scene." Stempel, *FrameWork*, 104.

19. Thomas, *King Cohn*, 104–5.

20. Maurice Zolotov, *Billy Wilder in Hollywood* (1977; London: Limelight, 1987), 56–57.

21. Steven Maras, *Screenwriting: History, Theory and Practice* (London: Wallflower, 2009), 15–23.

22. Norman, *What Happens Next*, 136.

23. Corliss, *Talking Pictures*, 5, 176; Pauline Kael quoted in Corliss, *Talking Pictures*, 5; Stempel, *FrameWork*, 116, 118.

24. Norman, *What Happens Next*, 176.

25. "Julius J. Epstein: A King of Comedy Interviewed by Pat McGilligan," in McGilligan, *Backstory*, 190.

26. "W. R. Burnett: The Outsider," 33.

27. Richard Glatzer, "A Conversation with Frank Capra," in Glatzer and Raeburn, *Frank Capra*, 34.

28. *Click Magazine*, March 1941.

29. Glatzer, "Conversation with Frank Capra," 34.

30. Eric Smoodin, *Regarding Frank Capra: Audience, Celebrity & American Film Studies, 1930–1960* (Durham, NC: Duke University Press, 2004), 238.

SELECT BIBLIOGRAPHY

Primary Sources

The Robert Riskin Papers are part of the Fay Wray Collection at the University of Southern California Cinema-Television Library. The Charles Bickford Collection, housed in the same location, was also consulted. The USC Warner Bros. Archives provided legal documents and memos pertaining to Riskin's work, especially during the period of Frank Capra Productions' existence. Materials on Riskin can also be found at the Margaret Herrick Library of the Motion Picture Academy of Arts and Sciences. Some materials documenting the origins and early work of the Screen Writers Guild are held in the James R. Webb Memorial Library of the Writers Guild of America, West. The library's collection of the *Screenwriter*, the Screen Writers Guild's official magazine, is particularly useful in this regard. Official correspondence of the Office of War Information and materials on Riskin were obtained from the National Archives and Records Administration. The author conducted personal interviews with Riskin's family members.

Secondary Sources

Barsam, Richard M. *Non-Fiction Film: A Critical History*. Rev. ed. Bloomington: Indiana University Press, 1992.

Belton, John, ed. *Movies and Mass Culture*. London: Athlone, 1996.

Bergman, Andrew. *We're in the Money: Depression America and Its Films*. Chicago: Ivan R. Dee, 1992.

Bernds, Edward. *Mr. Bernds Goes to Hollywood*. London: Scarecrow Press, 1999.

Capra, Frank. *The Name above the Title*. New York: Macmillan, 1971.

———. "One Man, One Film—The Capra Contention." *Los Angeles Times*, June 26, 1977, Calendar.

Carney, Ray. *American Vision: The Films of Frank Capra*. Hanover, NH: Wesleyan University Press, 1986.

Cawelti, John. *Adventure, Mystery, and Romance: Formula Stories as Art and Popular Culture*. Chicago: University of Chicago Press, 1976.

Ceplair, Larry, and Steven Englund. *The Inquisition in Hollywood: Politics in the Film Community, 1930–1960*. Berkeley: University of California Press, 1983.

Childs, James. "Capra Today." *Film Comment* 8, no. 4 (November 1972): 22.

Corliss, Richard. "Capra & Riskin." *Film Comment* 8, no. 4 (November 1972): 18–23.

———. *Talking Pictures: Screenwriters in the American Cinema*. New York: Penguin, 1974.

Custen, George F. *Twentieth Century's Fox: Darryl F. Zanuck and the Culture of Hollywood*. New York: Basic Books, 1997.

Dewey, Donald. *James Stewart: A Biography*. London: Little, Brown, 1997.

Dick, Bernard F. *The Merchant Prince of Poverty Row: Harry Cohn of Columbia Pictures*. Lexington: University Press of Kentucky, 1993.

———. *The Star-Spangled Screen: The American World War II Film*. Lexington: University Press of Kentucky, 1996.

Doherty, Thomas. *Projections of War: Hollywood, American Culture, and World War II*. New York: Columbia University Press, 1993.

Dunne, Philip. "The Documentary and Hollywood." *Hollywood Quarterly* 1, no. 2 (January 1946): 166–72.

———. "The Issue of 'Politics.'" *Screenwriter* 11, no. 7 (December 1946): 10.

Edgerton, Gary. "Capra and Altman: Mythmaker and Mythologist." *Literature/Film Quarterly* 11, no. 1 (1983): 28–35.

Elley, Derek, ed. Variety *Movie Guide 1993*. London: Hamlyn, 1992.

———, ed. Variety *Movie Guide 1997*. London: Hamlyn, 1996.

Eyman, Scott. *"Print the Legend": The Life and Times of John Ford*. New York: Simon and Schuster, 1999.

Frank, Sam. *"Lost Horizon*: A Timeless Journey." *American Cinematographer* 67, no. 4 (April 1986): 30–50.

Gabler, Neal. *An Empire of Their Own: How the Jews Invented Hollywood*. New York: Doubleday, 1988.

Gallagher, Brian. "Speech, Identity, and Ideology in 'Mr. Smith Goes to Washington.'" *Film Criticism* 5, no. 2 (Winter 1981): 12–22.

Gallagher, Tag. *John Ford: The Man and His Films*. Berkeley: University of California Press, 1986.

Gehring, Wes D. *Mr. Deeds Goes to Yankee Stadium: Baseball Films in the Capra Tradition*. Jefferson, NC: McFarland, 2004.

Glatzer, Richard, and John Raeburn, eds. *Frank Capra: The Man and His Films*. Ann Arbor: University of Michigan Press, 1975.

Hamilton, Ian. *Writers in Hollywood, 1915–1951*. New York: Carroll & Graf, 1991.

Hillenbrand, Laura. *Seabiscuit: The Making of a Legend*. London: Fourth Estate, 2001.

Hollows, Joanne, Peter Hutchings, and Mark Jancovich, eds. *The Film Studies Reader*. London: Arnold, 2000.

Horten, Gerd. *Radio Goes to War: The Cultural Politics of Propaganda during World War II*. Berkeley: University of California Press, 2002.

Koppes, Clayton R., and Gregory D. Black. *Hollywood Goes to War: How Politics, Profits and Propaganda Shaped World War II Movies*. New York: Macmillan, 1987.

Krome, Federic. "The True Glory and the Failure of Anglo-American Film Propaganda in the Second World War." *Journal of Contemporary History* 33, no. 1 (January 1998): 21–34.

Lingeman, Richard R. *Don't You Know There's a War On? The American Home Front, 1941–1945*. New York: Capricorn Books, 1976.

Lourdeaux, Lee. *Italian and Irish Filmmakers in America: Ford, Capra, Coppola, and Scorsese*. Philadelphia: Temple University Press, 1990.

Maland, Charles. *Frank Capra*. New York: Twayne, 1995.

———. "*Mr. Deeds* and American Consensus." *Film and History*, February 1978, 9–15.

Maltby, Richard. *Harmless Entertainment: Hollywood and the Ideology of Consensus*. London: Scarecrow Press, 1983.

Maras, Steven. *Screenwriting: History, Theory and Practice*. London: Wallflower, 2009.

May, Lary. *The Big Tomorrow: Hollywood and the Politics of the American Way*. Chicago: University of Chicago Press, 2000.

Mayer, Arthur L. "Fact into Film." *Public Opinion Quarterly* 8, no. 2 (Summer 1944): 206–25.

McBride, Joseph. *Frank Capra: The Catastrophe of Success*. London: Faber and Faber, 1992.

———. *Frankly: Unmasking Frank Capra*. Berkeley: Hightower, 2019.

McGilligan, Pat. *Backstory: Interviews with Screenwriters of Hollywood's Golden Age*. Berkeley: University of California Press, 1986.

———. Introduction to *Six Screenplays*, by Robert Riskin. Berkeley: University of California Press, 1997.

Meryman, Richard. *Mank: The Wit, World, and Life of Herman Mankiewicz*. New York: Morrow, 1978.

Mordden, Ethan. *The Hollywood Studios: Their Unique Styles during the Golden Age of Movies*. New York, Fireside, 1988.

Morgan, Iwan, and Philip John Davies, eds. *Hollywood and the Great Depression: American Film, Politics and Society in the 1930s*. Edinburgh: Edinburgh University Press, 2016.

Moss, Marilyn Ann. *Giant: George Stevens; A Life on Film*. Madison: University of Wisconsin Press, 2004.

Mulvey, Laura. "Visual Pleasure and Narrative Cinema." *Screen* 16, no. 3 (Autumn 1975): 6–18.

Neve, Brian. *Film and Politics in America: A Social Tradition*. London: Routledge, 1992.

Neve, Brian, and Philip Davies, eds. *Cinema, Politics, and Society*. Manchester: Manchester University Press, 1981.

Nichols, Bill. *Introduction to Documentary*. Bloomington: Indiana University Press, 2001.

Norman, Marc. *What Happens Next: A History of American Screenwriting*. London: Aurum, 2008.

Phelps, Glenn Alan. "Frank Capra and the Political Hero: A New Reading of 'Meet John Doe.'" *Film Criticism*, Winter 1981, 49–57.

———. "The Populist Films of Frank Capra." *Journal of American Studies* 13, no. 3 (1979): 377–92.

Poague, Leland. *Another Frank Capra*. Cambridge: Cambridge University Press, 1994.

Regev, Ronny. *Working in Hollywood: How the Studio System Turned Creativity into Labor*. Chapel Hill: University of North Carolina Press, 2018.

Renov, Michael, ed. *Theorizing Documentary*. New York: Routledge, 1993.

Riskin, Robert. "The Canine Era." *Hollywood Reporter*, December 31, 1934.

Riskin, Victoria. *Fay Wray and Robert Riskin: A Hollywood Memoir*. New York: Pantheon, 2019.

Roffman, Peter, and Jim Purdy. *The Hollywood Social Problem Film*. Bloomington: Indiana University Press, 1981.

Rollins, Peter C., and John E. O'Connor, eds. *Hollywood's White House: The American Presidency in Film and History*. Lexington: University Press of Kentucky, 2003.

Sarris, Andrew. *"You Ain't Heard Nothing Yet": The American Talking Film; History and Memory, 1927–1949*. New York: Oxford University Press, 1998.

Schatz, Thomas. *The Genius of the System: Hollywood Filmmaking in the Studio Era*. London: Faber and Faber, 1998.

Schwartz, Nancy Lynn. *The Hollywood Writers' Wars*. New York: Knopf, 1982.

Schwartz, Stephen. *From West to East: California and the Making of the American Mind*. New York: Simon & Schuster, 1998.

Scott, Ian. "Frank Capra's *State of the Union*: The Triumph of Politics." *Borderlines: Studies in American Culture* 5, no. 1 (1998): 33–47.

Self, Lois, and Robert Self. "Adaptation as Rhetorical Process: 'It Happened One Night' and 'Mr. Deeds Goes to Town.'" *Film Criticism*, Winter 1981, 58–69.

Shindler, Colin. *Hollywood in Crisis: Cinema and American Society, 1929–1939*. London: Routledge, 1996.

Shipman, David. *The Story of Cinema*. 2 vols. London: Hodder and Stoughton, 1982–84.

Sinclair, Andrew. *John Ford*. New York: Dial Press, 1979.

Sklar, Robert. *Movie-Made America: A Social History of American Movies*. New York: Random House, 1975.

Sklar, Robert, and Vito Zagarrio, eds. *Frank Capra: Authorship and the Studio System*. Philadelphia: Temple University Press, 1998.

Smoodin, Eric. *Regarding Frank Capra: Audience, Celebrity, and American Film Studies, 1930–1960*. Durham, NC: Duke University Press, 2004.

Stacey, Jackie. *Star Gazing: Hollywood Cinema and Female Spectatorship*. London: Routledge, 1994.

Starr, Kevin. *The Dream Endures: California Enters the 1940s*. New York: Oxford University Press, 1997.

———. *Endangered Dreams: The Great Depression in California*. New York: Oxford University Press, 1996.

Stein, Elliot. "Frank Capra." In *Cinema: A Critical Dictionary; The Major Filmmakers*, edited by Richard Roud, vol. 1, 62. London: Secker & Warburg, 1980.

Stempel, Tom. *FrameWork: A History of Screenwriting in the American Film*. 3rd ed. Syracuse, NY: Syracuse University Press, 2000.

Thomas, Bob. *King Cohn: The Life and Times of Hollywood Mogul Harry Cohn*. Beverly Hills: New Millennium Press, 2000.

Thomson, David. *The New Biographical Dictionary of Film*. 4th ed. London: Little, Brown, 2002.

———. *Rosebud: The Story of Orson Welles*. London: Abacus, 1997.

Walker, Joseph, and Juanita Walker. *The Light on Her Face*. Hollywood: ASC Press, 1984.

Wexman, Virginia Wright. *Hollywood's Artists: The Directors Guild of America and the Construction of Authorship*. New York: Columbia University Press, 2020.

Willis, Donald C. *The Films of Frank Capra*. Metuchen, NJ: Scarecrow
    Press, 1974.
Wolfe, Charles, ed. Meet John Doe: *Frank Capra, Director*. New Bruns-
    wick, NJ: Rutgers University Press, 1989.
Wray, Fay. *On the Other Hand: A Life Story*. New York: St. Martin's Press,
    1989.

INDEX